STRAND PRICE
5 23
5 00

D1301572

REBUILDING AN ENLIGHTENED WORLD

REBUILDING AN ENLIGHTENED WORLD

Folklorizing America

BILL IVEY

INDIANA UNIVERSITY PRESS

This book is a publication of

INDIANA UNIVERSITY PRESS
Office of Scholarly Publishing
Herman B Wells Library 350
1320 East 10th Street
Bloomington, Indiana 47405 USA

iupress.indiana.edu

© 2018 by Bill Ivey
All rights reserved

No part of this book may be reproduced
or utilized in any form or by any
means, electronic or mechanical,
including photocopying and recording,
or by any information storage and
retrieval system, without permission
in writing from the publisher.

The paper used in this publication
meets the minimum requirements of
the American National Standard for
Information Sciences – Permanence of
Paper for Printed Library Materials,
ANSI Z39.48–1992.

Manufactured in the
United States of America

Library of Congress
Cataloging-in-Publication Data

Names: Ivey, Bill J., [date] author.
Title: Rebuilding an enlightened world :
    folklorizing America / Bill Ivey.
Description: Bloomington : Indiana
    University Press, 2018. | Includes
    bibliographical references and index.
Identifiers: LCCN 2018017508 (print) |
    LCCN 2018018375 (ebook) | ISBN
    9780253030153 (ebook) | ISBN
    9780253029690 (cl : alk. paper)
Subjects: LCSH: Cultural awareness—
    United States. | Politics and culture—
    United States. | Enlightenment—
    Influence. | Folklore—Study and
    teaching. | United States—Relations. |
    United States—Cultural policy.
Classification: LCC E169.12 (ebook) |
    LCC E169.12 .I94 2018 (print) |
    DDC 306.0973—dc23
LC record available at https://
    lccn.loc.gov/2018017508

1 2 3 4 5   23 22 21 20 19 18

For Susan

"A vigorous culture capable of making corrective, stabilizing changes depends heavily on its educated people, and especially upon their critical capacities and depth of understanding."

JANE JACOBS, *Dark Age Ahead*

"To understand the present is not altogether a minor achievement, and indeed may be the best we can hope for in gaining a vision of what is to come. . . . If we can really know what today is like—if we can penetrate its depths, distinguish what is superficial and transient from what is enduring—we are at the edge of prophecy; we are at least in the realm where predictions can be made."

AUGUST HECKSCHER, *The Flow of Time*

"The only people who see the whole picture are the ones who step out of the frame."

SALMAN RUSHDIE, *The Ground Beneath Her Feet*

Contents

REBUILDING AN ENLIGHTENED WORLD

PROLOGUE

SUDDENLY, IN 2017, EVERYBODY IN WASHINGTON SEEMED TO
be speaking my language. Josh Earnest, in his final appearance as Obama
White House spokesman on MSNBC's *Morning Joe,* was asked by host
Mika Brzezinski about reports that the incoming Donald Trump White
House would close the pressroom, relocating correspondents to a space
in the Eisenhower Executive Office Building next door. Earnest an-
swered that it was important that the new administration "maintain
traditions." A week later, Ron Nell Andersen Jones and Sonja West, both
professors of law, elaborated on Earnest's point in a *New York Times*
opinion essay, noting that there was one pillar of press freedom that
Trump, "now seems most keen to destroy: tradition." They continue, "It
is primarily customs and traditions, not laws, that guarantee that members of the White House press corps have access to the workings of the
executive branch.... This is why we should be alarmed when Mr. Trump,
defying tradition, vilifies media institutions, attacks reporters by name
and refuses to take questions from those whose coverage he dislikes."[1]

This got my attention. Of course, like millions I agreed that "we
should be alarmed," but mostly I was startled to hear America's punditry
framing political analysis in the terminology of my chosen academic
discipline, folklore studies. After all, *custom* and *tradition* are folklore
words, standing at the center of what folklorists pay attention to when
observing the ways people work and talk in communities and groups.

In the fall, when NFL owners and players linked arms or "took a
knee" in an act of protest and solidarity, we learned that although the law
offered guidance on respect for the national anthem, there was no legal

penalty for violating "customary" behavior. In late 2016 the *New York Times* critiqued the incoming Trump administration by observing that "democratic institutions must be protected by strong informal norms," by "unwritten rules of the game."[2]

In an October 11 opinion piece, political scientist Greg Weiner sounded like a folklore scholar:

> Customs are the punctuation marks of republican politics, the silent guides we follow without pausing to consider their authority. They operate in a space that is difficult for formal rules to codify. That the president of the United States speaks with caution and dignity, that he exercises the pardon power the Constitution grants him soberly rather than wantonly, that he respects the independence of law enforcement, and that, to the extent reasonable politics permit, he speaks truthfully—these are all *customs*, not laws [my italics]. Law is powerless to impose them and powerless without them.[3]

Folklore scholar Lynne McNeill frames custom this way:

> If you just openly picked your nose while your boss was talking to you, or if you greeted your date's parents by passionately kissing them, or if you sat down at McDonald's and tried to flag down a server to come and take your order—these are all things that our informal culture tells us are incorrect. . . . This informal or unofficial level of cultural understanding is the "folk" level. . . . Instead of laws we have customs; instead of guidebooks we have experience and observation.[4]

For more than a year, President Trump had ignored and demeaned both democratic customs and their behavioral equivalent: long-established *norms* that established acceptable, traditional practice in politics and government. Just as customs memorialize critical behavior, norms constitute the *accepted standard* against which behaviors can be measured and critiqued. Just as customs and traditions are beliefs and practices sustained by informal communication, a norm represents a standard, model, or pattern: an accepted behavior that may be explicit—such as candidates releasing tax returns—or implied—such as the need for moderation, respectful exchange, fairness. Trump disdained daily security briefings, ignored long-standing protocols framing relations with China, and equivocated when asked about his plans to divest himself of investments and business—a widely accepted and important norm (and a matter of law for most government officials) designed to eliminate the appearance or reality of conflict between the new president's public and private commitments.

New York Times columnist David Brooks weighed in, invoking a more expansive folklore idea, lamenting the corruption of "America's true myth." His take on the genre surprised me; it is close to what a folklore scholar might say:

> Myths don't make a point or propose an argument. They inhabit us deeply and explain to us who we are. They capture how our own lives are connected to the universal sacred realities. In myth, the physical stuff in front of us is also a manifestation of something eternal, and our lives are seen in the context of some illimitable horizon.

Brooks then takes aim at an elusive target—the American myth: "America is . . . at the vanguard of the great human march of progress. America is the grateful inheritor of other people's gifts. It has a spiritual connection to all people in all places, but also an exceptional role. America culminates history." Nice try, but Brooks's formulation feels more "mythic" than real "myth." Still, he is drawn toward a version of folkloric thinking.[5]

My folklore studies colleagues understand the pervasive importance of unwritten tradition, but mainstream commentators seemed shocked to learn how much of our "government of laws, not men," was in fact not memorialized in legislation at all, but rather inhabited a realm of assumed practices maintained through speech and face-to-face demonstration, passed through imitation and anecdote from one generation of leaders to the next. Political analysts once content to study law, treaties, and regulations now tracked affronts to "custom," "tradition," and "norms." Throughout 2017 it appeared Americans had suddenly acquired an appreciation for the critical role traditional practice plays in the effective functioning of democratic society. Greg Weiner concludes that while most political theory "elevates contemporary reason . . . above all else . . . rejection of the authority of custom is more dangerous than we realize because without custom, there is no law."[6] In turbulent times, when the thin conceits of civilization seem weak, we instinctively and wisely fall back on the communal reassurance of folk belief and practice.

This new prominence of traditional knowledge and behavior, and a related retreat from science, history, and other hierarchies honored by civilization, isn't just happening here. In fact, contempt for law and established order reflects a new set of challenges facing both international engagement and domestic authorities everywhere. But today we can clearly see the power of traditional knowledge in our own behavior, and the behavior of antagonists—revolutionaries and zealots determined to undermine Western influence. We have lived as though the official vocabulary of modern society and government—reason, science, law—frame all understanding, shape all behavior. But if our *real* life of culture and community is, in a sense, "off the books"—in a space of oral tradition beyond the hegemony of official rules, formal learning, and scientific evidence—we must step back and reconsider the way we see ourselves, understand other people, assess motives, and engage alternate realities. The persistent authority of traditional knowledge and action demands a critical approach to our stories, assumptions, and dreams and to the narratives and hopes of others.

Hints of a realignment were offered a decade ago. In a *New York Times* opinion essay in the summer of 2011, author Neal Gabler lamented the absence of new, big ideas that "could ignite fires of debate, stimulate other thoughts, incite revolutions and fundamentally change the ways we look at and think about the world." For Gabler, big ideas are those that can be grasped intuitively, on their merits, not built up from assembled evidence. And big ideas should explain many things, not just one or two, should be universal or nearly so—strong enough to help us understand many things in many places. Noting that today what passes for big themes is usually little more than "observations," Gabler advances names from the past—Carl Sagan, Daniel Bell, Reinhold Niebuhr, Betty Friedan, Marshall McLuhan—as architects of ideas that could "penetrate the general culture."

As he measures the shrinkage of big thought, Gabler himself, almost in passing, puts forward a big idea of his own:

> It is no secret, especially here in America, that we live in a post-Enlightenment age in which rationality, science, evidence, logical argument and debate have lost the battle in many sectors, and perhaps even in society generally, to superstition, faith, opinion and orthodoxy. While we continue to make giant technological advances, we may be the first generation to have turned back the epochal clock—to have gone backward intellectually from advanced modes of thinking into old modes of belief.[7]

Gabler's observation was an aside—a tossed-off explanation of *why* in the summer of 2011 big ideas seemed to have faded from our American intellectual scene. But even then his notion of a "post-Enlightenment world" seemed just right. Here in the United States and around the world, official truth cowered, "old modes of belief" were on the rise. Subnational actors and transnational movements rejected the Enlightenment and its Western heritage. Thoroughly modernized China had experienced the Enlightenment only through the movement's relentless Western enabler, imperialism. Once free of alien intervention, the venerable society sped from imperial autonomy to vulgarized Marxism in a brief half-century. Alternative models of knowledge, philosophy, politics, and society advanced by a rising China increasingly challenged enlightened, Western understanding. Widespread religious fervor, the spread of global terrorism, and the growing influence of China demanded fresh thinking. No longer living in a Reaganist, triumphalist post–Cold War era, America now required a big idea strong enough to frame a new role in the world—an idea that could both explain and give us the tools necessary to cope with and respond to a daunting new reality.

We *are* living the essence of Gabler's shorthanded observation. For two centuries, the Enlightenment provided the underpinnings of Western assumed wisdom. It was the source of rationality and scientific analysis, harnessing the power of technology and market economies to improve the human condition and make democratic ideals real. But from the Taliban in Afghanistan to the Tea Party in Des Moines, Enlightenment assumptions have lost authority, are under attack. The Enlightenment has lost its hold on the world; the standing of science, secularity, human rights, inclusive politics has been undermined. It's our own fault. Rhetorically compassionate, Enlightenment ideas were all too often *imposed* on previously suppressed peoples. Outside the boundaries of civilization, the traditions and values of ordinary people were denigrated and dismissed; whole societies were forced to simply conform to enforced frames of government, language, learning. I clipped Gabler's *Times* piece and kept it with me.

This book is premised on the end of the Enlightenment, but my argument is about how we deal with the reality of a reconfigured, challenging present. It is my contention that Enlightenment assertions about individual agency, human rights, participatory government no longer fire the imaginations of the public. As a result, the world is witnessing a return to notions of community, faith, authority grounded in ancient traditions held by rural groups and tribal, oral societies. If Enlightenment values are to find renewed life, civilization must craft a new relationship with regular people by embracing new insights and a new *moral stance*. For many decades the West has grounded its perception of the world on Enlightenment principles. But abstract ideals aren't operational; it takes movements to convert values to actions. Through nineteenth-century ideologies and tenets of related human sciences—economics, sociology, psychology—Enlightenment ideals were distilled and distorted into ideological wellsprings of what would become conventional wisdom. Communism, capitalism, social Darwinism, fascism winked and promised "human rights." A smug Enlightenment consensus grew up around democracy, capitalism, competition, race, human capacity. This consensus justified imperial conquest, colonial occupation, postcolonial struggles for power and economic hegemony. But beyond the West, nations, societies, believers have always possessed alternative knowledge; now that the Enlightenment consensus has weakened, long-suppressed ancient ways are quickly filling the emptying space.[8]

Let's be clear: it's not Trump, it's that America is *not* immune to emerging reality. In its suspicion of science, distrust of Washington elites, the press, and highly educated leaders of business and government, the Trump campaign offered nothing more than a distinctly American rendition of an anti-Enlightenment sentiment sweeping the globe. In valorizing ethnic and racial distrust, trivializing women's rights, dismissively suggesting that opposing voices be silenced or "removed from the hall," Trump was not only marginalizing key legal and constitutional principles, he was the American face of the collapsing Enlightenment consensus—the final rejection of the West's postwar effort to impose its dream on ordinary people. It should have been no surprise that, to an extent unanticipated even by opponents, the Trump administration quickly institutionalized contempt for both long-embraced Enlightenment values and even the administrative state itself—the proud purpose of which, after all, is to convert visionary ideals into deployable public policy.

Implemented through the careless and oppressive march of imperial ambition, Enlightenment promises of equality, participation, respect today produce only frustration, anger. Angst is everywhere, and Trump's message bottled that resentment, then let it out, dramatically shifting the tone of political engagement. No surprise—while invoking the Trump brand, a white supremacist gathering in northern Virginia produced deadly acts of domestic terrorism.

Political scientists, historians, pundits—gloomy in the wake of a startling election—questioned the fate of America's democracy in the age of Trump. In one way or another they asked, "Can our institutions survive the presidency of an impulsive celebrity hostile to the press and entirely unschooled in the workings of our government?" Nativist, nationalistic anger targeting immigrants, Muslims, educated "elites," and mainstream media was normalized—even validated—overnight. Millions turned away from print and television to folklore-like online rumor and emotionally reinforcing "fake news." This destabilizing new order felt homegrown, but it was in fact a digital extension of global hostility to the customs, traditions, norms—the essential *authority*—of liberal democracy. Around the world political traditions prized by civilization were under attack, frequently by adherents of ancient societies, tribes, and religious groups, by the traditional communities and peoples who had for centuries been embraced in the enlightened rhetoric of human rights, social justice, participatory government. What is happening; why did they turn on us; what can we do?

: : : : :

I had been thinking hard about the meaning of folklore studies since the fall of 2007. In October of that year, members of the American Folklore Society (AFS) gathered for their annual meeting in a high-rise hotel hugging the edge of Old Quebec, the famous walled city in Canada's francophone province. I was wrapping up my two-year term as president of the society and had brooded for weeks about Saturday's required presidential address—it was not coming easily.[9] Now it was late Friday night and I'd spent the afternoon on the seventh floor of the Hilton, writing and rewriting, rushing from suite to business center to room again, printing, revising; one version, then another. I knew where I wanted the talk to go but couldn't quite get there.

My mental block was no fault of folklore studies. The field provided plenty to talk about. The venerable AFS could trace its origins to the 1880s—famous early leaders included humorist Mark Twain and anthropologist Franz Boas; the raw stuff of folklore had inspired purveyors of pop culture from Walt Disney to Bob Dylan. For most of its history the society had been home to university teachers and scholars—professionals in the field of folklore studies dedicated to collecting and analyzing songs and tales, legends, quilts, jokes, cabins, myths, and recipes. In more recent decades, the AFS welcomed an expanding cohort of folklore professionals who worked outside the academy—consultants or heads of state and city nonprofits specializing in oral traditions—such as customs, storytelling, and songs: the expressive lives of communities defined by ethnicity, nationality, work, race, or gender.

I knew what I was trying to say to society members: *Folklore studies is very important!* In all my years in country music—with the NEA and in a major university—my training in folklore had been critical to making the best of each situation, each opportunity. It was the study of folklore that gave me a practical sense of how the complexity of American culture fit together, and it was folklore studies that provided insight into the passions, motivations, prejudices, and assumptions that energized the colleagues, competitors, critics, and adversaries who populated my professional life.

In the end, my talk went fine—garnering what my friend Chet Atkins labeled "a crouching ovation." But something was missing; the speech felt like a beginning, not an end. So over months and then years my incomplete effort to value folklore studies continued to nag even as I was on to other things: teaching, university life, writing about culture—and especially culture in public policy.

I developed a taste for politics and became a real Democrat during my four years serving the Bill Clinton administration as chair of the National Endowment for the Arts. I carried my fascination with government and its relationship to culture into my work directing an arts policy center at Vanderbilt University. In early 2008 something nudged me to contribute a little money to the nascent campaign of Barack Obama. The young and inspiring Illinois senator secured the Democratic presidential nomination, and during the campaign my Clinton administration boss John Podesta asked me to conduct research on America's cultural agencies. A team worked secretly to assemble documents for the new president; fingers were crossed for an Obama victory. He won.

A year after my AFS speech, I moved back to Washington to work in the Obama presidential transition. The excitement of crafting new government was tempered by a shadow of hard times: the 2008 collapse of banks, housing, markets had triggered a global financial crisis, and even as the transition team gathered in DC to staff up our new administration, in the background our US economy was falling off a cliff.

In the end we didn't hit rock bottom. But the United States that staggered back from what came to be called the Great Recession had been transformed into a scary fun-house-mirror distortion of long-trusted assumptions. Anger and suspicion now ruled, undermining confidence in universal values, human rights, scientific rationalism, secular society, the primacy of market capitalism. The international system shuddered: Terrorism incubated in the volatile Middle East infected the world, providing fundamentalist nonstate actors and their converts with expanded, disruptive power. China—an ancient civilization grounded in Confucian philosophy driven by a centuries-old desire to reject foreign influence and achieve wealth and power—emerged as a leading international player of uncertain intent. In the United States, long a bastion of diplomacy, consensual government, and trust in science, Tea Party activists challenged expertise, the authority of elected officials, and the legitimacy of their new black president. At home and around the world, the established order trembled. Our post-Enlightenment age seemed closer—and more menacing—than ever before. Philosopher François Jullien put it this way:

> The culture that has become dominant over these past centuries (the "Western" one) has been forced to recognize that its sovereign position is being chipped away and it can no longer assert its pre-established legitimacy so dogmatically. ... The conditions for an *intelligent* dialogue, between cultures, are far from being assured.[10]

Scroll forward: A decade beyond the Obama transition, the election of Donald Trump confirmed that the United States was not safe from a global tilt toward populist nationalism, nor to the impact of the Enlightenment's end.

My set-aside fascination with the meaning and power of folklore and folklore studies was rekindled. The challenges of our new age of disarray seem especially amenable to the insights, perspective—the *stance*—of folklore studies. Across the globe, from the Taliban to the Tea Party, new disrupters were often the very villagers, rural populations, ordinary people who were the much-admired and much-examined objects of folklore studies. For nearly two centuries folklore scholars had maintained a critical but sympathetic connection with ordinary people. Insights of colleagues and mentors in the field had provided me with the keys to understanding identity, artistry, community, belief, ethnicity—even race. How must we respond? What new knowledge and what new engagements can breathe new life into Enlightenment ideas? These questions led me back to an argument I had advanced for years in books, essays, and lectures: Folklore constitutes a critical realm of human behavior; folklore studies explains how traditional practice works in the world, insight critical to understanding and engaging realities unsettling our current global order. Had a recently reconfigured global order suddenly assigned unique value to folklore knowledge? Nothing is more important to a scholarly discipline than the way it moves in the larger world. Could the way folklorists engage deep difference, and the way folklorists build meaning from this engagement, hold the key to understanding where we are today and how we must now move forward? Can this argument suggest specific achievable actions to counteract destructive forces afoot at home and around the world?

Gradually my search for understanding became an argument for change. We must abandon the conceits of colonial and imperial thinking, envision and build new relationships within the metaphorical border where the world of literacy, sophistication, and manners intersects the oral world of tribal practice and ancient religious belief. Folklorists have been there; maybe folklore studies can provide the knowledge and insight essential to forging this new, attentive relationship between globalized wealth and power and the billions who live in other ways.

Great uncertainty chills the air, around the world and in America. Worldwide disarray has been explained as a response to globalization, instability in a post–Cold War era, the fecklessness of modern governments, the rise of ancient societies, and the collapse of the hegemony of liberal democracy. This modern dilemma has been assigned to religious extremism, economic decline, or the frustrations of underpaid workers resentful of both governments and wealthy elites who have taken their livelihood. But it seemed to me that these were symptoms: the deeper challenge was an overarching collapse of a commitment to shared values that had defined purpose and quality of life for centuries. I was drawn toward a big idea. Yes, folklore studies possessed meaning beyond predictable boundaries of scholarship and presentation, but I now believed that folklore studies held the handbook of perceptions and prescriptions critical to solving the dangerous puzzle of our disrupted age. I came to a big question: If the end of the Age of Enlightenment is the best frame in which to analyze and understand a world in disarray, how can the approach of folklore studies—the *stance* of the field—help policy actors understand the present-day crisis and mark the smartest path forward?

:   :   :   :   :

No society is forever; no movement is permanent. This truth offers no comfort, for the end of the Enlightenment portends the painful loss of aspirational values in place for centuries. The shared assumption that freedom, social justice, and secular, citizen-directed government are permanent, unquestionable features on the horizon of human development is deeply embedded in rhetoric and policy throughout the West and beyond. The Enlightenment advanced a powerful sentiment—We Are All In This Together. Enlightenment thought inspires the universalized, heartwarming imagery of Edward Steichen's *Family of Man* and justifies the declarations and conventions of UNESCO and the United Nations, programs of the US government, US aid agencies, and NGOs. There has been little inclination to contest Enlightenment givens, and little understanding that the intellectual constellations essential to navigating modernity could be challenged and overturned.[11]

The Enlightenment stands as civilization's great gift to a world—every life has meaning, rationality and science validate action, and governments enable dreams. If a centuries-old Enlightenment consensus is eroded, life-shaping problems will no longer be considered within a context of agreed-to moral frames. We are in a new situation that we must try to understand; questions long-answered must now be taken up again. As columnist Beverly Gage wrote, "Issues once assumed to be settled—the desirability of racial tolerance, a general preference for democratic processes—now appear, suddenly and ominously, to be up for debate. For many, this has created a sense of rupture, a disconnect between what they had assumed would be happening at this moment in history and what is actually taking place."[12]

But even a cursory look at enlightenment's arc reveals a tragic truth: civilization's inclusive dream of universalized values failed not in vision, but in execution. In the advancement of lofty ideals, ordinary people were missionized, exploited, suppressed. Today, Enlightenment's seemingly fixed lessons are resisted; a beautiful vision has finally succumbed to centuries of bad behavior. A strident nationalism advances, even as an aggressive transnational tribalism fuels global terror. Fractious pluralism threatens cultural authority. An especially muscular capitalism—empowered by advertising, digital media, global manufacture and trade—exacerbates the real and perceived suffering of the have-nots.

Scholars of political science and history have done their best to characterize our present-day troubles. For some history simply stopped at the end of the Cold War, leaving liberal democracy poised for permanence; others assert we are caught up in a "clash of civilizations," pitting emerging societies against our Western establishment. Or perhaps we can calm a "world in disarray" by committing governments to a new comity among established nation-states. But these and other explanations advanced by experts are mired in old, inadequate understandings—military options, economic systems, trade, cultural distinctions, reconfigured national objectives. We need a *new* big idea—a broad framework of shared understanding within which to interpret changing circumstance.[13]

As my study of folklore's essential value led me to pioneers and their essential, evolving theories, the wisdoms coined by America's anointed policy actors seemed increasingly wrong—helpful at times but ultimately far short of the mark. In truth we are immersed in transformation that extends beyond politics and official power, and, like the Renaissance, the Dark Ages, and the Industrial Revolution, our age will one day have its own name. But that will take time. Now we must simply do our best to understand where we are. Today Gabler's "post-Enlightenment age" has finally emerged as a popular trope of cultural criticism, a phrase that if true insists that we take the time to understand just what is implied—what is lost, what is at risk, what can be done.

And what of folklore studies, the field of inquiry I wish to celebrate? In its earliest rendition folklore was "stuff"—tales, songs, practices: the *lore* of ordinary people. Writing in *Cultural Democracy*, Bau Graves defines folklore as "an expression of tradition within its own community. It is the way tradition manifests itself in the creative acts of daily life." Richard Dorson's 1968 definition fits my argument especially well: "the hidden submerged culture lying in the shadow of official civilization." In the early 1970s folklore scholar Dan Ben-Amos sidestepped the foundational notion of folklore as essentially an aesthetic product; it is instead simply "artistic forms that are part of the communicative process in small groups." For Lynne McNeill it is, just as simply, "informal, traditional culture." So folklore doesn't just belong to the past, to rural people, ancient tribal societies. As humor specialist Elliott Oring observed, "There has been a long-standing effort by folklorists to strip the term *folk* of any mandatory historical or social footing." To me this is a good thing, as there has been a parallel and equally persistent effort to shift the focus from folklore as a body of material toward an understanding of folklore as a *process* that offers a way of framing experience and organizing behavior that stands outside the formal conventions of civilization. Over decades, folklore scholarship gains both relevance and authority as its focus shifts from exploring folklore as a product of civilization's shadow toward tradition-making as a universal process that organizes experience in important ways. These changing perceptions and understandings will be an important part of my argument.[14]

Where does folklore studies belong? The field has sipped the Kool-Aid of social science, but for the most part is comfortably planted in the humanities. In fact, although it is not my purpose, some might interpret my celebration of the folklore perspective as a critique of economics, sociology, psychology, and their pervasive, overblown stature. The social sciences have exerted profound and often pernicious influences on public policy. If my argument chips at the margins of this sad reality, that is fine with me.

I have organized this book around aspects of folklore knowledge that can illuminate critical issues facing America today. Key big-idea questions: What is the Enlightenment idea? How was it extended into the twenty-first century and how has it lost authority? What is America's true character; what challenges are inherent in who we are? How do we explain the thrust of terrorism—the inexplicable willingness of sheltered youth to pursue a risky religious quest? How do we understand and engage inescapable difference and diversity? Most important, what is the special *stance* of folklore studies? How can the underlying values of a humble discipline help us understand why our modern world seems so undone; how can the observant, patient, critical insights of a venerable field help the Enlightenment dream begin again?

: : : : :

A note about terminology. Like *history*, folklore names both an academic discipline and an area of study. Unlike history, many terms used to designate specific genres of folklore also have everyday meanings—myth, legend, folksong, "folklore" itself. There exists a popular perception that folk stuff is old, unsophisticated, a product of a rural primitivism. It's what we had before we had television. It is made up, simple, maybe—or even probably—not true. Songs that lack complexity; stories that convey a moral center; proverbs, "A word to the wise . . ." There is truth here, but much of the work of folklore studies is not known at all or resides in a bubble of misunderstanding. Early on specialists realized that expressive activity that lived without print had a special character—a close connection with the past, a deep bond with community. But folklore studies also reveals the unspoken, hidden beliefs and understandings that shape behavior in even the most civilized context. A year into Donald J. Trump's presidency, it is clear that all kinds of people—rich, poor, intellectual, powerful—learn through tales, the observation of custom; they act on informal understanding, not rules or evidence. Folklore scholars know this, and through sympathetic engagement with many forms of modernity, it is the folklore scholar who argues that there is more than one valid way for human beings to live. This book is about the way the insights and practices of folklore scholars can frame a new approach to international engagement, understanding, human rights. When discussing the discipline, I will use the phrase *folklore studies*.

Of course, my title contains a made-up word. *Folklorizing* is an invented verb (*gerund* to be precise) that conveys an important point: our reflexive understanding of human behavior is too constrained by legal, scientific, ideological frames; too inattentive to the influence of informal culture. To *folklorize* is to reconfigure our frame of observation and interpretation to emphasize the influence of traditional practice, oral narrative. When a political pundit laments the impotence of law and regulation when measured against the force of custom, precedent, tradition, she is *folklorizing* her view.

The study of folklore was born in the Enlightenment; over centuries the discipline has developed a unique capacity to map both the "what" and the "why" of an important realm of human endeavor. It engages the actual situations of ordinary people, and, in honoring difference, exhibits an especially generous cosmopolitanism. Folklore scholars travel into what they call "the field," living with the communities and artists they study, celebrating what Dell Hymes called universal "human symbolic competence."[15] Folklore studies celebrates positive aspects of everyday life, while admitting that the traditional can also be cruel and at times evil. It is idealistic but not ideological, immune—or at least highly resistant—to civilization's impulse to reform, improve, exploit. Folklore studies has developed an attitude of respectful attentiveness and apolitical advocacy. Folklorists look at everyday society to acquire knowledge of difference and a deeper understanding of ourselves: What does that story mean? Why do they do that? Why don't we? If folklore scholars had been charged with implementing the Enlightenment, it might have worked.

This book opens a large and persistent question: How does *civilization*—global society's permanent but thin upper crust of sophistication, literacy, wealth, and power—interact with what has been called *the Other*—ordinary people, small groups, the public? It will suggest the ways the stance of folklore studies can transform this interaction. My sense of civilization is very close to the dictionary definition—"a high stage of cultural and technological development." Civilization is that elite segment of society that manipulates wealth and power, defined by literacy, written records, sophistication, refinement, internationalism, manners. Civilized society is a stratum found in every era, in all nations, in every culture. Civilization may be characterized by commercial activity; by the pastimes of royalty; by literature, painting, theater; or by philosophy, inquiry, history. In the past, civilization embraced literacy, politics, the intermarriage of competing royal families. Today, it is Davos, globalization, and harried businessmen cloistered in private airport lounges, piling up frequent-flyer miles. Civilization is where new technologies blossom and transforming ideas originate, but not necessarily where they are primarily put into practice.

Civilization created folklore studies, but folklore's songs, tales, legends, myths, proverbs—oral tradition itself—are the province of mass populations, ordinary people. (It is these often-suppressed people who have historically been viewed through a folklorized lens.) In English our understanding of *civilization* is clear; but its opposite is the blurry and inherently pejorative Other. I will avoid that word, and instead refer to the public, traditional communities, regular people, oral societies, villagers, subnational groups, suppressed peoples, small groups, ethnic groups, tribes, and, ordinary people. As the context at hand demands, I will use these terms interchangeably.

Worth repeating: Although the language of folklore studies is part of the intellectual currency of a scholarly discipline, our terms can be found scattered throughout popular media every day. In casual conversation, *myth* is usually something believed but not true, similar to a *belief*; a *folksong* is a musically simple composition, penned by the performer, accompanied by acoustic instrumentation; a *ballad* is a popular, sentimental love song; a *folktale*, conventional wisdom. And so on.

Even broad concepts that frame fundamental understandings are nagged by shifting meaning. *Culture* can mean fine art or "the sum of all human behavior." *Civilization* can mean "a people" or sometimes "a country" or "a culture." A *society* might designate an entire culture, sometimes a subset. Or society can mean the group that defines a nation— "French society" probably encompasses politics and social groups like farmers or factory workers, while "French culture" may lean toward the arts, cuisine, fashion. So, even when clearly defined, the language used to map identity and the character of groups and their expressive life is easily muddled. To make things more difficult, even expert observers frequently toss around terms without first working through problems of definition.

The language of the Enlightenment embraced everybody—well, maybe not slaves or Indians or women. But everybody that the eighteenth century accepted as *mankind* was now admitted to the human experience—the march of history, human rights. For centuries rural people lived in a cyclical world dictated by weather and the relentless rhythms of birth, death, planting, harvest. To the extent there was a past, it resided in myth and legend; to the extent the future offered promise, it was a heavenly afterlife. Enlightened assertions of universal rights, participatory government, scientific rationalism, a secular notion of the arc of existence brought subnational groups into the mainstream of history. Peasants and workers once seen as trapped on a repetitive treadmill of planting, building, and crafting were joined in a journey of lifelong growth and purpose—not in the hereafter, but right here.

Through inclusive, empowering language, civilization extended a rhetorical welcoming hand to ordinary people. The promise of the Enlightenment, once it was deployed to frame and justify universalist ideologies, captured the imagination of millions. After World War II, with the West triumphant and western values ascendant, there emerged a consensus view of a shared future, described by journalist Pankaj Mishra: "The belief that Anglo-American institutions of the nation state and liberal democracy will be gradually generalized around the world; the aspiring middle classes created by industrial capitalism will bring about accountable, representative and stable governments; religion would give way to secularism; rational human beings would defeat the forces of irrationalism—that every society . . . is destined to evolve just as a handful of countries in the West sometimes did."[16]

But now it seems this will not happen. The ambiguous present is dispiriting, and multitudes have turned away from the perceived failure of liberal capitalism and its underlying Enlightenment values. Demagogues tap into drift and disarray; long-suppressed ethnic, tribal, and religious antagonisms are stirred. An imaginary past defined by heroism, virtue, and violence becomes the lodestar for millions who see no path to a life of meaning and purpose. Internet columnist Christy Rodgers put it this way:

> The Enlightenment was flawed from its inception, a product of collective relationship to the living world that has proven catastrophic. . . . The great error of the Enlightenment's founders and heroes was their attempt to narrow all relevant understanding of the world to the confines of rational thought. To dispense with all other ways of knowing, particularly those that had largely been practiced by women and other "primitives.[17]

Today there exists an unaggregated consensus in America and throughout the world that we are living with "the return of ethnic separatism, the rise of authoritarian populism, the retreat of liberal democracy, the elevation of a warrior ethos that reduces politics to friend/enemy, zero-sum conflicts."[18] This reality, and my search for the deep value of folklore studies led me toward a "big idea"—toward a grand narrative encompassing overarching themes that have shaped the first quarter of the twenty-first century, an argument that would bundle all evidence of disruptive, transformational change into a convincing sense of "where we are," then into an argument about what we must do. *Rebuilding an Enlightened World: Folklorizing America*[19] is an account of what went wrong while civilization marched beneath the banner of its many smug conceits, mishandling western ideals, fueling forces that have shaped the disordered world we confront today. A time of trouble but perhaps not the end. For if the movement of power, wealth, ideology in the world is reconsidered and reshaped, the Enlightenment dream can begin again.

ONE

ENLIGHTENED

SENATORS AND CONGRESSMEN SMILED; MICHELLE OBAMA hugged George W. Bush. On a sunny Saturday morning in late September 2016, President Barack Obama addressed a distinguished audience gathered near the northern end of the Capitol Mall, under the shadow of a looming, bronze-glass-and-steel structure, Washington's new National Museum of African American History and Culture: an important event, the culmination of a decades-long process dedicated to planning and funding an institution documenting and honoring black Americans—their bondage, struggle; their achievements in business, government, the arts. The occasion held special meaning for our first African-American chief executive, and the dependably eloquent Obama reminded his audience of congressional leaders, major donors, and former presidents that our newest Smithsonian museum tells a "story of suffering and delight, one of fear, but also of hope, of wandering in the wilderness, and then seeing, out on the horizon, a glimmer of the Promised Land."[1]

The museum is a reminder of the struggle to "reaffirm the promise of our democracy," a reminder that "all of us are created equal." Although a "clear-eyed" story of black America "can make us uncomfortable," it is "because of that discomfort that we learn, and grow, and harness our collective power to make this nation more perfect." Today "does not prove that America's perfect. But it does validate the ideas of our founding. For this country born of change, this country born of revolution, this country of 'we, the people,' this country can get better."[2]

President Obama was quoting and paraphrasing key elements of America's democratic heritage. The argument was pure Enlightenment, invoking principles of equality, participatory government, human rights, individual achievement, and progress that sparked the American experiment more than two centuries ago. The Enlightenment—a period of intense philosophical and political innovation that began in the late eighteenth century—provided the intellectual underpinnings of democracy; it has remained a subject of fascination for public intellectuals. Writers like Steven Pinker and Gregg Easterbrook celebrate the Enlightenment and the positive impact of science and rational thought on material well-being for millions around the world. But the Enlightenment has been both lodestar and corral, offering ideas and language that inspire while at the same time setting hard boundaries limiting our social, political, and cultural imagination.[3]

The president celebrated America's capacity to wrest "triumph from tragedy," through our ability to "remake ourselves again and again, in accordance with our highest ideals."[4] But this notion—that despite centuries of enslavement, decades of prejudice and extra-judicial police killings, the enlightened American ideal had achieved a long-anticipated embrace with the African-American community—was open to challenge. The handsome new museum memorialized a shallowly hidden truth: the people it celebrated had crafted their potent culture with virtually no help from enlightened power. In truth, even as President Obama celebrated a visible marker of human progress, venerable ideals of equality, social justice, participatory government were at risk throughout the world. From the Middle East to Asia, and in France and Germany, principles assumed to be permanent were under threat. And in the United States, police encounters with our black citizens gave ample evidence that the dream of human rights, equality before the law, government by consent had been realized for the few, not the many.

What was the Enlightenment; what *is* enlightenment? The term denotes two things: First, the Enlightenment was a specific historical period during which human rights came to play a new and defining role in government and society. Political historian John Robertson offers this compact and straightforward definition: "A distinct intellectual movement of the eighteenth century, dedicated to the better understanding, and thence the practical advancement, of the human condition on this earth." Second, the Enlightenment introduced language and ideas that became commonplace in Western politics, justifying and inspiring political action, diplomacy, and inevitably, war. Robertson's deceptively simple sentence is the iceberg-tip of a more elaborate philosophical whole—an intellectual framework that honors science and rational thought, advances concern for the wellbeing of all mankind. Enlightenment assertions were painted in broad strokes—individual rights, democratic government, equality—life, liberty, the pursuit of happiness.[5]

Enlightenment celebrates the individual, believes in the power of reason, honors scientific truth—and this is important—believes that a heavenly destination is not enough—society and government should be rightly judged by the quality of life afforded citizens here on earth. Enlightenment principles were famously memorialized in Thomas Jefferson's assertions that "all men are created equal," endowed with "inalienable rights," and that governments derive "powers from the consent of the governed." As historian Vincenzo Ferrone explained, enlightened thinkers envisioned "a society without slaves, that was cosmopolitan, egalitarian, and founded on justice, the rule of law, and the rights of man."[6] And Enlightenment ideals required neither demonstration nor proof—they were, as the lawyers say, a priori, or, in Jefferson's phrase, self-evident. As writer Pankaj Mishra put it, the Enlightenment introduced "the earth-shattering idea that human beings could use their own reason to fundamentally reshape their circumstances." Enlightenment's broad assertions, memorialized in our Declaration of Independence, attained a permanent foundational role in discussions of the American experience, in the American Dream, and in worldwide efforts to improve the lot of the masses. They leaven the language of every US president.[7]

Enlightenment was the intellectual invention of eighteenth-century civilization, the product of a small group of elite, educated, secular-minded men insulated within the literate, wealthy, internationalized upper crust in England, the United States, and a few European countries. Accelerated by technology—the printing press played a critical role in the spread of Enlightenment argument—the ambitions of an expanding cohort of urban sophisticates fueled intellectual inquiry in Europe, England, and America. Their shared vision linked a new secularism with confidence in reason and science into a set of universal principles grounded in a vision of human progress and perfectibility. The

Enlightenment morphed to *enlightenment*—the intellectual legacy of a distinct period of history was distilled and memorialized as a permanent state of mind unique to the West.

Though on its face respectful of religious authority, enlightenment encouraged critiques of church intolerance and clerical pretension; an approach that was ultimately subversive. Assumed triumphant, reason made religious observance optional, arguing convincingly that a good, secular society offered the real possibility of human betterment—here on earth rather than in an afterlife; now rather than in some promised, magical future—no intervention by priest or pastor required. Enlightenment offered moral and intellectual autonomy—the ability of individuals to do good and think big thoughts independent of clergy and royalty. Truths could now be thought through, becoming both more expansive than religious edicts and more analytical than mere observations. Wise human beings could reason their way to universal principles of human interaction and government, and these could be enacted for the benefit of all. As Mishra puts it, absent religion, the world would now be subject to a "quasi-religious belief in continual progress"—progress realized through the efforts of "the self-affirming autonomous individual who, condemned to be free, continually opens up new possibilities of human mastery and empowerment."[8]

The Enlightenment promised that beneath earthly manifestations of difference, there exists a fundamental unity that might enable mankind to negotiate difference, misunderstanding, motives. As Ferrone notes, from the time of the Enlightenment forward, "man and his faculties were at the origin of all knowledge."[9] But man-at-the-center was understood in two distinct ways: as a subject to be engaged by hard, rational science and as an object of sentimental, nostalgic curiosity—Voltaire versus Rousseau. These two sides of the Enlightenment coin—the rational and romantic—lived cheek-by-jowl in late eighteenth-century thought.[10] When interest in the expressive lives of everyday people stirred in the nineteenth century, it was no surprise that curiosity about "the folk" mixed scientific investigation with sentimental enthusiasm for the virtues of premodern rural life. The distinction remains a feature of folklore studies today.

By the late nineteenth century, the rhetoric of enlightened policy had not only captivated a generation of intellectuals but had rationalized both the American revolt and the French revolution. As everyone knows, it was the United States that placed Enlightenment ideals at the heart of the nation's founding documents. Having thus memorialzed its faith in individual achievement and commitment to Enlightenment principles, the United States can make a legitimate claim to standing as *the* "Enlightenment nation." We still talk about ourselves using Enlightenment language. Columnist Paul Krugman recently restated our familiar defining trope: "What makes America America is that it is built around an idea: the idea that all men are created equal, and are entitled to basic human rights."[11] When Barack Obama affirms "the promise of our democracy," he is exercising the legitimate US claim to its enlightened inheritance.[12]

For more than two centuries, the handshake between enlightened thinkers and everyday people produced an inspiring but mostly rhetorical commitment to social justice, human rights, civility in the conduct of nations, citizen participation in government. As we have seen, this Enlightenment consensus has framed human aspiration. It is honored in founding documents and the language of government around the world, institutionalized in the United Nations, UNESCO, the World Bank, the Clinton and Gates foundations. The Enlightenment consensus promised the benefits of science, holding out the hope that well-imagined secular societies could offer a workable version of heaven on earth for all.

Enlightenment didn't come with an instruction manual. The big, rational, inclusive dream floats like a constellation up high above real life; there were no specifics about how a lofty vision could be brought down to the everyday world of institutions, policies, process. It's one thing to imagine equality, quite another to figure out how to realize the dream. And, unfortunately, inspiring language is adaptable; over centuries we've been accepting of enlightened rhetoric attached to pretty much anything—the constitution of every authoritarian state is "democratic"; Ho Chi Minh quoted Jefferson in a 1945 address. And in the dream, everybody was said to have rights. But scratch beneath the surface and "mankind" turned out to be a pretty select "everybody"—no slaves, women, rural masses, dark-skinned peoples. And the achievement of an enlightened society would seem to require significant measures of tolerance, mutual respect, reciprocity—but those implementing values are strikingly absent from Enlightenment arguments. No surprise that critics have continually zeroed in on disconnects between enlightened language and grim reality—the cynical distance between vision and failed implementation. Reacting to the familiar American-character trope employed, in this case by Senator Jeff Flake of Arizona, to keep violent, right-wing protests at a distance, "Hate and bigotry have no place in this country," opinion writer Lindy West wrote, "Really? Which America is that? Surely not the America that was stolen from indigenous peoples, that was built by slaves, that interned the Japanese, that has the highest maternal death rate in the developed world, . . . that has had one black president, zero female presidents, zero Jewish or Muslim presidents. . . . There might be freedom and love and audacity in the weft of our national fabric, but hate and bigotry are in the warp."[13]

So *if* the United States is the Enlightenment nation, what does that mean? Is it what we believe, or what we've done? America's founding documents offer a gauzy vision of a new social order; but a vision is not a program—eighteenth-century civilization told us what to *believe*, but not what to *do*. Once the French and American revolutions had forever disrupted the prerogatives of royalty and church, what was to be done; how would change be achieved?

: : : : :

Ferris, the central character in John Hughes's famous 1986 movie, *Ferris Bueller's Day Off*, dodges a test on European socialism, explaining, "Isms, in my opinion, are not good. A person should not believe in an ism, he should believe in himself."[14] Bueller—the charming, risk-taking, instigating, authority-challenging rogue may well have been right. Enlightenment came without an instruction manual. The world needed explanations, objectives, programs, and it was the nineteenth-century world of isms that stitched Enlightenment ideas into banners of belief, understanding, organization. The Enlightenment does not come to us directly, but through an interpretive framework of a few key nineteenth-century isms that converted (sometimes *perverted*) the inclusive dream of eighteenth-century thinkers and dreamers into a set of broad explanations and action-oriented interventions.

The big three—Darwinism, Marxism, Freudianism—are so deeply embedded in the recesses of Western thought that we can't see them as in any way conditional. The reflexive, almost automatic understandings we apply when confronting change and progress, human desire, the workings of society, the character of life itself, are anchored not in Enlightenment values, but in Enlightenment language interpreted and put in play by ideological intermediaries devoted to specific understandings, practices, outcomes. So when we observe the Enlightenment and its collapse, the failure is not in the original dream but in Darwinism, Marxism, Freudianism (and a few additional isms) that converted Enlightenment principles into rules for engaging the world.

The Merriam-Webster dictionary declared *ism* its Word of the Year in 2015, but it was the nineteenth that could be called the "century of isms."[15] Take a noun, attach *ism*, and you've got something more—a theory, doctrine, movement; an ideology justifying action; something to believe in; something to follow. Isms define religious faith (Mormonism), bundle public policies (protectionism), rally loyalties to a group or cause (feminism). Dozens and dozens of isms exist, but only five or six took up enlightened ideas of human rights, individual achievement, democratic government and made them operational.

This is what matters; this is what has collapsed. Although eighteenth-century moral arguments and lively debates fascinate, let's turn to the situation today: How have the real-world applications of Enlightenment language and ideals, filtered through various doctrines and movements, failed to secure anything resembling an equitable, stable world order, instead delivering multi-century misery, wars big and small, disruptive interventions in the lives of everyday people? How has enlightened language enabled and justified actions and interventions that subvert long-established values of the public, disrupting centuries-old communities, suppressing venerable ways of living? Ferris Bueller was right: "isms are not good." They offer fun-house-mirror distortions of the Enlightenment dream but today form the undiscussed, unchallenged intellectual frame of policy imaginings in the West. So when the brilliant French intellectual Michel Foucault set out to expose "the less commonly

understood historical consequences of the power exercised by rationality and knowledge," he was attacking not the Enlightenment but its
nineteenth-century ideological offspring—the century's isms.[16]

Consider Darwin: Charles Darwin's brilliant research reached deep
into Western society and resonates today. Evolution spawned a cornu-
copia of ideas that not only reconfigured our understanding of man's
place in the world but advanced explanations of change, progress, competition, achievement that could be quickly reconfigured to explain the
dynamics of history, society, government. Darwin's argument advanced
a rational, secular view of the how and why of mankind, an idea of progress in which both biological and cultural standing was achieved through
competition and struggle.

Darwin's study of the animal kingdom was perfectly timed to establish a framework for implementing enlightened understanding. He
gathered data in the early 1830s—two decades later he was lecturing on
his findings. His book *On the Origin of Species* was published in 1859 and
was a sensation, especially in the United States, gaining authority far beyond its original scientific frame of biological evolution. Civilized elites,
unsettled by decades of disruptive challenge to long-held prerogatives,
were quick to seize on the unarticulated potential of the great scholar's
argument—a scientific understanding of cultural difference and social
dynamics, especially a theory that justified their status: "They invoked
key Darwin phrases—'natural selection,' 'survival of the fittest,' and 'the
struggle for existence'—to assert the innate superiority of the era's 1 percent, and to declare people at the bottom of the social order as innately
ill equipped to succeed in the competitive race of life."[17]

This turn—"social Darwinism"—felt scientific but mostly legitimated assumptions (or prejudices, or folkloric beliefs) about innate
ability, ambition, the virtue of competition, and most important, the
confidence that a rational, scientifically demonstrated process brings
the most worthy, most capable people to the top. Individuals and whole
groups—tribes, societies, communities—could now be placed at a particular stage of development, assigned space on a continuum from savage
to civilized. Similarly, cultural difference could be linked to physical
characteristics—race, gender—handing the powerful reasons to ignore
or even suppress entire peoples. This arrogantly deployed justification
for embedded social hierarchies comforted elites, providing exploitative

realities with a cover story of reform and improvement targeting the conditions and capacities of ordinary people stuck on lower rungs of evolutionary progress. All could now be couched in the smug, rational authority of science. Of course, social Darwinism lost authority decades ago, but when we frame racial conflict, consider the plight of refugees or needs of hurricane victims today, deep, firmly held beliefs about development, progress, individual capacity, social organization still shape understanding. In the spring of 2018, *National Geographic* accepted a University of Virginia report documenting the publication's racist heritage. Urban, educated blacks were never featured. Instead, "Black people were presented as static, primitive, and non-technological, often unclothed or presented as savages."[18] Such Darwinian assumptions of struggle and difference have become especially reflexive and strong in the age of ISIS, Trump, and the Tea Party.

Karl Marx (with Frederic Engels) published his *Communist Manifesto* in 1848. A disappointed mid-century revolutionary, Marx relocated from Germany to England and set out to develop a natural science of history and society that would help justify dramatic political change. Observing the harsh conditions of early industrial production in England, Marx theorized that family and community life were determined by the economy—wealth and work—and that economic standing divided every society into distinct classes. Thus long-established reservoirs of identity—culture, religion, politics—became mere subsets of the economy. For Marx, history traced progressive change—various economic models arose, were dominant for a time, collapsed; the inexorable trajectory of society was forward: a march toward a stateless, classless society.

A word about progress—Darwin repurposed by Marx. The notion of human progress over time, the assumption that economic factors have the biggest role in human motivation and human identity, the sense that life is a competitive struggle for limited resources, is perhaps the most deeply embedded, the most influential, and at times the most pernicious aspect of our Western worldview. As Marxist historian Eric Hobsbawm put it, the Enlightenment's champions "believed firmly (and correctly) that human history was an ascent, rather than a decline or an undulating movement about a level trend."[19] Progress moves mankind toward an earthly heaven; progress is essential; progress is good, justifying intervention, coercion, control.

The demise of the Soviet Union discredited Marxism as a model for historical change and dispensed with the utility of communism as an approach to organizing society. But like Darwinism, elements of Marxism burrowed deep into Western consciousness, and the idea of economic man—motivated and defined by income, work, consumption; the notion of class defined by wealth—remain features of the way we reflexively invoke isms' corrupted Enlightenment legacy.

Marx interpreted the social dimension of the Enlightenment's promise. Sigmund Freud codified the movement's focus on the individual. Our understanding of the character and motives of economic man—dog-eat-dog competition, survival of the fittest, the inevitable tilt of progress, the power of markets, was significantly enhanced by Freud's theories about the formation of the unconscious and its subterranean role in adult life. Freud taught us "how our childhoods echo through us, sometimes trapping us, or how our identifications with early figures in our lives shape the complicated humans we become."[20] This powerful idea blended with notions of competition, economic motive, progress. The mystery of human impulse and action could be explained not by race, gender, or ethnicity, but by childhood experience—experience hidden away in the unconscious, a lurking influence powerful enough to shape adult behavior. If our ordinary worker or elite capitalist manager acted out in some way, we could look to greed, envy, or ambition, but now observers might just as easily seek the cause of disruption in bad parenting, schoolyard bullying, or early sexual abuse.

The isms spawned not only argument but research—capitalism and Marxism gave us modern economics, social Darwinism sociology, Freudianism psychology: Enlightenment themes, gathered up in ideologies, empowered by social science. It is the civilized oral traditions from these movements and disciplines—the folklorized norms, tropes, and customary explanations—that are the deep knowledge of the West, fixing the limits within which we interpret and engage the distant, unfamiliar world. The embedded assumptions of Darwinism, capitalism, Marxism, Freudianism have shaped understanding. Nationalism and colonialism have shaped the way we link understanding to action and power. Ferris Bueller was right.

Once enlightened thought was explained and empowered by ideology, some kind of action was inevitable. Now, at last, government, society, mankind could be better—people could be happier, more fulfilled, immune to the prejudices and superstitions that plagued earlier times. It might have been otherwise. Consider: once the masses were made part of history, once enlightenment advanced the idea of equality, it might have seemed appropriate and opportune to engage difference in a new way, exploring and even embracing alternative forms of knowledge, engaging distant strangers to expand ways of understanding. But things did not go that way. In practice, equality quickly gave way to hierarchy, openness was replaced by authority, the need to listen and learn was sidelined by arrogance. The nineteenth century took up Enlightenment rhetoric, forced it into a scientific frame that reconfigured it, slyly reintroducing old beliefs about race, distant societies, alternative knowledge, exotic cultural practices. Once government embraced science, progress, ideology, the West's new rendition of the Enlightenment dream would be truly dangerous.

: : : : :

In the fall of 1966, as a first-year graduate student, I enrolled in "Folklore and Anthropology," taught by John Messenger, specialist in the folk and lore of the Aran Islands, dots of isolation featuring farm settlements rich in tradition, close beside Ireland's west coast. Messenger, a burly, garrulous lecturer, spoke constantly of his Irish experience, but our first assigned reading was about Africa, novelist Chinua Achebe's properly revered 1958 novel invoking the challenges of a Nigerian Igbo community encountering British imperial power, *Things Fall Apart*.

Achebe offers a sympathetic but clear-eyed window into the ambitions, jealousies, alliances of African tribal society, presenting the struggle for cultural authority within the border separating civilization from traditional lifeways in which the author's flawed hero, Okonkwo, navigates a complex network of ritual and custom that determines standing and influence within his village.

Okonkwo's friend, Obierika, tells him of the white man who comes to the village on a motorcycle:

> The elders consulted their Oracle and it told them that the strange man would break their clan and spread destruction among them. And so they killed the white man and tied his iron horse to their sacred tree because it looked as if

it would run away to call the man's friends. I forgot to tell you another thing which the Oracle said. It said that other white men were on their way. They were locusts, it said, and that first man was their harbinger sent to explore the terrain. And so they killed him.[21]

The struggle for cultural authority within the border separating civilization from traditional lifeways quickly becomes personal. Okonkwo resists and in an ultimate confrontation takes his own life. The British district commissioner defies Igbo custom by refusing to take down Okonkwo's body; such an act "would give the natives a poor opinion of him." The officer contemplates his experiences "bringing civilization to Africa."[22] Confident on reflection, he decides to write a book entitled *The Pacification of the Primitive Tribes of the Lower Niger.*

This is colonialism—the ism that elevated nineteenth-century assumptions about the character, potential, and rights of ordinary people to a central position in Western government policy. This was enlightened thinking corrupted and reconfigured as national ambition; economic expansion; alien language, law, and learning forced on the masses. It was imperial reach and colonial management that carried Enlightenment ideas into the modern age. Colonialism deployed military and economic power to dominate or subjugate ordinary people in societies considered by the West to be undercivilized. Colonialism bundled the assumptions of Enlightenment-empowered ideologies, combining the racial and ethnic hierarchies of social Darwinism, Marxian economic man, the understanding that Western society stood atop the ladder of cultural achievement—civilized, entitled, righteous.

We read Achebe knowing how Africa and colonialism worked out; we understand that while a few white strangers may be killed or captured, others will be back, in greater numbers, armed with laws, the conceits of civilization, powerful weapons. No matter that the Igbo can fight back at first; the die is cast, the West and its values will conquer, marginalize, and ultimately eliminate whole societies grounded in orality, folklore, tradition.

Achebe's district commissioner is a stand-in, a metaphor, for a century of colonial rule, the always confident and sometimes cruel face of imperial power in remote tribal settings. By foreshadowing the destruction of Igbo society, the author intends *Things Fall Apart* as tragedy, and he is correct; it is an insensitive reader indeed who does not grieve for

Okonkwo, his good friend Obierika, the Igbo, and the subtle complexities of tribal life soon to be shattered by imposed Western ways. Charmed and romantically nostalgic for the richness of village lives lived "close to the ground," we lament the permanent loss of innocence, charm, and dignity; Achebe would agree.

The conceits of colonialism—the sense of cultural superiority and entitlement that framed the West's engagement with the masses—enjoyed remarkable staying power. The British in India, the United States in its oppression of blacks and suppression and dislocation of Native Americans, the French and then Americans in Southeast Asia, and Americans, again, in Vietnam and Afghanistan—these and many other Western nations claimed territory, imposed government institutions, extracted resources, relocated peoples, confidently expressing faith in Enlightenment principles while acting out very old tropes of race, ethnicity, nationality, power. It was a paradox highlighted by historian Edmund Morgan: "The rise of liberty and equality in this country was accompanied by the rise of slavery. That two such contradictory developments were taking place over a long period of our history, from the seventeenth century to the nineteenth, is the central paradox of American history."[23]

Morgan's American paradox was by no means limited to slavery. David Reynolds, writing about the removal of Native Americans to the West, the deportation of blacks to Africa, observes that the paradox was generalized, characterizing the relationship between "the nation's egalitarian ideals and its unjust treatment of ethnic minorities."[24] The British colonized India, not only imposing English as an official language, but similarly installing educational, legal, and governmental functions just like those at home. All this accomplished with an enlightened rhetorical flourish, driven by notions that the Indian people were "like little children," untrustworthy, lacking in self-discipline, hard to educate, exemplary of a culture that was better than savage but by no means civilized. As historian Alan Greenberger pointed out, "the image of the Indian as a child fitted in very nicely with the British image of himself as a strong all-knowing leader."[25] This sense of the colonial spirit—armed with what historian Alain Peyrefitte describes as "the West's virtually messianic faith in itself"—was both oppressive and paternalistic, curious about exotic ways but closed off to real new knowledge. Peyrefitte shorthands the tragic irony of interaction between Europe's universal principles and the reality imposed on global publics: in the end, "the populations subject to European domination were denied liberty, equality, and fraternity."[26]

· · · · ·

"Once upon a time there was a rich man who lived happily with his wife for a long time, and they had one little girl together." Yes, these old stories really started this way. In fact, this "once upon a time" (translated from German) begins the famous tale of "Cinderella" as it appears in the first volume of *Children's and Household Tales*, published in Germany by Jacob and Wilhelm Grimm in late 1812. This narrative, famously interpreted by Walt Disney Studios in its 1950 animated feature film, concludes just as we would expect: The prince, seeking his mysterious dancing partner, proffers the golden slipper. Cinderella, maligned and mistreated by her wicked stepsisters, tries it on. "After she pressed a bit, her foot fit as though the slipper had been made for her. And when she stood up, the prince looked at her face and recognized the beautiful princess once again and cried, 'This is the right bride!'"[27]

Most of the plot was transferred directly to film—magical, helpful animals, elegant gowns, a menacing midnight deadline. Although the Disney creative team cute-ified birds and rabbits, and fabulated gowns, they excised edgier content: In the Grimm original, Cinderella's mother dies; her father's remarriage is the source of stepsisters who "did everything imaginable to cause her grief and make her look ridiculous," forcing her to "lie next to the hearth in the ashes." When the prince travels the countryside seeking the woman whose foot will match the golden slipper, her desperate stepsisters, encouraged by their mother, take a knife to heel and toe in the hope of fitting the slender shoe. "It will hurt a bit. But what does that matter? It will soon pass, and one of you will become queen." But the prince, appalled that "blood is spilling out of the slipper," quickly figures out that he is being deceived.[28]

The Grimm brothers were students of German linguistic history and were among the first scholars to gather stories told by maids and footmen, farmers and rustic tradesmen. This is the beginning of what came to be called folklore, and the Grimms were pioneers—an 1816 publication date places their collection as one of the earliest attempts by educated, urban scholars to sympathetically connect with rural creative practice.

The collection and publication of these old tales should be viewed as an enlightened endeavor—respect for peasant culture was a new idea in the early nineteenth century. Like the work of earlier Enlightenment intellectuals, the Grimms' collecting was greatly aided by technology; specifically, eighteenth-century advances in printing and publishing. Communication technology enabled civilization to spread new ideas within literate society and across borders, creating for the first time a kind of global salon devoted to advancing and debating the very ideas that would give the Enlightenment its firm hold on the thinking of Western elites.

The term *folklore* was coined in England in 1846. Like the Grimm's folktale collections, English interest in the expressive life of the masses was one of the earliest applications of Enlightenment inclusiveness to scholarly work. In England, the *Athenæum* was this kind of periodical. Appearing weekly, the size of a modern tabloid, the journal published notes, short articles, letters on a variety of subjects in featured sections— music, literature, the fine arts, and science. It was in two consecutive issues of the *Athenæum* that William John Thoms reframed and recombined the terms *popular antiquities* and *popular literature* into a fresh concept denoted by a new hyphenate—*folk-lore*.[29]

For decades an understanding had existed that rural populations sustained exotic examples of homespun music, beliefs, tales, and customs. The romantic strand of enlightened thinking—nostalgic, sentimental, concerned—elevated the standing of amateur scholars devoted to collecting examples of these songs, stories, and practices. In 1838 Thoms was elected a fellow of the Society of Antiquaries, a position that gave weight to his inquiries into oral narrative and its relationship to literature of the day. Thoms had also encountered the Grimms' collection of German folktales and was mightily impressed. Like many antiquarians, Thoms proceeded from an assumption that modernity—print, transportation, communication—was pressing down upon ancient myths and ancient ways. This was the inevitable obverse of enlightenment's commitment to progress. Progress was good, but progress too often meant simple, rural culture would be left behind. Within enlightenment's romantic wing lay a powerful sense of responsibility for collecting and preserving evidence of the character of a vanishing way of life.

In early 1846, Thoms suggested that the *Athenæum* begin gathering and reproducing "old-world manners, customs, and popular superstition."

Athenæum editors quickly agreed, and it was Thoms himself who introduced the idea in consecutive issues in August of the same year. (Appointed clerk of the House of Lords in 1845, and no doubt sensitive to the constraints implied by his government post, Thoms published his *Athenæum* columns under the pseudonym "Ambrose Merton.")[30]

Framed as a call to fellow antiquarians to gather the tales, beliefs, and festival practices—"subjects not undeserving attention"—Thoms's *Athenæum* columns also introduce concepts that would remain important to future scholars and practitioners. First, of course, is the term *folklore* itself. Foreshadowing Richard Dorson's definition by a century, Thoms neatly reconfigures popular antiquities into something that is about people—folk—and about things—lore. He instructs correspondents to collect narratives from living people—no hint of then-prevalent library research—and suggests that folk lore is movable and changeable, that individual tales, rhymes, or beliefs "become of importance when they form links in a great chain." These were among his key ideas—that folklore was sustained by specific people, that to be true its sources had to be spoken and heard, not read. Finally, while individual bits of lore might be fragmentary and apparently of little import, all lore of the people gained significance as a part of a process that extended over time and space. Although not completely worked out, concepts Thoms introduced would energize sympathetic scholars for the next hundred years.[31]

Two especially important ideas: First, setting aside the exploitative interventions of early explorers and missionaries, the study of folklore was the earliest attempt by civilized society to understand the vast, global public—the millions of previously suppressed peoples who were brought into the mainstream of history by the practice of enlightenment. Second, despite its provenance as the pioneering engagement connecting civilization with oral societies, early folklore studies never gained standing equal to philosophy, literature, or history. Armed with hindsight, it seems that the absence of standing has not been a bad thing. Folklore scholars sensed that too much intervention—the conceits of colonial projections of wealth and power—might well upset the apple cart. The voices of ordinary people, inducted into some partisan or reformist cause, would quickly lose their distinctive character, the very elements that made their art and understanding so valuable. Folklore studies never embraced "folklorism," never framed its own ideology, and was from the beginning tentative in promoting public policy or political movements. With a couple of dramatic exceptions (to be discussed) folklore studies kept a certain distance, was rarely embraced by political leaders as a methodology for understanding or manipulating the multiple, diverse oral societies contained within national boundaries.[32] But as we will see, it may be time for change, and change will take work. If the insights of folklore scholarship possess special value, how can we shift critical knowledge out from beneath the shadow of anthropology, sociology, and other disciplines that dominated cultural thinking through the twentieth century?

We've already seen that the definition of *folklore* and the work of folklore studies has changed over the years. In the early nineteenth century—the era of the Grimms and William Thoms—folklore could be categorized as interesting curiosities: folktales, songs, recipes, customs discovered in the lives of tribes and rural peasant communities. For the first generation of enlightened scholars, folklore was understood as product and creative practice—what might be termed the "accumulated expressive life"—of what were then called tribal and peasant communities. Enlightenment embraced these societies—the men, women, families who for centuries lived outside the civilized, cosmopolitan mainstream of history, literacy, and sophistication. The excitement of early discovery was accompanied by a powerful sentiment that traditional artistry and practice were threatened by the forces of modernity—technology, literacy, commerce. This threat of loss meant the dedicated scholar must first gather up as much as possible. Much collecting was completed, and by the late nineteenth century, once this amassing of traditional materials was well under way, folklore studies gradually shifted focus from things—tales, songs, quilts, cabins—to process: How was traditional knowledge preserved and slowly transformed? How did music and oral literature originate; how did they move from place to place?

Folklore studies learned that tribes and villages possessed history; a special kind of historical knowledge embedded in memory, sustained by oral tradition. While tradition, unlike the written history of civilization, was subject to revision over time, this change-in-public occurred slowly, at the margins of myth, legend, and belief. Even as the nineteenth century configured the new spirit of Enlightenment into rational explanations of human behavior, arguments for social and political reform,

scientific analysis of business and trade, folklore scholarship was patiently gathering traditional expression, gradually advancing toward a
new way of engaging the complexity and variety of human experience.[33]

:   :   :   :   :

But what of the big idea? If Neal Gabler and I are correct—if America
and the world *have* entered a "post-Enlightenment age"—the insights
and stance of folklore studies are essential to understanding where we
are today. If what folklore teaches us is true, a fresh engagement with
the ways folklorists found meaning in the products and process of oral
tradition and traditional communities can inform policy actors in government and business. We are in a global struggle to craft policy that
accommodates or deflects the increasing authority of tribalism, fundamentalist religion, distrust of science, and the rise of societies with different and competing values—forces that reject Enlightenment articles
of faith. An understanding of "the folk" and "lore" can provide us with a
critical insight—a sense of where we are.[34]

We've seen that folklore studies is a child of the Enlightenment.
But early on the work of folklore separated from its evolving parent.
Enlightenment, empowered by colonialism, imperialism, the ideologies
and isms that slotted the public into categories and classes, pathologies
and needs, was not welcoming to a discipline that was observational,
collaborative, non-threatening. The intellectual discomfort was mutual;
as social science acquired the mantle of enlightened rationalism, folklore studies was off to the side. Scroll forward: though colonialism has
faded, the impulse to extend control remains. The United States has
more than two hundred thousand troops deployed in one hundred and
forty countries; two thousand Department of Homeland Security staff
work outside our borders; the US dollar still dominates world commerce.
As Pankaj Mishra notes, Rousseau had it right. In practice the Enlightenment turned out to be "a game rigged by and in favour of, elites: a recipe,
in other words, for class conflict, moral decay, social chaos and political
despotism." This truth shadows us today.[35]

The Enlightenment has foundered, its brilliant conception was undermined from the outset by misunderstanding, by insincere implemen-

tation, and by a cynical suppression and exploitation of folk communities that extended over centuries. Now ordinary people are pushing back. They do not hate us because we are free, humane, or rich, but because we have ignored and suppressed the voices and values of traditional societies. If we are to avoid a future of institutionalized disarray, we must start again—reaffirming a commitment to essential Enlightenment values, but tempering our beliefs by listening to everyday voices from beyond the assumed truths of civilization. If modern civilization still embraces enlightenment, we must begin again with a commitment to social justice, civility in conflict, human rights, and democracy through a genuine cosmopolitanism—one that respects traditional societies and their values, one that understands the limits of our nineteenth-century enlightened ways of thought.

Let's be clear: Enlightenment principles are not circumscribed by the ideologies and ambitions that have corrupted them; its principles readily accommodate humility, restraint, respect for alternative ways of living and thinking. But for nearly two centuries, enlightened ideals have been linked to dismissive intervention, demeaning analysis, the ambitions of wealth and power. Over the same period, folklore scholarship has mostly worked another way—assuming little, asking quietly, "Why are they like that? How are they different from us? What do they really want?" Can we look at, and listen to, traditional expression in order to map assumptions and beliefs; can we determine what fixed perspectives and likely responses are sustained by tradition; finally, can we develop interventions tailored to belief in specific settings, to specific populations? If we move beyond our own confidence in economics, psychology, and a universal desire for progress to *listen*, mapping what is true, critical parts of the Enlightenment dream can be preserved.

Enlightenment got us here, but our challenge is still twofold—to first understand where we are today, and then to find a way to reinvigorate the more generous opportunity long ignored but still resident in Enlightenment ideals. We must consider who we are and what we need and then find our way to a new, genuine cosmopolitan spirit—a spirit of respectful curiosity toward the expressive lives of ordinary fellow citizens and uncelebrated people around the world.

TWO

IDENTITY

"That's not who we are."

> Congressman Paul Ryan on October 2, 2017, the day after a horrific
> assault during which an assassin armed with automated rifles
> murdered nearly sixty country music fans at a Las Vegas concert

THINK ABOUT IT. SAY IT AGAIN: "THAT'S NOT WHO WE ARE."
We've heard the phrase again and again—evoked when some stark reality that runs counter to our presumed American values rears its head. It comes at us from all sides. Tracking presumed liberal soft-headedness, the conservative online political report the *Washington Free Beacon* counted forty-six times that President Barack Obama deployed "what we're not" language during his eight years in office.[1] Applying our folklore-studies perspective, the assertion could be labeled "almost traditional." Columnist Tim Dowling, writing in the *Guardian*, demeans the "not-us" claim as "a catchy way to encapsulate outrage, to address the gap between American ideals and American realities." He notes that when University of Oklahoma president David Boren went public after fraternity members were filmed chanting racist epithets on a bus, he explained (you guessed it), "This is not who we are." Dowling offers a wry clarification: "This is *not* who we are" should be understood as "This is *sort of* who we are" [my italics].[2]

If nothing else, this way of hedging failure and responsibility is grounded in an underlying obsession with identity, although perceptions are muddled. Who are we? Is there a shared *something* in the American situation—values, religion, respect for law—that provides a framework that can encompass American ingenuity, generosity, bravery, and our society's all-too-frequent descent into mayhem, dishonesty, deplorable behavior?

Enlightenment ideals, memorialized in founding documents, made active by nineteenth-century ideologies, categorized and measured by social science, provided an identity template. Wealth, education, race, nationality, sex, childhood experience could be tracked, assessed, and, when crunched as data, could tell us who we were—smart or dull, Democrat or Republican, generous or pinched, successful or failing. But the "that's-not-who-we-are" trope persists. It seems that our unsettled times—the collapse of our Enlightenment consensus, the rise of tribal passions, multiple dislocations—have shaken our sense of ourselves, giving questions of America's identity a fretful urgency. There's been plenty of recent speculation on the subject. Editorial writers of all stripes— sometimes quoting outside authority, sometimes on their own—have taken up the challenge of defining who we are. Americans are variously defined by our shared adherence to a set of founding egalitarian principles, or by our roles as pioneering settlers perpetually seeking and subduing some real or metaphorical frontier, or then again as a cohort of white, Christian English speakers, although we *say* we're defined as a country at ease with diversity.

Consider the ways we still think about the Enlightenment's embraced *other*—ordinary people welcomed into the flow of history. How do we figure out who these different people really are? The reductionist conflation of Muslim faith with violence, even terrorism; our easy assumption that Syria or Iraq are hotbeds of sectarian conflict; or even the notion that urban blacks are defined by economic misfortune that then converts to violence or drug use—each trope exhibits hallmarks of externally crafted identity. Simple but inevitably incomplete. You get my point: a propensity to craft identity using one or two broad strokes characterizes—and constrains—the ways we see each other and the outside world.

In a smart *New York Times* "Interpreter" newsletter in late 2017, Max Fisher and Amanda Taub turned the tables, imagining American leadership and policy explained by outside observers deploying the same sketchy labels we routinely apply to everybody else. Perhaps foreign experts might see Washington as "driven by sectarian grudges against certain tribes," or view us as "obsessed with outdated imperial ambitions," or even conclude that American leadership is "personally insane." To us these stereotypes are far off the mark, but this is exactly the way we talk about countries like Iran, France, and, of course, North Korea.[3]

This truth should not be surprising. Enlightenment thinkers posited a set of ideas that, if honored, would have afforded everyday people an unprecedented opportunity to claim a respected place in a global narrative, advancing the lives of individuals, small groups, and tribes into the mainstream of human history. But as I've argued, although the Enlightenment provided rhetorical commitment to engaging difference and distinction, that legacy was almost immediately reconfigured and then promulgated by its derivative, explanatory, activist isms, converting moral authority into civilized scientific policy and understandings that rationalized venerable stereotypes. Darwinism, Freudianism, Marxism, economics gave Westerners whose thinking never left the back porch plenty of snappy concepts that could easily characterize everyday people as unevolved, neurotic class actors or money-addled hopefuls.

Bolstered by confidence in scientific principles, belief in change and progress, the nineteenth century gave us a hierarchy of human types: Was a distant community or tribe "savage," "primitive" (better), or even somewhat "civilized"? The next hundred years expanded the ability to craft identity from the outside, as the Enlightenment's minions—Freudianism, Marxism, Darwinism—promulgated rational, positivist explanations for identity, behavior, motivation. It was these Enlightenment-enabled movements and their accompanying analytical frames that grew into building blocks we use reflexively to assemble identity today. Now identity didn't reside in the soul or spirit but instead could be divined by mapping an array of factors that, taken together, tell us who we are. Add troubled childhood, economic deprivation, level of education; stir in gender and race—voilà! Identity!

Rather than initiating an exchange between civilization and previously suppressed peoples—a dialogue between urbanity and markedly different ways of life—Enlightenment ideas became fixed in static analytical frames that were imposed on rural and ethnic people. As we have seen, whether in India, China, Africa, or the wilderness of an expanding United States, tribal people were dishonored, subjugated, and exploited in pursuit of objectives suited to the desires of dominant Western societies. Centuries-old cultural practice was forcibly pushed aside to be replaced by corrupted or hybridized renditions of European and American tropes—democracy, judiciary, market economies, public education. Although Enlightenment values are secular at their core, in practice enlightened colonists intent on improving the lives of ordinary people enthusiastically bundled Western policy with the expansion of one form or another of European Christianity. Native languages gave way to French, German, English, Spanish, Dutch; wealth was extracted through one-sided, tightly enforced economic systems. It is this ironic juxtaposition of Enlightenment ideals against oppressive, contemptuous, and often violent suppression of non-Western cultural values, beliefs, practices, and sentiments that gradually earned the permanent enmity of previously ignored peoples now saddled with foreign occupiers.

Set in place by the force of arms and economic might, the imposition of Western values on rural people lasted a long time—for centuries, in fact. No surprise: spotty resistance to colonial authority showed up almost from the beginning. As soon as various renditions of colonial power were secured in the Middle East, India, China, and Southeast Asia, grass-roots political movements worked to extract indigenous populations from the imposed frameworks that served imperialist ambition. But a century of efforts by local leadership to gain control of governments set up by colonial powers have not produced long-term success; today global anger is no longer aimed at government reform, but instead embraces the transnational or subnational tribal passions that define the character of our post-Enlightenment order.[4]

So identity is a source of meaning, pride, and sometimes conflict. European countries and many tribal societies define identity through common language, shared history, and ancient, heroic mythology. A unifying nationalist narrative brings a sense of identity to large populations; the same elements unite smaller groups. Native American tribes are rich in tradition: they assemble identity from shared internalized custom, spiritual belief and practice, ancient tales, music, ceremony, a powerful sense of place. But America's rendition of enlightened values featured little interest in tribal ways of life. While expansionist passions pushed Native Americans to the margins of American civilization, the mainstream, elite society that consolidated power lacked a deep historical and linguistic coherence of its own; lacked the sense of identity that tribal peoples and European nations derived from a sense of shared, deep heritage. Instead, over the years, there arose a conventional wisdom that American identity was constructed directly out of Enlightenment ideas memorialized in our Declaration of Independence. Columnist Paul Krugman again: "The real, real America is a multiracial, multicultural land of great metropolitan areas as well as small towns. More fundamentally, what makes America America is that it is built around an idea: the idea that all men are created equal, and are entitled to basic human rights."[5]

No nation's sense of self is more closely aligned with Enlightenment values than is the United States. Faceless, rural masses were suddenly assigned lives of meaning and purpose. But Europe was different. Unlike America, Europe's identity was grounded in language and history. European folklore scholars worked this frame, mining the culture of rural peasantry, gathering stories and songs assumed to represent the surviving genius of civilized society's forebears. Ancient tales in a shared language came to define what it meant to be French, German, English, and much folklore research was directed by the desire for a venerable, shared, nationalistic identity; folklore scholarship and patriotism merged. But as we will see, an intensifying link between folklore scholarship and nationalism made European folklore scholarship an instrument of state policy and government intent; the discipline would be pulled off center.

America lacked a peasantry and the continent's indigenous peoples were removed from the conversation—marginalized through war, relocation, the suppression of language and cultural practice. Official America was defined by the Enlightenment's familiar universal principles, but the United States lacked an ancient, mythic past, lacked both a shared, expansive history and a common language. Lofty principles by themselves were an insufficient substitute for the unifying force of romantic nationalism. Around the world, enlightened imperialism turned ordinary people into enemies of elite society, while here at home, the Enlightenment dream simply benefited too few for too long, and today our American alternative—the very legitimacy of shared identity grounded in abstract notions of democracy, equality, human rights—is threatened. As Beverly Gage wrote in the *New York Times Magazine*, "Operational standards of our enlightened democracy are open to challenge—the arc of history no longer seems certain." This confusion disrupts, unsettling America's exceptionalist confidence. Suddenly mere difference implies danger; finger-pointing at un-American behavior erupts across the political spectrum; racial resentments rise; foreigners threaten. But to be "un-American" suggests that an American identity is understood. Historian Gage continues: "On the surface, 'un-American' implies consensus: It carries a punch only when everybody agrees what 'American' is. But the word has historically gained traction at moments when national consensus seems the most wobbly and uncertain."[6]

Today the continual invocation of founding principles takes on a defensive tone. But just as enlightened abstractions only made a difference after ideology took them up, principles of individualism, democracy, and social justice can't shape identity. Is the vision sufficiently firm; are documents strong enough? *New York Times* columnist Ross Douthat suggests that the idea that America is "a propositional nation bound together by ideas rather than any specific cultural traditions" is inadequate, because it forces us to transcend, or at least give up, "all non-universalist forms of patriotic memory." Douthat argues that the particular is also part of identity, that we are a "settler culture," dependent on a "Christian moral consensus." This is the America of "Pilgrims and the Founders, with Lewis and Clark and Davy Crockett and Laura Ingalls Wilder," an America that prefers "the melting pot to multiculturalism." Douthat concludes that leaders today must reach "for a story about who we are and were, not just what we're not." But "maybe no unifying story is really possible."[7]

Samuel Huntington, having advanced his notion that our age is defined by a "clash of civilizations," took on the question of American identity. Noting that the Germans, French, and British "define themselves increasingly in terms of ancestry, language, or culture," Huntington argues that the United States lacks a "racial or ethnic national identity." He begins his book *Who Are We?* with an exhaustive litany of rhetorical questions:

> Are we a "we," one people or several? If we are a "we," what distinguishes us from the "thems" who are not us? Race, religion, ethnicity, values, culture, wealth, politics, or what? Is the United States, as some have argued, a "universal nation," based on values common to all humanity and in principle embracing all peoples? Or are we a Western nation with our identity defined by our European heritage and institutions? Or are we unique with a distinctive civilization of our own, as the proponents of "American exceptionalism" have argued throughout our history? Are we basically a political community whose identity exists only in a social contract embodied in the Declaration of Independence and other founding documents? Are we multicultural, bicultural, or unicultural, a mosaic or a melting pot? Do we have any meaningful identity as a nation that transcends our subnational ethnic, religious, racial identities?[8]

Whew! More than three hundred pages later, admitting that we are in "an age of vulnerability," threatened by "external attack and by a new turn to religion," Huntington still doesn't know who we are.[9] He offers no real answers.

America lacked a deep heritage grounded in common language and culture; there was no rural peasantry—realities that at first glance seemed hostile to traditional culture. But the United States quickly emerged as a uniquely fertile environment in which the full potential of folklore studies could be realized. America's shallow history insulated research from the corrupting influences of nationalist pride and government meddling. And in an urbanizing, multilingual immigrant nation, scholars from the beginning were forced to engage the way folklore adapted, reconfigured, and ultimately flourished in multiethnic city communities, cheek-by-jowl with fine art and popular culture. Absent the luxury of identity grounded in the nostalgia and passions of romantic nationalism, students of America's complicated folklore environment were forced to move away from European assumptions, teasing new commonalities by engaging the yeasty brew of a diverse, even disparate cultural scene.

In the late 1950s, two early-career folklorists working in strikingly different settings published research offering unique insight into the way America's situation defines its character. Neither was especially inclined toward theoretical assertion, and neither set out to address the big question Huntington would pose a half-century later—defining an American experience shaped by a unique engagement with nature, community, family, work. Instead, each sought to gather and interpret the expressive life of two distinct regions, and though the theoretical underpinnings of their research were modest—*humble*, in a sense—their insights take us a long way toward defining the identity that all Americans share.[10] Both folklore scholars, working alone, in different regions of the country, approached the question of identity in a new way, reframing the question "Who are we?" to ask, "Where are we?" And with this shift in perspective each came close to defining America's common identity.

:   :   :   :   :

The Upper Peninsula (UP) of Michigan is a harsh-climated near-wilderness at the northern extreme of the Upper Midwest. Running east and west along the south coast of frigid Lake Superior, the UP includes one-third of the total area but just 3 percent of the population of Michigan. Bordered by three Great Lakes, even today slenderly linked to the rest of the state by a single, impressive single-span bridge, the peninsula has a lifestyle shaped by isolation and distance from the relative prosperity and urbanity of Detroit, Flint, or Grand Rapids. Optimistic geographers, intent on enlightening the American public, sometimes use the size and shape of the UP as a simile for Israel—a dubious tactic since the outlines of northern Michigan are no better known than is the configuration of the Jewish state. The economy—based on logging and mining—enjoyed a successful run in the late nineteenth century; as early as 1920 decline had settled in. But despite its persistent obscurity, for Richard Dorson, a Harvard-trained folklorist and historian, Michigan's Upper Peninsula would serve as an arena of discovery and professional opportunity.

Dorson was a New York City kid from a well-to-do family whose elite early education led straight to Harvard University, where by all accounts he flourished. Sporting below-average looks, Dorson compensated by deploying a gregarious personality, both charming and self-confident. He dressed with style. He landed at Harvard a talented prep-trained athlete, and in less than a year captained Harvard's squash team; at the beginning of his second semester he nosed out Bernard Ridder of Princeton to capture the National Intercollegiate Squash Racquets Championship. Dorson worked summers in the family's New York City furniture business, but two years into his undergraduate career, he turned firmly toward the academic life and to the advanced study of American history and culture. While his career would be shaped in research and in the classrooms of Midwestern universities, he carried the competitive spirit of a big-city entrepreneur into the world of scholarship.[11]

Dorson began graduate study at an exciting time. The Jazz Age had morphed into the era of big-band swing; the Harlem Renaissance had secured the power and artistic merit of the vernacular African American voice in poetry and fiction. Literary scholars had shifted focus from England and Europe to the United States; the stature of Melville, Twain, and other US authors grew; in 1939, historian John Truslow Adams coined the phrase, "the American Dream." As in other times of stress and disruption (I include our own), the Great Depression had prompted fresh curiosity about the nature of American identity.

Constance Rourke's 1931 study, *American Humor: A Study of the National Character,* surveyed popular literature, identifying three distinctive American types—the Yankee peddler, the backwoodsman, and the Negro minstrel. Rourke made a convincing case that the nation's expressive life was shaped by the American experience, and that taken together the figures featured in vernacular tales, legends, and songs offered evidence of a unique American character. Rourke's study validated grassroots artistry, linked it to a growing national pride and self-consciousness. Most important, Rourke influenced a generation of scholars eager to turn their talents toward a homegrown cultural scene.[12]

Even elite Harvard University was not immune to this early-century fascination with down-home, rural American culture. When the university approved a degree in what could be termed "Americanism"; no surprise that Richard Dorson was one of the program's first students. As an undergraduate Dorson had already followed Constance Rourke's lead, studying printed versions of tall tales attached to the career of Tennessean Davy Crockett (Rourke's archetypal backwoodsman). His doctoral dissertation was another compilation of folk-stories from printed sources—a collection of New England folktales and legends, published in 1946 as *Jonathan Draws the Long Bow*.[13]

As a graduate student and young scholar, Dorson's work in American folklore had concentrated on stories, jokes, and legends collected by others or published in newspapers and regional magazines. Dorson was an anomaly in folklore studies in the 1940s. The American Folklore Society had been around for a half-century but was at first dominated by anthropologists and later included many amateur writers, collectors, and performers who lacked the intellectual rigor and methodological underpinnings of real scholarship. Folklorists of the day like Stith Thompson, Archer Taylor, and Ralph Steele Boggs approached material from the perspective of literature; Dorson was the first to arrive from history, a "whole civilization" approach grounding folklore work in the American experience.

Dorson stayed at Harvard, earning a master's degree in 1940. Drawn to a promising new curriculum in American history and civilization, he added a PhD in 1943. After a year as an instructor in Harvard's Department of History, he accepted a position in folklore and history at Michigan State University. He would remain at Michigan's land-grant university for more than a decade, publishing several books and rising to the rank of full professor.

Dorson was not much for advancing bold new theories, perhaps from caution bred in his study of history, a field in which most theory was long settled. And he was not a memoirist—he never wrote about underlying enthusiasms that might have revealed the "why" of his research. But a sense of Dorson's personal motivation and purpose can be divined from his professional life and from a close reading of his many publications. Above all, his academic choices had been bold: American civilization was a new Harvard PhD that offered no assurance of professional success. His conversion to folklore studies—a discipline with deep European roots but only a marginal place in American scholarship—was similarly risky. Research in Michigan would also break new ground.

Established in his Michigan State career, Dorson decided to collect traditional narratives in person, visiting the homes, taverns, church socials where tales were conveyed, face-to-face, from person to person, generation to generation. Face-to-face research—"fieldwork" in the parlance of folklore studies—was by the 1940s a marker of legitimate scholarship. Unlike the sociologist armed with surveys, categories, and trends, and unlike the anthropologist drawn to remote tribal societies—closed, functional systems—the folklorist travels to a town or urban neighborhood, settles in, and gains the trust of knowledgeable locals in order to sit, watch, and listen as singers and tale-tellers perform.

The work that defined Richard Dorson's career would be done in the field. His visit to Michigan's Upper Peninsula (UP) was the first important step in what would be a landmark folklore studies career. Remember, Dorson had cut his teeth studying texts based on oral sources. He doubted that the US cultural setting—already saturated by mid-century print and broadcast media—could actually sustain unadulterated oral tradition. That changed in the spring of 1947 when he traveled to the remote and sparsely populated northern region, a territory of miners, loggers, and small-plot farmers living nearly next door to Ojibwa tribes. The pre–Mackinac Bridge UP of Dorson's era was accessible only by auto ferries traversing five miles of open water at the confluence of two Great Lakes, Michigan and Huron (the admired bridge opened in 1956). Once a vibrant timber and mining region, over-logging and competition from new mining technologies in the western United States had tipped the peninsula into a slow decline.

Dorson described folklore in northern Michigan this way: "From my own fieldwork I can suggest some generalizations about the folk-culture complex of the Upper Peninsula. The boundaries are fairly well fixed by the geographical encirclement of the Great Lakes on all sides save the Wisconsin border. . . . The Peninsula is compounded of occupational groups—the lumberjacks, iron and copper miners, and Great Lakes sailors; immigrant groups—the Finns, French-Canadians, and Cornishmen primarily, with a sprinkling of most European nationalities; and the Ojibwa Indians scattered on small reservations."[14] In truth Dorson was "exhilarated and astonished" to discover "one of the great storytelling regions in the United States.[15]

He was delighted that the UP's multiple groups sustained a variety of traditions—local historical narratives, occupational tales that "never cross" from miner to lumberman, dialect stories, tall tales of fighting men and epic feats of stamina, as well as tales, beliefs, and legends with Old

World antecedents. In truth, Dorson was studying an entire region, one that contained many sealed fraternities—homogeneous groups united by race, occupation, neighborhood, ethnicity. For Dorson, each sealed fraternity is a folk. It's the folk who create and sustain the lore—stories, proverbs, songs, beliefs that "come by word of mouth, and are told among closely knit groups." Unlike fixed texts of civilizations, the lore of the folk lives in oral tradition, and the subtle changes introduced through face-to-face transmission gives folklore texts special validity, a truth forged through shared expression refined over time: "We ask that lore live in people's mouths for at least several generations, that it be shared by many, that it bear the marks of much handling."[16]

Decline had begun decades earlier, but the region Dorson explored in the late 1940s had been hit especially hard by the Great Depression. Although mining lived on into the 1960s, and some hardwood logging is practiced even today, the UP never regained its early standing as a center for extractive industries. As early as 1911, business leaders in Upper Michigan and northern Wisconsin actively pursued business opportunities that might free the region from industries subject to resource depletion and the vicissitudes of shifting demand. They settled on tourism, and the image of an isolated pristine north woods blessed with unique scenic beauty, fishing and hunting, clean air, and a cool summer alternative to big-city grime and heat became a marketing theme and an internalized self-image.[17]

So Richard Dorson was taking on an interconnected set of challenges. The setting was rural and isolated, but everybody read newspapers and listened to local and national radio broadcasts. Attempts to attract tourists driven by a generalized local boosterism had established a set of made-up folk-like tales designed to charm tourists. Upper Michigan had a promoters' sense of self and an "official" history—real oral tradition was hidden from the casual glance.[18] And even when plumbed for legends, tall tales, Ojibwa myths seasoned by oral transmission over time, the region was a jumble of ethnicities, nationalities, and non-English dialect; apart from Ojibwas, everybody was from somewhere else and no single group had the cultural upper hand.

Dorson devoted five months to face-to-face fieldwork in northern Michigan. He encountered traditional storytelling right away. A few hundred miles north of the car-ferry ride across the Straits of Mackinac, the folklorist stopped at a roadside zoo that offered an opportunity to feed the bears in order to question the bearded proprietor, Spike Horn, who approached with a slight limp:

"Why do you limp, Spike?" Dorson asked.

"One night I shot two deer, both bucks, one in the light of the moon and the other in the dark of the moon. I skinned them and made me a pair of buckskin pants. The leg made from the deer I killed in the light of the moon kept shrinking. I cut off the extra length and sewed it onto the short leg but still it shrunk faster than the other one grew, till it shriveled right up and I caught rheumatism from walking around bare."[19]

This is a special kind of folklore: not quite a joke, but amusing; short of mythological but touching on the magical influence of dark and light moons; not a complete tall tale but an obvious exaggeration. "These are folk narratives," Dorson wrote, "folk documents of a sort, filled with the raw stuff of life and filtered through imaginative minds."[20] He found folk tales with European analogues and the creation myths of the Ojibwa, but most of Dorson's Upper Peninsula collecting yielded stories of this sort—narratives grounded in the UP's unique, hardscrabble lifeways, peppered with traditional belief, crafted into a compelling oral performance, and served up to make a point. Often a point about *difference*: who are *we* in comparison to *them*.

Native American jokes make this point. Living in relative poverty in an impoverished region, the Ojibwas looked at white neighbors with a degree of both condescension and bemusement: "Some dude hunters from Lower Michigan stopped off at a reservation on their way to Canada. . . . One spoke to the chief through an interpreter, and asked the nature expert what the winter would be like. 'Going to be long hard winter.' 'How do you know?' 'White people have big wood piles.'"[21] The chief, assumed by slickers to be "close to nature"—an oracle of omen and prophecy—is instead a shrewd observer of white behavior, more than willing to slyly subvert both a pervasive Indian stereotype and the presumption of white sophistication and competence.

Dorson was collecting traditional narratives, but he was also following the trail set by Constance Rourke, searching out an American character, answering the question Samuel Huntington would reprise a half-century later, "Who are we?" Dorson had engaged folk, gathered lore, and in his ten-year effort to assemble evidence into an organized narrative, he had discovered a secret to America's shared identity.

Dorson's insight: Americans live in a border society in which authority is dispersed, where hierarchies are shifting and uncertain, where every citizen is continually forced to establish identity by politely—sometimes humorously—positioning himself or herself in a community where difference is paramount, negotiation a constant, and no single group had been granted an upper hand. While border societies grow up along physical and political barriers, Richard Dorson had discovered border as metaphor—a place where isolation, economic stress, and persistent difference defines region: where holding your position demands continual negotiation and discomfort, where a skilled storyteller can use a familiar tale to define both belonging and independence.

Richard Dorson took years to edit and organize five months of northern Michigan research. Published in 1956, *Bloodstoppers and Bearwalkers* was an important contribution to American folklore studies. Although Dorson found many already-recognized folklore genres—creation myths, fairy tales, legends—in the end he structured his book around traditional historical narratives of the folk groups who together defined separation and belonging in the UP. Chapter titles—"Indians Stuffed and Live," "Canadiens," "Cousin Jacks" (Cornish), "Finns," "Townsfolk," "Miners"—distinguish people, not the stories they tell. Dorson did not set out to describe the American character, he did not mention the border nature of the UP, nor did he speculate about the culturally complicated region as a metaphor for America's borderland nature. But the underlying insight jumps from the page. Dorson understood that folklore was the essential currency of comparison, exchange, and identity in the complex reality of the American experience. He sensed that in America real life was local, and that government and the concerns of civilized modernity had little hold on the imaginations of everyday people: "For the most part the community cares little, and talks less, about past-presidents and power politics; what concerns it deeply, and flavors its "yarning," is the memory of township crises and the neighborhood characters."[22]

Unlike the European model of linguistically and culturally mono-lithic nations (consider France or Germany), US society has always ex-hibited the character of a perpetual border—a place where "distinct cultural formations come into contact and stimulate a search for novel combinations of available resources."[23] Although it can feel like a fron-tier, a frontier is different—distant, shifting, always "over there." A bor-der isn't about exploration, movement, or new territory. Instead we live together in our border nation over the long haul, fated to continually ne-gotiate difference, diversity, security. Dorson's sense of border is almost entirely positive—a place of sharing, pride in distinction, tolerance for difference. In truth a functional border offers unity and pride in times of adversity or great achievement—America in its Great Depression, World War II, the civil-rights movement, our manned space program, Dorson's struggling UP communities. But today America's confidence in the most essential attributes of border is breaking down. The divi-sion is partisan: 57 percent of Americans say "they are outraged enough about an issue to carry a protest sign for a day." Engagement, to be sure, but for Democrats the issue is "gun control," for Republicans, "protect-ing our borders and limiting immigration" and the "right to bear arms." More alarmingly, while 74 percent of Democrats are "comfortable with changes in America," only 29 percent of Republicans agree.[24]

: : : : :

Bloodstoppers and Bearwalkers was published in 1957. The next year Américo Paredes, a newly minted University of Texas folklore-studies PhD, published a revised version of his doctoral dissertation. *With His Pistol in His Hand: A Border Ballad and Its Hero* was a study of the music of the Texas-Mexican border in the isolated, international culture of the lower Rio Grande, or the "Lower Border." For Richard Dorson, the Up-per Peninsula of Michigan was a kind of metaphorical borderland, an iso-lated landscape with limited access to modernity where multiple groups jostled to secure identity and meaning. For Paredes, the Rio Grande bor-der was every bit as isolated as the UP but was a *real* border—half was in the United States; half in Mexico—a river marking political and cultural fault lines that had generated real shooting battles pitting popular Mexican bandits against Anglos like the legendary (but mostly despicable) Texas Rangers. This was (and is) a border defined by dividing lines. In contrast to Dorson, Paredes highlights the conflict, power disparities, violence that can shape the character of border, a cautionary insight that sharpens our understanding of this defining American metaphor, elevating its importance.

Américo Paredes was born in 1915, a year earlier than Richard Dorson. If Dorson's path to folklore studies was direct and privileged, Paredes's journey was gradual and meandering. Son of the Texas-Mexican border, Paredes was an aspiring poet and novelist who performed Spanish-language folksongs on a powerful border radio station. Drafted into the army late in World War II, Paredes served as a correspondent for *Pacific Stars and Stripes*. He remained overseas after the war, covering the complex social and political issues that defined the US occupation of postwar Japan. He was still there when Richard Dorson completed his Michigan research.

Accompanied by a Japanese bride, Paredes returned to Austin to write and study literature. He soon fell under the spell of Robert Stephenson, Mody Boatright, and other folklore studies faculty at the University of Texas, and the field quickly became his passion. He completed his MA and in 1954 received a research fellowship to tape-record music along the Texas-Mexico border. His study of ballads memorializing the exploits of Gregorio Cortez was completed two years later and Paredes earned his PhD. After a short stint at Texas Western University in El Paso, he joined the University of Texas faculty.

Paredes studied a single ballad of the Rio Grande border, "El Corrido de Gregorio Cortez." Here are the first and last verses:

In the county of El Carmen
A great misfortune befell;
The Major Sheriff is dead;
Who killed him no one can tell.

Then said Gregorio Cortez,
With his pistol in his hand,
"Ah, so many mounted Rangers
Just to take one Mexican!"

Of course, the killer is Gregorio Cortez, who rides away, is pursued by vicious Texas Rangers and their equally vicious dogs, and is gloriously martyred in a heroic last stand. The song is the tip of a folkloric iceberg, a small representation of the legendary tales that surround Cortez—a real historical figure who shot and killed Sheriff W. T. Morris in 1901. For Paredes, the Cortez *corrido* and the newspaper accounts and legends that surround Cortez are an entry point into border culture and into the volatile mix of stereotypes, prejudices, and imbalances of power that shape ethnic relations in a remote and isolated region. Here oral tradition, singing, and storytelling performance are windows into the realities of oppression, crime, heroism illuminated by Paredes's folklorist perspective and journalistic instincts.

Dorson's work was observational; Paredes—son of the Rio Grande Valley—was more attentive than Dorson to the ways race, language, nationality could be politicized in a border setting. Although the context and motivation are markedly different, Paredes's description of the lower Rio Grande is remarkably like Dorson's characterization of the Upper Peninsula: "The Lower Rio Grande people lived under conditions in which folk cultures develop. They lived in isolation from the main currents of world events. They preferred to live in small, tightly knit communities that were interested in their own problems. Their type of social organization was the family holding or the communal village, ruled by patriarchal authority under a kind of pre-eighteenth-century democracy. And their forms of entertainment were oral."[25] But there were important differences. "The Rio Grande people lived in tight little groups—usually straddling the river—surrounded by an alien world."[26] If Michigan's metaphorical border was a space of accommodation and negotiation, the Rio Grande was primed for conflict. From the north came the English-speaking *gringo*, which meant "foreigner," and from the south the *fuereno*, or "outsider," the term designating Mexicans of the interior. And these two dominant groups were separated not only by language, but by a set of prejudices and stereotypes that cast the American as trigger-happy and violent, the Mexican as sedentary but inherently cruel.

A close observer of the Texas-Mexican border, an advocate on behalf of Mexican culture and identity, and a journalist-student of postwar relations between the United States and Japan, Paredes always understood the complexities of difference in political terms. As biographer Ramón Saldívar noted, "Paredes was observing, thinking, and writing about the power of national cultures, languages, and literatures."[27] A close observer of cultural interaction in both Texas and Japan, he was convinced that borders are unique environments, populated by multicultural persons whose lives define an environment in which singular notions of political, social, and cultural identity are insufficient.

For Paredes, the border is modern in the sense that old orders of identity and meaning don't work, and new structures must be made up, or imagined. For Paredes, this imagined identity must be transnational; for Dorson, multinational. But the similarity of perspective is striking. Borders are places where unique folklore expressions emerge—narratives shaped by history, elements of tradition, individual imagination and talent. The character of borderland expressive life is not determined by external authority but is invented and sustained by the citizens who continually negotiate a shared set of identities, values, beliefs.

Though disinclined to speak in theoretical terms, Paredes and Dorson together introduce themes of real theoretical import that influenced folklore studies into the twenty-first century. Each understood that the European approach—a rigorous brand of textual scholarship stalked by prideful nationalism—simply didn't apply to the American situation. Further, the United States lacked the rural peasantry that defined "the public" for much of the Old World. In America, the most interesting and instructive American folk communities were often ethnic or racial enclaves within some larger community or city. Responding to disparate cultural realities, Dorson and Paredes present compatible understandings. The two made little effort to trace the historical origins of songs and tales; little attempt to link newly collected materials with European or British analogues. Instead, both scholars focused on the way oral expressive life combined traditional elements with historical events, and the way songs and tales created this way helped protect individual identity while providing a collective sense of belonging in a specific region. Dorson "went broad," sampling a range of oral historical narratives reflecting the ethnic diversity of Michigan's isolated Upper Peninsula. Paredes "went deep," mining the content and context of a single folksong to expose the hierarchies, conflicts, loyalties of the isolated Rio Grande Valley region.

Together, Dorson and Paredes posed a new question: How do disparate groups, lacking shared history and common language, forced together by geography and societal necessity, convert experience into meaningful narratives? Why does this process seem critical to creating and sustaining identity? The two scholars established a new benchmark with special relevance to the complexities of urban modernity. It would take decades for a new generation of folklore scholars to map the essential underlying process by which the lived past is organized into stories and songs that can be repeated, remembered, and performed.

But their insightful questioning gives folklore studies standing and utility in the larger world. It was Dorson and Paredes who defined a true American character—a vision of "who we are." *Americans are residents of a perpetual border; this truth shapes our shared identity.* A state with boundaries but no fixed hierarchies of ethnicity or nationality, a place where identity is fluid and continually reworked by experience, recrafted through negotiation, the border is a space where stereotypes flourish, where individuals are separated from hierarchical assumptions of ethnicity and nationality; it is a space inclined toward a natural equality, where disparate groups negotiate a new, shared identity. It is the often-painful perpetual creation of orally performed stories, practices, and songs within the borderland—artistry crafted in the company of people not like us—that defines the American character.

Borders are regions of cooperation, collaboration, resistance. Americans cooperate in cuisine, and we share and sample the music, art, fashion of many small groups. The border forces contact with difference, and Americans are noted for the face-to-face helpfulness that inevitably follows tragedy. Witness the surge in charitable gifts and blood donation after the 2017 mass shooting in Las Vegas. And from time to time borderland sensitivity to the character and needs of strangers is memorialized in law; our Americans with Disabilities Act set a global standard for the way a society should treat its compromised citizens.

But border life is demanding—continual exposure to alternative knowledge and alien practices; forced negotiation with the values, attitudes, pretensions of strangers. Collaboration and learning can result, but also resistance. To the degree that the United States can be characterized as a metaphorical border, it's obvious that some residents just won't play. Distinctions of wealth, religious belief, ethnic and racial difference can fuel ambition and a distinct cultural vitality admired around the world. But suspicion, frustration, a willingness to demonize strangers are also part of border life—a retreat into tribal loyalties, nativist resentment, even mass murder.

Witness the "gated community"—self-segregated housing organized to screen neighbors, offer privatized security and recreation, reinforce commonalities of wealth and prestige. If a vibrant border is the marker of America's unifying alternative identity, the gated community undermines our essential character: "One of the most important elements in democratic societies is respect for and maintenance of heterogeneity. Communities need all age groups and lifestyles to remain viable places. Gated communities, however, tend to be homogeneous. . . . This lack of diversity makes the communities brittle and too easily harmed."[28] Writer Rich Benjamin waxes caustic: "Gated communities churn a vicious cycle by attracting like-minded residents who seek shelter from outsiders and whose physical seclusion then worsens paranoid groupthink against outsiders."[29] Maintaining quality of life in a borderland requires patience, courtesy, respect, empathy, and modesty. Difficult. No surprise that America's persistent doubts about difference pioneered the gated community in the 1980s.

The border is also a place of inevitable cultural exchange. Sometimes the process is framed positively as "borrowing" or "acculturation." Folklore scholars have favored the term *creolization,* extending the identifier of racially mixed populations in Louisiana to denote a two-way street of cultural exchange, a process that in the end produces something entirely new. A New Orleans–style *blend.*

But in recent years such freewheeling cultural exchange has come under a cloud. If the gated community manifests one symptom of borderland anxiety—fear of the other—the debate over cultural appropriation exemplifies a different apprehension—the fear that some powerful group will work its way inside, stealing your creativity, exploiting your legitimate, authentic expressive life to generate wealth and prestige for somebody not of your group.

Theft of cultural assets had been a problem for centuries. Even as artistry was increasingly commoditized in the West, colonialism promulgated the fiction that music, costume, traditional medicine, artifacts of subjugated peoples belonged, absent compensation, to representatives of dominating nations. In more recent times, folksongs were gathered, recorded, sold as commercial releases without paying or crediting folk artists or their traditional communities. In 1974, when the president of Peru learned that the Simon and Garfunkel recording of "El Cóndor Paso" had been part of a Grammy-winning album, he complained to UNESCO authorities that the royalties should be paid to the nation where the song originated. His objection started a process that generated a UN Convention on the Preservation and Protection of Intangible Cultural Heritage. Exploitation of folk stuff is not a new concern.[30]

But the current US fascination with appropriation as a symptom of domination and exploitation is especially intense, extending the notion of cultural theft to encompass fiction writers who invent characters whose ethnicity, race, sex are different from those of the authors. Criticism, much of it on campus, challenges teachers of yoga who aren't Indian, the service of "culturally appropriated food," the fiction writer's excursion into the minds of imagined alternative demographics, economic strata, sexual orientations. Bari Weiss, in a *New York Times* opinion essay, puts the problem this way:

> Charges of cultural appropriation are being hurled at every corner of American life: the art museum, the restaurant, the movie theater, the fashion show, the novel and, especially, the college campus. . . . The accusation of "cultural appropriation" is overwhelmingly being used as an objection to syncretism—the mixing of different thoughts, religions, cultures and ethnicities that often ends up creating entirely new ones. . . . The point is that everything great and iconic about this country comes when seemingly disparate parts are blended in revelatory ways.[31]

The bedrock beneath charges of appropriation is cultural commodification—the deep Marxism that infects American thought with the assumption that all behaviors are subsumed beneath the economy—where every action, every person, every thing derives meaning from economic value, from price. It's not my intent to enter the "appropriation fray" (although I would say while theft is bad, extrapolation and imitation are, well, flattery), my point is to position this intense argument as another example cementing the borderland character of the American scene—in this case through the breakdown of borders' tenuous, generous civility. It is the in-your-face proximity and intensity of our society that makes the United States a refuge of egalitarian cohesion in times of war, tragedy, or natural disaster, but that very closeness is continually threatened by the gravitational pull of tribalism, suspicion, racism, fear. It is hard to live appropriately on the border. Just as gated communities break border trust, appropriation commoditizes difference, making routine give-and-take a kind of theft. Both attack the spirit of tolerance, openness, and sharing that border life requires.

Dorson and Paredes figured this out; they understood the character of borderlands. Their borders were worlds unto themselves, shaped by cultural complexities, uncomfortable proximities, linguistic confusions. Often deeply resistant to law and regulation, the border breeds its own hierarchies and connections distinct from obvious cultural authority. To live well on the border is to continuously compare and negotiate. Standing and status are diffuse, power transitory; assertion, respect, restraint, creativity, fear coexist and are intensified.

Are Americans citizens of a vast borderland; does the idea of borders best capture our strength and frailties, our resilient allure? Of course, Paul Krugman is right—the United States *is* a nation defined by "the idea that men are created equal, and are entitled to basic human rights." We're also (to ape political rhetoric) the "richest, happiest, most powerful nation on the earth." *That's* who we've said we are. But principles are abstract and distant, a Big Dipper floating high above the messy reality of the American borderland; campaign talk is boilerplate, not to be believed. Our enlightened dream is fading. Today, when it comes to who we are, we're not so sure.

America is a border of intense contradictions, where generosity, respect, and cooperation are offset by distancing suspicion and a too-easy retreat into violence. A border where shared humanity shines, where tolerance too often collapses into hostility. A border with no single hegemonic cultural authority; a border easily manipulated by fear but also inspired by the opportunity of transcendent purpose; a border where the expressive life of an oppressed black minority can rise to influence

world culture. When it works, a borderland rich in respect for difference, open to competing voices, can satisfy the ambition of residents
and be powerfully attractive to outsiders. This is our challenge: The attributes that make America work are easily marginalized by unscrupu-
lous, manipulative leaders, but are as easily strengthened toward unity
and shared effort in the face of natural disaster, external threat, or bold
opportunity. It is the responsibility of leaders to *interpret* and *translate*
the dream of enlightenment—honoring abstract democratic principles
by making them real, crafting smart public policies that advance the
respect, neighborliness, and collaboration that are the best qualities of
our American borderland.

Two folklore scholars, working decades ago, in isolation, in different regions of the United States, independently identified the value and
risk of a nation living its border metaphor, where engagement forced by
proximity can at once breed understanding and empathy, distrust and
deep resistance.

THREE

UNDERSTANDING

"IT IS COMMON TO FIND RADICALIZATION AMONG ADOLES-
cents and young adults who experience traumatic dislocations in childhood, some abrupt move across continents or cultures that takes the
child from a known environment where they must rely on the nuclear
family, with both mother and father suffering their own transitional dif-
ficulties." So explains the expert psychologist in Laleh Khadivi's novel, *A
Good Country*, her account of a young American's conversion to Islamic
extremism.[1] A diagnosis offered by *New York Times* columnist Roger
Cohen, in an opinion piece devoted to Manchester, England, terrorism suspect Salman Abedi, is even more concise: "It's unclear just what
combination of gangs, drugs, sexual frustration, inadequacy, political
and religious indoctrination, cultural alienation and personal failure
pushed him to kill twenty-two people, including an eight-year-old, by
blowing himself up."[2]

Of course, this is standard fare. The rational, causalist scientific
method, applied to humanity through sociology, psychology, and economics, explains behavior this way all the time—explicating childhood
trauma, the effects of class, race, gender, and nationality, and especially
the assumed power of wealth, as markers of failure or success. As I have
argued, Enlightenment ideas were deployed in nineteenth-century ideologies—Ferris Bueller's isms—which promptly spawned scholarly and
scientific practices purpose-built to support belief with evidence. Even
in today's post-Enlightenment world, what passes for insight defaults to
the social scientific—to the external forces that we are convinced not

only shape identity but also trigger action. If somebody robs, steals, or engages in some other form of mayhem in our American borderland, reporters and scholars reflexively probe childhood and family, schoolyard insults, online rejection, and, over and over, the presence or absence of money. The ordinary life of mass killer Stephen Paddock—okay childhood, plenty of money, no early crime, no obvious psychosis—produced confusion and dismay in the ranks of law enforcement and experts in behavior. We know that real, hard science—biology, physics, mathematics—is predictive. But unfortunately, as clinical psychiatrist Richard Friedman noted, "as a general matter it is very difficult, if not impossible, to predict who is likely to turn violent."[3]

So, despite its name, *social* science, lab-inspired techniques applied to human beings, continually fails to predict, fails to be replicable. Even political polls and analytics come up short—we can aggregate voter characteristics like income, race, gender, religion, employment status, and yet what individuals will do in the privacy of a voting booth remains mysterious. Cause and effect just don't add up: we know many children are bullied, many are poor, many suffer cultural and social dislocation and the dangers of physical and emotional abuse. But in the end only a few steal and murder and even fewer follow the path of violent terrorism. Like our attempts to define singular identities out of demographic data, rationalist constructions of human motivation and behavior remain pervasive and their advocates relentless. But as in defining identity, applying the methods of science and the beliefs of economics, sociology, and psychology to map human motivation and predict future actions always comes up short.

This weakness is especially obvious as we attempt to track the arc of youthful terrorism, notably those kids mysteriously "radicalized" while coddled beneath the umbrella of affluence, capable families, good educations, decent jobs. How could this happen? we wonder. How could someone for whom all the externals were positive give up a good or at least respectable life to pray, train, fight, and very likely die in a seemingly quixotic politico-religious adventure? What can account for the actions of a lone-wolf terrorist who conspires in a dingy apartment; gathers guns, bombs, military garb; and then murders coworkers, classmates, and neighbors in the name of a distant religious ideology?

Here we go: "traumatic dislocations" are advanced as one explanation, or perhaps "trampled identity," "perceived loss of significance," or the perennial "hopeless economic conditions." Root causes of terrorist conversion can be traced to frustration and especially to factors shaping childhood and youth. The answers are found in assessing "anger and alienation. In this we must look to the family, school upbringing and society as a whole."[4] But if a willingness to engage in the same failed activity over and over while expecting a different result is a popular definition of insanity, this belief in the predictive authority of economics, sociology, and psychology fits. It's all about "push" factors—hardship and deprivation leading to despair and a desperate need to belong. Skepticism has yet to take hold, but Americans today have every right to be leery of tired social-scientific and economic explanations, knowing full well that sufferings of childhood and angst of youth do not dependably forecast violent behaviors, to say nothing of the peculiar to-the-death loyalty of a killer pledged to an imagined struggle on behalf of religion and an almost nonexistent Muslim pure state.

Folklore studies recognizes the legitimacy of alternative knowledge—artistry, values, motives that are grounded in ancient wisdom and the practices of oral transmission. Could it be that civilization's understanding of the terrorist impulse is wrong? Might a commitment to extreme sectarian violence be based not on slights and deprivation, but on a universal desire for achievement, recognition, meaning? Harvard historian Odd Arne Westad provides a hint: "People, especially young people, need to be part of something bigger than themselves or even their families, some immense idea to devote one's life to."[5]

Literary historian Denice Turner calls this a "universal cultural imperative"—"the idea that one should rise above certain things: adversity, anonymity, and monotony."[6] The human objective is to engage forces that are spiritual, eternal, dynamic, while leaving mundane temporal life—corrupt and uninteresting—behind. ISIS and its ilk offer this kind of promise—a journey into an imagined geography, a space where extraordinary performance is honored, a world not accessible to ordinary human beings.

This is the idea that Benjamin Dueholm explores. Writing in *Aeon*, he offers a similar though less transcendent metaphor—fascination with swordplay and chivalry. For Dueholm, the quest for the caliphate is a form of "cosplay"—a "dress-up festival of blood-soaked nostalgia whose very pretensions to antiquity mark it as the rankest kind of modern innovation." For Dueholm, murderous devotion to ISIS is a kind of "nerd's fantasy," a dream of "legitimate authority vouchsafed by blood and virtue, by descent from, and imitation of, the heroic past." A fantasy, he concludes, very much like J. R. R. Tolkien's "sprawling, leisurely epic," *The Lord of the Rings*.[7]

But Dueholm's explanation is itself mundane; shy of the mark—ISIS is not simply a game made real. Instead, as Graeme Wood writes in the *Atlantic*, the Islamic State is grounded in "coherent and even learned interpretations of Islam." It is a movement that "requires territory to remain legitimate"—territory acquired by military tactics passed down in the Koran and employed by fighters "faithfully reproducing its norms of war." US Special Operations commander Major General Michael K. Nagata admitted that "he had hardly begun figuring out the Islamic State's appeal. 'We have not defeated the idea,' he said. 'We do not even understand the idea.'"[8] Folklore scholarship can help. Just as Dorson and Paredes discovered America's identity and its borderland character, the work of another specialist in the storytelling of tribes and rural people, Joseph Campbell—student of world mythology and spiritual guru to generations of truth-seekers—offers a path to understanding the terrorist's quest. Campbell offers an alternative to behavior explained by economic insecurity, social dislocation, some hidden psychological upset. Campbell sets aside push factors to map the irresistible pull of an adventurous quest—a quest that overpowers the ennui induced by a modern world crippled by what Dueholm calls the "slow drift toward shallow belief and low stakes."[9] Campbell is well known—today maybe just shy of famous—but beyond celebrity his work on the power of myth has exerted a powerful, underappreciated influence on American culture. For just as Disney gave the world its beloved G-rated *Cinderella*, Hollywood movies discovered, adapted, and finally used Campbell's insights in crafting compelling story lines for countless films.

Joseph Campbell advanced the idea of an overarching *monomyth*— a set of universal themes hardwired into human consciousness, hidden but strong enough to influence belief, understanding, action. And that's where folklore studies and Hollywood again came together. The mythologist's influential 1949 book *The Hero with a Thousand Faces* reached film director George Lukas just as he was completing the screenplay for his 1977 film, *Star Wars*: "It was very eerie because in reading *The Hero with a Thousand Faces* I began to realize that my first draft of *Star Wars* was following classical motifs. . . . It seemed that these deep psychological motifs are all there in everybody, and that they've been there for thousands of years. The general psychology of mankind doesn't seem to have changed much."[10] Lukas then went deeper, consciously shaping his evolving film idea around Campbell's universal model of the heroic journey—a *quest* marked by separation, conflict, achievement, and return.[11] Much has been written about the phenomenon, but it is fair to say that the vast "Star Wars" franchise, advanced through sequels, prequels, and massive marketing and merchandising campaigns, relies on the universal appeal of mythic models—folkloric narrative removed from traditional roots and embedded in a completely modern art form.

A decade after George Lucas discovered Joseph Campbell, screenwriter and script consultant Christopher Vogler noticed it was not only *Star Wars*, but many successful films that plotted conflict and resolution through Campbellian stages in a generic hero's journey. Vogler, then a staffer with the Walt Disney Company, drafted a seven-page internal memo compressing Joseph Campbell's framework into a concise sequence of actions, citing examples of successful movies that had (unconsciously, it seems), closely followed the progression of a global monomyth. Arguing the value and applicability of universal mythological themes in creating stories with lasting appeal, Vogler's memo became Hollywood legend and the basis for many screenplays—good and bad. A Campbell-enabled, highly successful, folklorized model of plot construction shaped decades of film, from the *Star Wars* franchise to *Finding Dory, Coco,* and *Black Panther.*[12] Vogler himself deployed Campbell's insight in crafting the script for Disney's *Lion King* and in the 1990s expanded Campbell-derived principles into an influential film-school screenwriting text, *The Writer's Journey.*[13]

What are the key elements of Campbell's heroic monomyth? Here's a quick outline: The hero lives in the ordinary world but receives a call to adventure. Though the hero at first refuses, reservations are put aside by the teachings and wisdom of a mentor. The hero leaves home to encounter tests, forge alliances, confront enemies. Inspired by more mentors, aided by allies, the hero endures an ordeal, seizes a reward, journeys back to the ordinary world. He (or she) returns transformed, bearing a treasure that benefits all people. Stated simply, the hero is called to adventure, enters an alien, magical world, assembles a team, defeats enemies, and returns with knowledge and power that benefits society or even all humanity. The *Star Wars* narrative tapped into the pull of a powerful, ancient, universal theme embodying hope, challenge, and achievement. The hero's journey resonates; might it also *motivate*?

Richard Dorson was of the first generation of home-grown scholars captivated by the emergent fascination with America's indigenous history, values, artistry. Campbell was more than a decade older than Dorson, coming to intellectual pursuits just before the American studies phenomenon gained traction. He completed his Columbia University MA in 1929, years before Dorson entered Harvard and nearly a decade before our most prestigious university validated the study of American civilization with a new PhD. Engaging the intellectual opportunities of his day, Campbell was drawn to heroic tales of kings, knights, and princesses, and to the explanatory traditional mythologies maintained by tribal societies.

Campbell was good-looking, an Olympic-level distance runner and capable musician, talented with languages. Drawn to the study of historical narratives of vast scope (his MA thesis was on Arthurian legend), Campbell became a scholar of myth—the vast traditional stories that recount the supernatural history of a people, the battles of gods and goddesses, heroes, the narratives that hold and pass along community's essential values. Like early folklore scholars in Europe and England whose close observation and inquiry into the artistry of ethnic people defines the modern day importance of folklore studies, Campbell—a mythologist—was passionate, ambitious, highly productive.

In 1934 Campbell joined the faculty of Sarah Lawrence College, the experimental institution for women in Bronxville, New York. His first course was built around his fascination with cross-cultural folklore themes. Delighted that at Sarah Lawrence "I can teach the way I want to," Campbell's early classroom objective encapsulates his life's work:

"The first thing I am going to try . . . is to break through the crust of the Middle Ages into the well of human mythology that lies beneath it and I'm going to help them to see the connection of that mythology with the deepest places in themselves." Campbell's career would be a search for "life wisdom," and while he published extensively, his mastery of myth and a related understanding of multiple religions, his willingness to engage wide audiences on popular themes of spirituality and quality of life enabled a career mostly outside the academy.[14] He nurtured links to prominent spiritual leaders, public intellectuals, and a range of practitioners determined to employ ancient wisdom in the pursuit of personal spiritual growth and transformation. Campbell's relationship with Sarah Lawrence provided him with an academic home base for decades; the imaginative, "seeking" style of the school was a perfect fit for the romantic side of Enlightenment inquiry. For Campbell, it was not science, but curiosity and sensation that led to learning, and ancient mythological wisdom offered the path to revelation.

Early folklorists had studied myth—it was one useful "entry point" to the study of tribal culture in the nineteenth century. But by the twentieth century folklore research focused on genres found in towns and small groups in cities—jokes, tales, urban legends, folksongs. Extracting life lessons and spiritual insight from ancient myth, Joseph Campbell was a presence on the scene but off to the side of folklore studies. Cognizant of the ways folksongs and fairy tales could be distorted, reinvented, commercialized in popular culture, folklore studies has always been especially sensitive to, and critical of, scholars who achieve broad attention. Although Campbell's insights helped codify and validate value-rich, epic stories and fueled parts of a modern, self-realization movement, popular success meant he would never be fully embraced by the scholarly community. Toward the end of a long and productive life he appeared onstage with the Grateful Dead, broke bread with Bob Dylan, and was the subject of a book and series of programs on public television—"The Power of Myth." As Elliott Oring wrote:

> Campbell's basic argument was that the myths and tales of peoples throughout the world contained a single, unified message: the material world is transitory, it arises from a source to which everything will return, this truth is only to be grasped by an inward turning, the journey is difficult, yet there is nothing to

fear. This is the lesson that the hero brings back to the world. . . . His work is and is meant to be a teaching for those who inhabit a material world in which they live without meaning and which they are fated to surrender at death. This is the source of Campbell's impact and popularity."[15]

So it is unfair to dismiss Joseph Campbell as a pop-culture celebrity—as an energetic, brilliant, but ultimately lightweight priest of self-discovery. His essential contribution to the importance of folklore studies was in synthesizing the form of myth from around the world—enumerating stages in the actions of heroic, mythological figures, constructing a framework in which to understand human motivation and action. For Campbell, myth is connected to our deepest places, underlying themes and understandings that shape behavior and, in an important way, inspire action rising above fear and ambition. Drawing on the work of early anthropologists and insights of Jungian psychology, he argued that behavior in myth exerts a powerful but unconscious influence on modern lives. For Carl Jung, myths identified constantly repeating energies and characters that occur in the dreams and myths of all people, everywhere. Like Sigmund Freud, Jung mapped the human consciousness, but where Freud explored the lasting effects of childhood longings and trauma, Jung argued that behaviors emerged from the influence of universal archetypes that were manifestations of a collective unconscious shared across the human race. Like Jung, Campbell observed strong similarities within the story lines of myths collected by scholars working in many cultures. By combining the psychological frame advanced by Jung with his own study of comparative mythology, Campbell produced the outline of basic, shared elements that together constitute a universal whole—a global monomyth.[16]

Let's get back to terrorism. It has evolved into the most vexing question of the twenty-first century. From the Irish "Troubles," through the Oklahoma City bombing, to the apparently widespread willingness of thousands to sacrifice themselves in order to advance perceived spiritual values in the face of modernity, terrorism feels like a place beyond the boundaries of civilization's rational conceits. We ask "why" every time, and too often no clear answer can be found.

But we try. Equipped with our tool kit of Enlightenment understandings, we apply the explanatory principles that were set in place more than two hundred years ago. Why do terrorists take up weapons; why do they hate us; why do young people leave home and school, join religious quests to fight and frequently die in grisly battles in bleak, remote regions? Terrorism disarms us, and disarmed, we reach back to the theories, assumptions, tropes of the isms that define the limits of our twenty-first-century imagination.

Eric Hoffer (paraphrased by David Brooks) argues that mass movements are not really *for* anything, but instead arise only "when a once sturdy social structure is in a state of decay or disintegration." People dedicated to mass movements "are driven primarily by frustration. Their personal ambitions are unfulfilled. They have lost faith in their own abilities to realize their dreams."[17]

John Graham for the *Huffington Post* proposes that ISIS targets the bewildered, threatened, disappointed: "people who feel inadequate, disrespected, full of unfulfilled ambitions, angry at real or perceived injustices, and who are blaming other people or institutions for their woes." ISIS offers "a way out of an insecure and undignified life." For many in the Middle East, nationalism and political ideology have failed, "leaving religion as an attractive alternative."[18] "Loss of personal significance," "hopeless economic conditions," and a persistent atmosphere of "pain and humiliation" open personalities to the manipulation of recruiters. To keep newcomers engaged, "The goal is to embed the feeling that, by the possession of a potent doctrine and a charismatic leader, they have access to irresistible power."[19]

Clearly such explanations fit neatly into the conceits of late-Enlightenment isms. Such explanations of terrorist motivation are rational, secular, and grounded in the vulgarized Enlightenment principles manifested in Darwinism, Marxism, and Freudianism—it's about weakness and absence and damage. And about a resultant longing—not a longing for transcendence, but for relief of the symptoms of suffering, failure, loss. So the lives of young terrorists—especially those who abandon promising urban lives to travel to remote centers of danger and lifestyle constraint—are probed for hints of motivation, not so often for motive. Did she do badly in school, perhaps bullied by classmates? Was her family too poor, too demanding, too remote? Was there, heaven forbid, evidence of sexual abuse? Was he unemployed; did he spend too much time online visiting nasty sites? In short, was she damaged in childhood (Freud) or disappointed in work (Marx), or was she perhaps falling short in the struggle for social success and economic survival (Darwin)? Look hard and deep enough, analysts say, and surely the cause will emerge—a cause that will, perhaps with a bit of bend and twist, fit the readily repeatable model we impose on failure whenever it erupts in modern life.

Joseph Campbell offers another way. The conventional enlightened wisdom of civilization sees youthful terror recruits as *pushed*: we invoke psychology, economics, ethnicity, education, to explain abandonment of friends and family, travel to remote, inhospitable settings, engagement with weapons and dangerous enemies, as efforts to resolve problems. But what if ISIS recruits are not fleeing hidden problems or troubled pasts, but pursuing a heroic quest; what if the pull of a global monomyth, its heroic narrative, and its strong links to fundamental universal archetypes is what's really at work? Then what do we do? Few question the idea that ennui pervades modern societies; does a cure reside in constructed adventure? When George Lucas linked the hero's journey to *Star Wars*, "it came to me that there was really no modern use of mythology."[20] The director filled that gap through film, offering adventure, collaboration, achievement, and reward—all exciting, all determinedly vicarious.

The potential terrorist recruit needs a quest, not a job; inspiration, not counseling. Policy actors, paying due attention to universal themes embedded in oral myths and society can begin to identify real alternatives to the promise of terror. As Christopher Vogler put it, "The values of the myths are what's important. The images of the basic version—young heroes seeking magic swords from old wizards, fighting evil dragons in deep caves, etc.—are just symbols and can be changed infinitely to suit the story at hand."[21] Even if the "story at hand" is about *jihad*. Writer Graeme Wood characterizes ISIS this way: "ISIS asked its followers to join not because it was fighting US troops . . . but because it had established the world's only Islamic state, with no law but God's, and with a purity of purpose that even the Taliban had not envisioned."[22] This is the hard-to-see truth that lives right in front of our noses: the dream of leaving home to take up arms to help establish a new Islamic state exerts a powerful, positive pull on young adventurers weighed down by boring, technologized consumerism in modern civilized living.

Joseph Campbell—prolific chronicler of myth and religion—is an ambiguous figure. Although grounded in the academy, his orientation, and therefore his work, always seemed aimed at a mass audience. Campbell's prodigious efforts to condense, compare, and synthesize myth and religion from around the world, and his ability to cast discovered principles in the language of personal discovery, attracted a circle of prominent artists and public intellectuals—individuals of influence in sophisticated, urbane society. His Sarah Lawrence students seemed more like devoted fans than engaged intellectuals, and phrases plucked from his books meshed perfectly with late-twentieth-century pop psychology and its self-improvement movement. Sentences like "Follow your bliss and the universe will open doors for you where there were only walls" could produce enraptured sighs of longing and recognition among spiritual pilgrims while at the same time triggering eye-rolling skepticism among academics.[23] But Campbell's assertion of universal motive illuminates a folklorized understanding of behavior.

: : : : :

On a comfortable, desert-dry Las Vegas night in early October 2017, sixty-four-year-old Stephen C. Paddock smashed two windows in his thirty-second-floor hotel suite in the Mandalay Bay Hotel. From the advantage of his elevated perspective, employing an array of long guns, some modified for fully automatic fire, Paddock sprayed bullets onto the audience of an outdoor country-music festival. Fifty-eight people were killed; hundreds more wounded. As authorities responded, the shooter took his own life. Within hours the inevitable, relentless process had begun: Why had he done it; what was his possible motive?

But the predictable media scramble to craft a narrative of blame led nowhere. Weapons had been purchased in multiple states in legal transactions—assault-style rifles modified with "bumper" stocks (also legal) that in effect transformed the one-shot-per-trigger-pull semiautomatics into machine guns. There were no immediate signs of money problems, and Paddock had no apparent history of mental illness, domestic violence, or childhood trauma. Once unlocked, his computers yielded nothing special—no contact with radical Islam and no interaction with US right-wing groups—no online rants, no threatening tweets. Paddock was a retired accountant, a seemingly successful gambler who had developed a winning approach to casino poker machines. He was quiet, taciturn, but generous with family. He had sent his girlfriend, Marilou Danley, to the Philippines on a family visit. Perhaps anticipating an abrupt end, Paddock had wired her $100,000. Danley remembered him "as a kind, caring, quiet man. I loved him and hoped for a quiet future together with him."[24]

As we have seen, social science defines identity by mapping forces and factors—psychological, societal, economic—that act on an individual, group, community. But as we have also seen, America's border identity represents a "given" of American identity—a circumstance of history and cultural complexity that constitutes a context that forces everybody to pay attention to everybody else, all the time. As social science explains identity, the isms attempt the same trick with motivation. Show me a young jihadist, or a black-clad serial killer, and just beneath the surface will be found the external roots of action—bullying, poverty, failure, domestic violence—rationalizing violence set in motion by the purred entreaties of radical Islam's recruiters. America's twenty-first-century conventional wisdom? In the face of evil, break it down, inventory the trauma, deprivation, defeat, suffering. Explain.

But this time it wouldn't work. One week out, Stephen Paddock was still unknowable. As CNN put it, "A shooter's reasons, however sick and twisted, usually become clear within a day or two. A suicide note, a manifesto, a series of social media screeds, a phone call—even police reports and court dockets can provide insight into what drives a warped mind to commit such a violent act. Usually, someone close knows something or realizes, in retrospect, that they missed the warning signs."[25] But Paddock flew under the radar, and when radar finally spotted him, it revealed only a nondescript "numbers guy."[26]

But the drumbeat went on. Paddock's father, Benjamin, an oft-incarcerated bank robber who did time on the FBI's most wanted list, apparently left the family for good when young Stephen was only seven. Two weeks after the Las Vegas shootings, "F.B.I. profilers are trying to construct a psychological makeup of Mr. Paddock, which probably includes the family history of mental illness." Absent the usual social-science narrative, the *New York Times* fell back on analyzing the senior Mr. Paddock almost as though *he* were the perpetrator. Paddock's father was an apparent unrepentant rogue who was "an only child, pampered by his mother and not disciplined by his father. . . . While Stephen Paddock was playing at the family's white ranch house, his father was robbing banks with a snub-nosed revolver and getting away in the family station wagon." But after detailing a father's life of crime, the *Times* backed away with a wan disclaimer: "The portrait of Stephen Paddock that investigators have assembled stands in stark contrast: Reserved, even boring, he was an accountant and investor who liked to gamble only after calculating all the risks. Before the shooting, the authorities say, he had never broken the law. Among the many questions that are unanswered is what influence, if any, his father's absence and infamy had on his life."[27]

So Paddock was well off, reserved but polite, a fair-minded, attentive landlord, caring to family and close friends, a smart investor and successful gambler. In short, a character who, despite efforts to shoehorn him into some rendition of an economic, sociological, or psychological pathology, just didn't fit. As a last resort, Paddock's brain was sent to the laboratory of Dr. Hannes Vogel, director of neuropathology at Stanford University. But "the chances of finding answers in the brain tissue" were slim, the *New York Times* reported, and multiple experts "sought to dampen public expectations." According to Dr. Vogel, most psychiatric illnesses are not currently discernible by this type of examination.[28]

Of course an obvious alternative exists: perhaps Stephen Paddock was simply evil—not evil in the sense of somebody turned bad by circumstance or experience, but just plain *evil*. Ism thinking doesn't incorporate evil apart from some set of discoverable causes that, given enough time and sufficiently deep research, will yield a rational explanation.

In Joseph Campbell's vision of the universal heroic quest, evil simply exists: "Horror is simply the foreground of wonder."[29] That's not our way. We want to know. But when rational, social-scientific explorations of cause and terrifying effect come up short, it's not just the unsatisfying absence of "why," but the sudden emergence of discomfiting reminders of the stickiness—the deeply embedded character—of our "ismetic" explanations. American Nazi Andrew Anglin, "the alt-right's most vicious troll and propagandist," manager of "arguably the leading hate site on the internet," began his peripatetic path to a menacing antigovernment, anti-Semitic, anti-immigrant ideology with a quest. As Luke O'Brien wrote in the *Atlantic*, in 2008 Anglin ended a short stint as university student. "He'd meandered through Asia until he reached the Philippines. He'd been reading Joseph Campbell, the writer famous for his work on mythology, and thinking about how to forge his own heroic narrative. Anglin wanted a tribe—a real one. And he'd been looking." In 2013 Anglin launched a new website, *The Daily Stormer*, a translation of *Der Sturmer*, a Nazi-era weekly read faithfully by Adolph Hitler. Andrew Anglin had left home, lived in the jungle, returned with his rendition of ineffable truth. A version of pure evil.[30]

∶ ∶ ⋮ ∶ ∶

The American borderland exists free of cultural hegemony. Multiple languages, races, legacies, nationalities compete for authority, respect, opportunity. Enlightenment principles can't quite replace Europe's romantic nationalism—too abstract, too remote, too difficult to apply in specific situations. The challenge facing American policy actors is to continually nudge the forces of the border in the best direction—toward sharing, accommodation, respect; away from suspicion, separation, violence. We know that our borderland can unite around challenge—natural disaster, war, terrorist attack. But folklore studies tells us that the power of quest—a challenge to character, temperament, ability—can also bring out the best in the American experiment. Most important, a renewed commitment to the *pull* of achievement, adventure, learning—NASA's manned space program, the Peace Corps—can be both inspiration and motivation to American youth too often consigned to a debt-burdened path of work and wealth. Manned space travel—the ultimate credential of a heroic nation—has gone the way of risk-averse economizing. The Peace Corps lives on, criticized for its cost (more than $50,000 per volunteer per year), and for its inability to achieve the agency's central goal of "help to the people of interested countries." But we need to rethink: the Corps is not about them; it's about us, and the opportunity for young, heroic American travelers to return home bearing achievement and new knowledge.

Despite the pop-culture celebrity that framed much of his career, Joseph Campbell provided key insights into human behavior by reminding denizens of civilized society of an essential truth sidelined by reason, secularism, and science—that modern lives are still directed by ancient, universal patterns of good and evil; by desire, aspiration, achievement, and recognition. Policy actors should explore alternative, traditional understandings. After all, today's hegemonic social sciences—psychology, sociology, economics—have time and again come up short when called upon to explain behaviors. Undaunted, these minions of Marx, Darwin, and Freud have only turned up the heat: assertions of authority are inflated even as their rational maps of causation dead-end. "We are living in an age in which the behavioral sciences have become inescapable."[31] Inescapable, we're told, but often wrong. But a demonstrated lack of success has not diminished our enthusiasm for tapping into the early life, the social life, or the economic life of perpetrators whenever somebody does something really terrible.

Christopher Vogler and George Lucas provide a distinctly American validation of the work of Joseph Campbell—movies. The mythologist's underlying explanation of the universal human quest has energized countless compelling dramas, and entertainment leaders have placed evidence of Campbell's insight "on the page." "Black Panther," the breakaway hit of 2018, features not only a heroic quest but an invented African nation, Wakanda—a high-tech but folklorized society free of colonial influence, hiding its technological sophistication behind a third-world ruse. So the compelling attraction of a journey toward imagined geography where heroism can forge alliances, advance good, vanquish evil, transcend the boundaries of ordinary life is clear, and not only in imaginative drama. Joseph Campbell takes us on a new path, suggesting that while motive and mood may be affected by childhood experience, community, peer influence, the absence or presence of work and money, there exists a unifying human mindset that exerts a strong, fundamental pull on the way we think and act. Campbell hints at a realm of alternative knowledge, a frame strong enough to shape human behavior. Folklorized thinking lets us engage a level of action that is deeper, more universal, and ultimately more revealing than the tired tropes of suffering, rejection, and deprivation. We are residents of a borderland, drawn to promise of unifying adventure.

FOUR

NEGOTIATION

IN NOVEMBER 2014, A HIGH-PROFILE INVESTIGATIVE TEAM
from Chicago published a report documenting and confirming long-
suspected collusion between officials of the American Psychological
Association (APA), the Department of Defense, and the CIA. According to the inquiry, a few months after 9/11 terrorist attacks, the APA
had adopted a "Resolution on Terror" "to encourage collaborations that
would help psychologists fight terrorism." The result was the application
of various theories of behavior and related psychological techniques to
the torture of suspects in terrorism investigations, including detainees
held in Guantanamo Bay.[1]

According to the report, "The APA secretly coordinated with officials from the CIA, White House and the Department of Defense to
create an APA ethics policy on national security interrogations which
comported with the then-classified legal guidance authorizing the CIA
torture program."[2] Once made public, the unsettling participation of
social-science professionals in the development and implementation of
"enhanced interrogation techniques" roiled the APA and the entire field.
Leaders of the organization resigned, new ethical standards were formu-
lated, the entire discipline was cast in shadow. As Tamsin Shaw wrote in
the *New York Review of Books*, "APA leaders were apparently motivated
by the enormous financial benefits conferred on the profession in the
form of Department of Defense Funding. The episode demonstrates
well the fragility of morality."[3]

Morality, to be certain, but also the susceptibility of the academic
ego to the allure of power and the sense of consequence that accompanies

real work carrying out the objectives of generals, spies, powerful elected officials. But no academic calculation is more critical than is the character of the relationship between scholarship and the influence of government and business. As we have seen, highly regarded social sciences are prone to stumble. Armed with apparently sturdy theory and reams of data certified by the conceits of clinical research, they seem especially susceptible to big money, flattery, the prerogatives of power. But if folklore studies is to help rebuild the Enlightenment legacy, it must reach beyond internal questions and debate to connect with public policy. I have characterized folklore studies as "venerable"—faint-praise positioning of the field as respected but not widely influential. Fundamentally a humanities discipline, folklore studies, like history, philosophy, and literature, lacks the trendy, lab-coated façade that automatically links to the priorities of government and corporate power, but while the relationship between the field and civic and corporate life has been more flirtation than embrace, folklore work has not been entirely immune to the ambiguous effect of activity outside the academy. Psychology was derailed by service to the demands of post-9/11 national defense and the manipulation of audiences and consumers. But from the nineteenth century forward, folklore studies has been unsettled by its own special relationship to an especially potent ideology—romantic nationalism.

Early folklore research never completely bought into the scientific, objective tenets of enlightened rationalism. Although the discipline was proud to bask in the rational authority of post-Enlightenment scholarship, it's obvious that early folklore scholars simultaneously viewed rural culture through the lens of sentiment and nostalgia—a departure from the harder edges of Enlightenment positivism. And this should be no surprise; from earliest encounters, the rural village was more than a container for traditional artistry. The simplicity, cohesiveness, obvious authenticity of farm and festival served as an appealing counterpoint to the superficiality, stress, pretensions of educated urbanity. Village life seemed *thick*; city life *thin*. The study of the stories, songs, and customs of everyday people always mixed intellectual curiosity with enthusiasm and respect. From the beginning, folklore scholars were drawn to both exotic songs, tales, and beliefs and to a charming alternative to society driven by wealth, status, technology. To this day, many folklore scholars proudly maintain a deep suspicion of the social effects of modernity.

It was Rousseau—the founding visionary of the romantic strain of Enlightenment thought—who believed common people (as opposed to city sophisticates) were the true repository of civilization. Rural people were studied, but also idealized; the notion of "a folk" elevated. Further, as Enlightenment ideals were integrated into Marxist political models in the nineteenth century, folk societies came to be seen as a distinct class—one that maintained a vital, primitive life-essence that, if engaged, could benefit all society. We have seen that Enlightenment principles were too abstract, too open to interpretation to transform the world on their own. Nineteenth-century isms interpreted the new, enlightened sense of mankind in the world. Romanticism was the specific disease that infected folklore studies in Europe.

Romanticism's belief in the virtue of ordinary people and their unlettered ways of life provided an argument—a justification—for assertions of national identity or character forged in the countryside, close to the soil. Sentimental nostalgia was joined by something new: rising patriotic sentiment among masses of ordinary people that were defined and promoted by nineteenth-century governments that replaced the faded influence of top-down royal authority. Leadership would now be empowered and legitimated by the passions of ordinary people who drew inspiration from their sense of national identity, shared language. This powerful but often toxic philosophical hybrid was *romantic nationalism*. The phrase derived from the writings of a German Enlightenment philosopher, Johann Gottfried Herder. Folklore scholar Bert Wilson describes the phenomenon concisely: "Romantic nationalism emphasized passion and instinct instead of reason, national difference instead of common aspiration, and, above all, the building of nations on the traditions and myths of the past—that is, on folklore."[4]

We have seen that nineteenth-century isms have interpreted Enlightenment ideas, making them real. None has been more consequential than romantic nationalism. In Germany and in Europe generally, iterations of this new ideology—defined by common language and by the idea of shared, heroic, ethnically uniform history—played an ever-expanding, defining role in legitimating government authority. Expert in the customs and traditions of ordinary people and conversant with the artistry and alternative knowledge of the distant countryside, folklore studies was a perfect resource for politicians and officials desperate to find and spread stories that could stir up and then maintain the spirits of a population united by nationalist enthusiasm.

Fascism required a general narrative that bundled meaning, purpose, and commitment in a heroic, unifying identity that expressed a sense of national superiority. German folklore filled the bill; the Third Reich swallowed folklore studies whole. Like many a warm embrace by powerful actors, disaster arrived dressed up as opportunity. National Socialists of Germany's Third Reich celebrated folklore—*Volkskunde*—as the academic field most capable of advancing the idea of "One People, One Nation, One Ruler." As folklore scholar Bill Nicolaisen put it, the alliance of collecting and research with Nazi aspirations enabled "all the consequences of territorial acquisition, ethnic cleansing, and derogatory stigmatization of 'others.'" As early as 1933, party leaders advanced strategies for creating and controlling cultural politics. All artists, publishers, composers, librarians, booksellers would be enlisted in the ideological training of German citizens. The objective was to link the fascist dream of a Thousand Year Reich to a golden past, grounding nationalistic goals in a heroic Nordicism, justifying violent and exclusionary racial mythology. Bill Nicolaisen again: The appropriation of folklore studies "for arrogant, xenophobic, political purposes in national-socialist Germany left the discipline so tainted that it took many years to imbue it with unchallengeable qualities of academic respectability again." Just as links to coercion and imprisonment taint psychology today, connections between folklore studies and Nazism haunt European scholarship. In fact, the German Folklore Society did not address the issue directly until 1986—a half-century after the demise of the Third Reich—when the society's biennial congress was for the first time organized around the theme of "Folklore Studies and Nationalism."5

Inflammatory populist nationalism still lives and has roiled recent politics, in America and around the world. From the presidential campaign forward, the Trump phenomenon exploited anti-immigrant sentiment and nationalist enthusiasms, stoked racial resentments. But while strident voices strive to define the United States as white and English-speaking, our nation's borderland character continually deflects or at least minimizes the most dangerous assertions of ethnic, linguistic, racial identity. As we have seen, America lacks both a common language and a deep, mythic past. If not immune, we're at least highly resistant to the forces of romantic nationalism. Unlike Europe, where cultural pride fuels political action, power in the American setting (our entertainment industries excepted) has never been especially drawn to traditional culture as a vehicle for organizing mass sentiment or political action. But that doesn't mean that folklore scholarship, like much of the academic world, hasn't gazed with envy at the attention and support that accompanies the public-policy big-time. How has the discipline worked with government and business? If the stance of folklore studies can revitalize fading Enlightenment values, how will folklore scholars behave?

∶ ∶ ⦙ ∶ ∶

In 1961, just when folklore studies in postwar Germany was barely beginning to confront the impact of a fascist heritage, Richard Dorson wrote a pleading letter to Senator Wayne Morse, chairman of the Senate Foreign Relations Committee. His reputation greatly advanced by his research in rural Michigan, by the 1960s Dorson had relocated to Indiana University as heir-apparent to the legendary Stith Thompson, master of the old-school branch of folklore research, where scholars mapped origins, the shared elements, and movement of folk stories and songs through time and distance. Dorson was a fine scholar but also ambitious, industrious, canny; in the years since the publication of *Bloodstoppers and Bearwalkers*, he had mastered the arcanery of university politics, forging strong bonds with Indiana's administrative hierarchy. When he drafted his letter to the senate, he was mere months away from a major achievement—departmental status for a folklore degree program that had until then been cobbled together as an "Institute."

However, Dorson had resisted bringing the discipline into the realm of mainstream public policy. In part this was practical; government operated outside his scholarly comfort zone. But more importantly, Dorson had witnessed and studied the decades-long corruption of folklore studies by romantic nationalism in Germany and other states, and felt that the field and government were a bad fit—that the objectives of law and regulation ran counter to core academic values in folklore studies, shoe-horning the field into political ambitions, undermining the discipline's fundamental commitment to research and authenticity.

But now a crucial engagement with policy leaders loomed and, ironically, it involved the Cold War—the national defense issue infused with American nationalism of the day. Dorson was then president of the American Folklore Society, and he had been directed by the society board to ask congress to reconsider cuts to graduate-student funding, and at the same time push back against congressional criticism and highly public assertions that folklore was too marginal, too frivolous to be included in the range of humanities research supported by the National Defense Education Act (NDEA). Passed by Congress a few months after Soviet Russia's successful launch of its Sputnik 1 artificial satellite in late 1957, the NDEA aimed to advance America's academic capacities—especially scientific achievement—in the face of the Cold-War menace. Foreign languages were in, possessing an obvious inter-national-relations benefit, and of course history was assumed to bolster patriotic agendas by solidifying understanding of America's principles and purposes, the nation's exceptional place in the world. But support for graduate study and research in nonscience was pretty thin, limited to students striving for university teaching careers. (No surprise, major NDEA priorities would today fit comfortably in a STEM curriculum.)

Folklore was especially disadvantaged. As we have seen, popular no-tions about the meaning of folklore's special terminology—*myth, legend, folksong*—made it easy to assume that the discipline was about the study of lies, popular perceptions, or the festival presentation of guitar-accom-panied songs. As would happen again and again, misunderstanding of folklore studies handed critical observers an opening for dismissive fun, the *Wall Street Journal* opining that the inclusion of folklore in the NDEA had secured America's "lead in boondoggling." In his letter to the senate, Dorson takes on this problem by alluding to his old "fakelore" argument, singling out "longhaired folksingers," "pseudo-heroes," and purveyors of the "quaint, cute, and the 'folksy.'" For Dorson, the field "has become contaminated by amateurs, entertainers, and charlatans."[6]

But most important, Dorson was negotiating along a fine line—arguing that while folklore studies would inevitably be diminished by politics and the intervention of governments, in *this* case, government support was appropriate and essential to advancing American objectives around the world. In his letter to congress, Dorson—writing to represent the interests of the American Folklore Society—places the study of folklore within a patriotic frame compatible with the Cold-War objectives of the NDEA. He highlights Nazi Germany and Soviet Russia as examples of the way governments falsify, distort, and manipulate tradition in order to justify policy and influence populations, arguing that "fascist and communist states have found in folklore a most effective propaganda medium." Dorson warns that if we "cold-shoulder" students in the United States and around the world who want to "learn the techniques and methods of collecting, archiving, and analyzing folk materials," the Soviet Union and others "will be delighted to explain to these students and scholars how folklore expresses the protest of the working people against the capitalists and imperialists."[7]

Dorson's plea didn't work; graduate folklore study would no longer be supported by the NDEA. It would be a decade before Richard Dorson would address congress again, when he would apply some of the same arguments to a very different matter.

:   :   :   :   :

Those who study mankind are inclined toward either understanding or action—toward listening or giving orders. To shape policy, ideas must intersect power—media, business, and especially government. But proceed with caution: psychology was poisoned by the vampiric embrace of national defense; folklore studies in Europe became tightly wrapped in nationalist rhetoric and values. The field would for decades be demeaned and dismissed as both rationalizer and enabler of Germany's Nazi regime. From the mid-nineteenth century forward, the discipline's collection and analysis of oral tradition, origins, language and ancient myth fitted well—sometimes *too* well—with the theories and ambitions of authoritarian leaders. Lenin and Stalin used Russian folk traditions to give distinct identities to minority populations in the Soviet Union;

modern China has embraced United Nations programs celebrating oral traditions as a way of honoring rural people and celebrating the nation's ancient heritage.

Folklore studies in America has been resistant to nationalist rationale and policies: mostly immune, but not entirely. If romantic nationalism's excess emerged as the key challenge for folklore scholarship in Europe, in America the challenge was choice—the choice between *inquiry* and *empathy and reform*. Working with rural communities, labor groups, ethnic neighborhoods, traditional artists and artisans, it was inevitable that folklore scholars would move beyond research, developing strong affinities for action aimed at improving the lives of ordinary people. From the 1950s forward, this inquiry-action division was manifest in US folklore studies, sometimes quite starkly. If nationalism was the near-bane of European folklore work, Marxism had a less definitive but still influential role on the American field. If the reader is to accept my argument that folklore studies offers the critical stance essential to understanding our post-Enlightenment age, it is important to place the perspective of folklore studies along the spectrum that runs between *scholarship* and *action*.

Richard Dorson, the great entrepreneur of academic folklore, distrusted public presentation, popular interpretation, and especially government intervention in traditional communities. But while Dorson could set standards for academic study and research, building university departments and institutes, he and his colleagues could not constrain access to the personalities and practices of traditional communities. Interest in the music, dance, tales of the folk was simply too widespread, and the rich reservoir of material too deep, to keep other approaches at bay.

From his youth, Alan Lomax studied folk music and dance in traditional communities, working on the academy's fringe. A prolific fieldworker (he had collected songs in Michigan's UP before Dorson gathered community traditions), Lomax was eager to use the star power of folk-based performers like Lead Belly and Woody Guthrie to increase understanding of traditional culture as central to the American experience. John Lomax, Alan's father, had taken his teenage son on folksong-collecting trips back in the 1930s. The father-son team, minimally funded by the Library of Congress, toured the sketchily-roaded South in an old sedan, lugging a weighty, primitive disc recorder. They recorded folk artists where they lived, favoring small towns. Father and son were especially drawn to prisons, reservoirs of folk expression maintained by inmates locked away from media and modernity. In African-American singers behind bars, the younger Lomax saw a "flame of beauty." As biographer John Szwed put it, these were "performances that asked the audience to link the singer with the song, to understand it as a naturalism that demanded that the singers draw on their own experiences." Lomax sensed that "the country was hungry for a vision of itself in song," and it was the masterful black artist who could present elite society with a sense of the challenge and promise of America's true identity. A famous example: the Lomaxes discovered Lead Belly in Mississippi's notorious prison, Angola. The charismatic singer (composer of, among other songs, "Goodnight, Irene") became an intimate part of the Lomax circle. As he did later with Woody Guthrie, Alan worked diligently to provide Lead Belly with the framework of a real career.[8]

Decades after Alan and John Lomax brought Lead Belly to a national audience, just as Richard Dorson was securing the future of academic folklore at Indiana, two alternative approaches to traditional culture were taking shape beyond the university. We've already encountered the first; it was strictly commercial: In addition to the Grimm brothers–based *Cinderella*, the Walt Disney Company had produced a number of successful animated features based on folktales. The patriotic, triumphalist frontier epic *Davy Crockett* was a live-action movie sensation in 1957. Over the decades, Hollywood has continued to find both story lines and inspiration in folk narratives. From folklike stories (*The Little Mermaid*; *Frozen*) to the adaptation of Joseph Campbell's framework for heroic quest (think *Finding Dory*), to Pixar's 2017 Day-of-the-Dead hit, *Coco*, Hollywood has been a consistent utilizer of simple, resonant traditional tales and overarching traditional frames.

The unprecedented popular enthusiasm for "folk stuff"—music, in particular—was different. Here commercial interests merged with a passion for rural music to produce what came to be called America's "Folksong Revival," a fusion of simple songs, Enlightenment ideals, sentimental rurality, left-wing politics. Lomax, Lead Belly, Woody Guthrie were part of this story, as were Pete Seeger, the Weavers, Harry Belafonte, Josh

White, Joan Baez, Bob Dylan, and thousands of imitating aspirants who took up the guitar. Yes, these were the "longhaired folksingers" disparaged in Dorson's senate letter, but the movement was really a complex creative and commercial environment (a border within a border?) where stars of stage and recording utilized and sometimes mimicked artists discovered by dedicated scholar-collectors. The revival celebrated the best of traditional performance and presented folk artistry to the widest possible audience, produced second-rate renditions of real folk stuff, and provided a launching pad for ambitious singer-songwriters intent on professional careers.

For the most part, these folklore scholars and folklore exploiters were populist without being highly political, activist without strong ideology, but in their own way, they were ready for action, willing to push the limits of folklore's benign stance. As European folklore work became an instrument of patriotism and identity, the United States folklore movement engaged politics. In particular, through the first half of the twentieth century, a sympathetic link grew between folk music and the American Left. After trying out classical and choral music composed to inspire worker solidarity and class consciousness, the American Communist Party (CPUSA) settled on traditional folksongs and political songs created in a folk style as an effective vehicle for political messaging that nurtured group solidarity. As folklore scholar Richard Reuss put it, the communist movement "consciously tied traditional folk songs and propaganda music composed mostly in folk-style into one collective genre, 'people's songs,' the true music of the working masses."9

Many folksingers of the era—Burl Ives, Will Geer, Woody Guthrie, the Almanac Singers, Pete Seeger—were committed to the notion that folk songs "offered a realistic reflection of the people's historical and social experiences," but they also were "infused with class consciousness."10 Alan Lomax touched every part of the folk movement. Combining deep engagement with oral communities, advocacy on behalf of folk performers, and sincere leftist politics, he came closest to connecting the dots separating folk music scholarship, commercial exposure, and politics. More a researcher than a teacher, viewing universities as mere reservoirs of support for his research, Lomax balanced academics with his media-based social and political activism. Like Pete Seeger and other leaders of the popularized folk-music movement, Alan Lomax was targeted during the anti-Communist moral panic that swept America in the 1950s; at the height of the Red Scare, he relocated to England.[11]

The music festival—a feature of folk music collecting and presentation from the 1930s forward—became a vehicle of popularization, protest, and politics. Modeled on a successful annual jazz event, the Newport Folk Festival was launched in 1963, capitalizing on folk music's newfound commercial standing. Ralph Rinzler, talented musician and passionate advocate for grassroots performers like Bill Monroe and Doc Watson, led the field research that populated the Newport Folk Festival with authentic voices. In the mid-1960s Rinzler signed a "special consultant" contract with the Smithsonian Institution and quickly became the artistic and political force behind the institution's Festival of American Folklife, launched in 1967.

There were other voices outside the academy. Joe Wilson led the National Council for the Traditional Arts—a nonprofit that produced recordings and live performances and in general lobbied government on behalf of folk presentation.[12] And a few PhD folklorists violated Dorson's prescript and worked both sides of the fence. Kenneth Goldstein helped grow the University of Pennsylvania Department of Folklore while producing recordings and leading the Philadelphia Folk Festival. Roger Abrahams was a PhD student at Penn while weekending as a folksinger in Lower Manhattan.

But the activities of talented researchers outside the university never coalesced as a movement that could influence the course of folklore work—especially work within the academy. Rinzler and Wilson lacked advanced degrees in folklore studies and didn't write much; a prolific writer, Lomax had rarely taught, instead focusing on recording, broadcasting, and the advancement of a few folk-artist careers. And personality played a role; while Lomax remained an influence throughout his life, up close he could be imperious, impatient, and abrupt; he was ill equipped and little inclined to front a movement.[13] Lacking an obvious center, and too far Left to be fully embraced by state and national governments, the folklore workers whose efforts spread a passion for folk music never shaped public policy. Mass-appeal performance and non-university scholarship could capture the attention of press and political leaders, but the relationship between government and folklore studies would be negotiated by the academy.

:   :   :   :   :

An opportunity to link the discipline with government in a big way emerged in the 1970s. It took initial shape as a challenge to the hegemonic authority of academic folklore, when hopes for a better position for folklore in public policy converged around a gadfly folklore scholar whose life had been the obverse of Richard Dorson's. Archie Green—a figure not yet on the horizon in the early 1960s—would lead a cohort of folklore activists toward real collaboration with mainstream public policy. In the end, it was the same Archie Green who would be critical to pulling folklore studies back from the brink of the biggest public project ever.

Metaphors for activism and academics, Green and Dorson are the bookends that set the limits of action within American folklore studies. As we have seen, Richard Dorson's path from elite private schools to Harvard and to a tenure-track teaching position had been sure and steady. He earned his Harvard PhD in 1942 and two years later was ensconced in a tenure-track post at a major midwestern university. By the late 1950s, Dorson was hard at work building Indiana's folklore program.

A different path. Just a year younger than Dorson, Archie Green earned his BA from UC Berkeley in 1939. Degree in hand, he then joined the Civilian Conservation Corps, returning to San Francisco after a year to begin work as an apprentice shipwright. While Richard Dorson was planning a research trip to rural Michigan, Green was launching his career as an all-in union man. In the 1950s, he caught the folksong bug and began collecting traditional and string-band music on vintage recordings, especially songs of labor and work. Like Lomax, Campbell, and yes, even Dorson, Archie Green combined passion for folklore with ambition sufficient to advance his career. His interests gradually led away from labor and unions toward the academy, where research, once underway, would always reflect his populist commitment to the situation of working men and women in America's diverse borderland society. Green eased away from manual labor, taking a behind-a-desk library job at the University of Illinois, which led to research, teaching, and then graduate work, still a sideline. In 1969 he earned his late-in-life PhD (at age fifty-two) and parlayed his degree and real-life experience into a career of research, but also of action and advocacy. If Dorson was the "scholar" of folklore scholarship; Green was the "public" in community work that was first labeled "applied," and today is called "public" folklore.[14]

The early 1970s were a heady time in Washington, DC. Culture was on the public-policy agenda, the Kennedy Center for the Performing Arts was up and running, a long-awaited renovation of Pennsylvania Avenue had begun, and the new National Endowments for the Arts and the Humanities had garnered significant budget increases from the mostly conservative administration of Richard Nixon. Although from the outset both US cultural agencies were focused on history, literature, and Europe-derived fine arts, government support signaled that official Washington's disdain for culture as a component of public policy had eased, at least a bit.

The nation's capital had established its own history with folklore—exactly the scattershot initiatives and small agencies we'd expect in a nation lacking a central, monocultural identity. The Library of Congress Archive of Folk Song was organized in the late 1920s, and it had greatly expanded its activities and its holdings during the New Deal. Additional arts programming under the Roosevelt-era Works Progress Administration featured grassroots creativity, laying the groundwork for future preservation and presentation programs recognizing all forms of American culture. In the seventies, those early commitments took on new meaning.

When S. Dillon Ripley became secretary of the Smithsonian Institution in 1964, he immediately set out to expand the size and reach of his multiple museums: "A museum should be an open experience," Ripley wrote. "People should be flowing in and out of buildings, experiencing a sense of connection between their own lives and the history of their culture."[15] In moving his institution outdoors, Ripley had a strong supporter in his arts director, Jim Morris. Morris in turn relied on the energetic talent scout Ralph Rinzler, who had departed the increasingly pop

Newport festival to serve as applied folklore consultant to the Smithsonian. The secretary's notion of a museum without walls was a perfect backdrop for the Festival of American Folklife, launched on the Capitol Mall in 1967, at the height of the Folksong Revival. Although benefiting mightily from the popularity of folk music, a folklife festival would be something different. As Rinzler put it, "The festival was designed to make a statement about as broad a range of traditions from different regions and ethnic groups and immigrant groups as possible ... to totally differentiate between the folk song revival, where you'd have a folk festival, and folklife continuity."[16] The Washington festival was Newport with credibility—seminars, scholarly introductions of performers, attention to craft and authentic traditional practice.

The festival proved timely. Just as the work of father-and-son Lomax had tapped a wellspring of interest in the culture of ordinary Americans, Rinzler's curated performances on the Mall served as a collegial presentation of borderland diversity, a useful reaffirmation of American unity in the aftermath of civil-rights unrest that also afforded a tantalizing look at what the nation had to celebrate in its looming bicentennial. Although the festival had its critics—mostly inside the Smithsonian—it was an immediate success with the DC press and the public. To frame performance and demonstration, Rinzler put together an academic conference, turning to sympathetic scholars like Alan Lomax, Kenneth Goldstein, and Roger Abrahams as academic advisers. Rinzler seeded advisory committees within the festival's parent institution with academics, giving the two-week summer event a higher profile than a flowchart might imply. Although never explicit, it was clear that Ralph Rinzler saw the festival as a launching pad for an expanded role for folklore (or folklife) within the Smithsonian's portfolio.

Capitol Hill took notice of the summer Mall event. Texas Senator Ralph Yarborough, prodded by staffer Jim Hightower, introduced "The American Folklife Foundation Act" in March 1969. Inspired by visits to festival performances, Hightower began to work closely with Ralph Rinzler. The 1969 act advanced Rinzler's agenda, aimed at expanding folklore programming within the Smithsonian and securing the financial future of the Festival of American Folklife, while at the same time

handing the institution a new and important function—the capacity
to make grants across the country in support of folklore projects. In
effect, the new entity would join the National Endowment for the Arts
and the National Endowment for the Humanities as a third US cultural
agency—this one devoted to supporting grassroots American culture.[17]

Archie Green was by then a new PhD, friendly with Rinzler. The
two shared a passion for traditional music and a purist's sense of what
was worthy in America's oral culture. To Green and Rinzler, the still-low
profile of traditional artistry within the nation's frame of law and policy
represented a failure of democracy. After all, it was not the refined performance of the concert hall but folksongs, legends, tall tales, tepees, five-
stringed banjoes that defined America's *real, authentic* expressive life. It
was natural for Archie Green to come aboard, helping to lobby on behalf
of the Yarborough bill. Everybody assumed this would be easy-to-pass,
nonpartisan legislation: an appropriate new investment in American
artistry as Washington ramped up toward bicentennial events. But what
appeared to be a brief endeavor to enact a noncontroversial measure
turned into a seven-year effort marked by agency infighting, disagree-
ment, and disarray in the folklore community.

At first the bill moved ahead rapidly. Introduced late in 1969, a hearing was scheduled in May of the next year—a fast pace. But things went
off the track. Because of his rapport with Ralph Rinzler and his expansive
vision for the Smithsonian, it was assumed that Dillon Ripley would
support the bill. After all, it would expand the institution's mandate and
place an important grant-making capacity where one had not existed.
But the secretary reported that the Smithsonian's Board of Regents had
recommended against the bill, arguing, in brief, that a grantmaking
function would add a challenging new function to the institution, one
that would "lie outside our characteristic historic role."[18]

Despite positive comments from a parade of folklore advocates, Ripley's negative testimony, which unfortunately led off the hearing, sealed
the bill's fate. Richard Dorson spoke last, restating the arguments he
had made a decade earlier in his effort to secure government funding
for folklore graduate students, driving in the final coffin nails. Dorson
suggested (without evidence, to be sure) that folklore scholars would

not support the new entity because they disliked its legislative pedigree. He characterized government intervention in folklife as "a dangerous area," once again arguing that reorienting people toward the proper way to execute a traditional life is what happened in Nazi Germany, Soviet Russia, and Eastern Europe: "You may say that it is a large step from our endeavoring to retrain the American people in their own folk roots, but it is not such a large step when you begin to use Federal agencies as instruments of national policy. So I am opposed to this concept of the revival and promotion of folklore through the staging of popular festivals."[19]

Although not scheduled to testify, Archie Green felt compelled to step forward, responding to Dorson. He invoked academic responsibility, a 1970 position framed by campus unrest surrounding the Vietnam War and the recent bombing of Cambodia. Green didn't see the academy and activism as an "either-or" choice:

> One of the central points of debate in almost every major American university now is what is the commitment of a scholar as a citizen? At what point does his conscience impel him into some form of action? . . . I think, for the record, it must be indicated that many folklorists have worked successfully with festivals, with performers, and have not sullied their standards. That is, it is possible to work at both levels if you have got yourself together, to use the vernacular. That expression, of course, comes out of folk speech.[20]

Archie was passionate in his support for workers, rural citizens, everyday people. But he played well with establishment leaders and worked enthusiastically within conventional systems—universities, nonprofit organizations, the US Congress. He was Left without the Leninist, interventionist, revolutionary anger that sidelined many like-minded folklore partisans. (In a sense, Green's leftism foreshadowed by a half-century the socialist-populist appeal of Bernie Sanders.) Archie's response to Dorson was neither shrill nor especially doctrinaire. Of course, it was unusual, almost unheard of, for a scholarly debate to break out in a congressional hearing: a painful indication that competing notions of exactly how credentialed folklore specialists should properly engage everyday people had by no means been resolved. The failed bill was also evidence that agencies of government—even semiprivate ones like the Smithsonian Institution—possessed their own values, assumptions, hierarchies,

and pretensions. A great idea could easily founder on the shoals of interagency jealousy and prerogative. And there was always scheming.
Dorson, to this point only a consummate academic politico, adopted
DC-insider tactics, meeting with Smithsonian insiders the night before
the hearing to craft disruption. Some senior staff wanted no part of an
expanded folklife footprint, and their objectives fitted Dorson's purposes
exactly. The congruence of Ripley-Dorson testimony was preset.

This fractious public performance turned out to be a setback, not the
end. In 1973 the legislation was reconfigured as the "American Folklife
Preservation Act," and Archie Green became the leader of a quirky, extended, methodical lobbying effort. Green walked the halls of Congress,
paperwork stuffed in a department-store shopping bag, meeting Hill
staffers (and members, when possible), patiently making the case for
federal support for traditional culture. A rumpled caricature of a slick K
Street lobbyist, Archie dressed in threadbare khakis, a tired sport jacket,
worn canvas tennis shoes. He was unfailingly friendly, always positive,
message delivered with a smile. The effort to advance the new legislation
took three years.

And new challenges arose. Although the original Yarborough bill
had been reworked, it still contained a grant-making provision. A new
government program—perhaps even an agency—authorized to support
the artistry of ethnic Americans presented an immediate threat to the
two endowments charged with supporting cultural work—the NEA and
NEH. The arts endowment's chairman, Nancy Hanks, understood that
grassroots expressive life could have broad political appeal that could
easily displace congressional enthusiasm for the NEA's fine-arts, big-
city agenda.

Archie Green, determined to advance his populist vision of a sup-
portive policy environment for the art of traditional communities, was
seeking allies wherever they could be found. Even as he tennis-shoed
his way around Capitol Hill, Green was also talking to the nation's established cultural funders. The NEH ignored him: the politically savvy
Hanks, along with her staff, paid attention to congressional enthusiasm
for the bill and to the handful of specialists who had teamed up to lobby
for the Preservation Act. As Michael Straight, Hanks biographer and

NEA deputy chairman, observed, "Nancy may not have been tuned in to folk culture in 1973, but she heard—loud and clear—voices raised on Capitol Hill.[21]

In early December 1973, Larry Reger, then NEA general counsel, hosted a meeting at the NEA's new Columbia Plaza offices. Green, Lomax, Roger Abrahams, Joe Wilson, and others were in attendance; Reger's claim that the NEA was already supporting folk culture generated disbelief and a fair amount of grumbling. Chairman Hanks joined the group late in the session, late enough to miss any fireworks but clearly able to sense tense criticism aimed at the NEA's indifference to everyday culture. Alan Jabbour, then head of the Library of Congress Archive of Folksong, summarized what had been said. Jabbour, famously articulate, made it clear that "it wasn't enough to just give grants, you really need a program devoted to this."[22] Jabbour had positioned himself as unofficial spokesman for the ad hoc group, and over the next few weeks he spoke with Larry Reger a number of times. The NEA launched its Folk Arts Program in the spring of 1974; in April, Alan Jabbour departed his Library of Congress post to become the program's first director. Nancy Hanks had deflected the threat of a folklore endowment on the outside by creating the Folk Arts Program inside the NEA.

Still, hearings on the bill were held by both the House and Senate in early May 1974. Smithsonian leadership had backed away from the new center, and the NEA had felt threatened. With no support from on high and the Smithsonian's grantmaking authority obviated by Nancy Hank's maneuvering, Ralph Rinzler's enthusiasm waned. Larry Reger, representing the NEA, announced the new Folk Arts Program and introduced Alan Jabbour as its director. The NEA effort justified Reger's objection to the funding authority included in the Preservation Act. Senators questioned Reger sharply; after all, in truth few folk arts grants had been made. But the interagency hand had been well played by the NEA. When the American Folklife Center was finally created and lodged in the Library of Congress, its grantmaking authority was gone.

Despite his absence, Richard Dorson's distrust of folklore activism exerted influence in both hearings. Wayland Hand, a senior voice among academic folklorists, was the last to testify on behalf of the Folklife Preservation Act. He responded to Dorson's argument directly, noting first that while traditional culture and folk scholarship had been subverted and ill served in fascist and communist regimes, such abuse was not inevitable:

> The supremely human values that are exemplified in America's folklore and folklife lead to such a deep and enduring love of country that a perversion of our national life and purpose through any misapplication of these historical studies and scholarly pursuits is unthinkable. . . .
>
> From these representations, it can readily be seen that folklore and folklife reveal a dimension of life not easily measured in other terms. In the stories, the songs, the beliefs and customs, the proverbs and sayings, and all the rest are mirrored human hopes and aspirations, fear and elations, and the myriad thoughts and impulses that give quality and zest to life.[23]

The NEA maintained its resistance to an outside grant-making agency focused on ethnic and rural culture. The American Folklife Preservation Act became law on January 2, 1976. There had been machinations and compromises to the end, but there was one good result: the American Folklife Center was created within the Library of Congress. Although many felt Archie Green had earned the center's directorship, in the end Alan Jabbour returned from the NEA to take the position. Folklore's long march to the heart of American public policy had come up short, but not empty-handed. Archie Green and compatriots had been heard, a new center was launched, and the NEA had been forced to embrace traditional artmaking. Within a decade the Arts Endowment would carve out an important role in connecting folk artistry with public policy.

:   :   :   :   :

Our tale has a coda. In 1971 funds were allocated by Congress for the excavation and construction of a 232-mile transportation project in the American mid-South—a canal connecting the Tennessee and Tombigbee Rivers. Advanced by powerful members of the House and Senate, in the day when seniority gave multi-term officials nearly unlimited powers, the new waterway was positioned as an economic development project. It would, coincidentally, flood thousands of square miles of land, submerging entire communities in the poorest parts of Alabama, Tennessee, and Mississippi. In an unexceptional Capitol Hill irony, the "Tenn-Tom," as it was called, moved forward at the same time as the American Folklife Preservation Act made its way through Congress.

In 1977, late in the game, the US Department of the Interior approached the still-new American Folklife Center about the development of a cultural impact study. One percent of Tenn-Tom was allocated for the study and mitigation of environmental impact, broadly defined, and Interior's invitation carried substantial funding—nearly $500,000. Such an undertaking would secure the standing of the Library of Congress's new center and engage many folklorists and graduate students—it would be the largest folklife research project ever in the United States.

An interagency agreement was signed between the Department of the Interior and the Folklife Center in late 1978. Engagement by the field was late—there was no hope that folklore research would turn back the disruption and dislocation built into the construction of a massive new waterway. Low expectations hovering, the Folklife Center board met in early 1979 to consider the project; outside comment was encouraged. The folklore community split along familiar academic-activist lines: Archie Green and his allies—Roger Abrahams, Ralph Rinzler, Joe Wilson—were against the project. Others, including the venerable Wayland Hand, were in favor. The final decision was left to Alan Jabbour. Facing worrisome press coverage and a sharply divided board and community of scholars, the director pulled out of the agreement. The project went forward without the advice of professionals best equipped to assess, collect, study, relocate, and protect communities, artifacts, and artists.

While maintaining respect and affection for those distant communities that are especially rich in the artistry of oral tradition, US folklore scholars have been restrained and cautious around efforts designed to yoke the discipline to reform, reconstruction, revitalization. Writing decades after the Tenn-Tom opportunity was set aside, American Folklore Society president Peggy Bulger revisited the controversy and its resolution. Acknowledging that she could "see both sides of the argument," she felt strongly that "despite well-meant impulses, folklorists missed an opportunity to be central to the work of cultural conservation and the environmental survey work that is still going on today. By demonizing powerful institutions such as the Army Corps of Engineers and refusing to deal with their agendas, our outraged sensibilities have kept us on the fringes of this important work, rather than in a central position with our colleagues from related disciplines."[24]

An observational discipline with strong public instincts, folklore studies has regularly found itself in the middle of America's great political dilemma. As Daniel Patrick Moynihan famously put it: "The central conservative truth is that it is culture, not politics, the determines the success of society. The central liberal truth is that politics can change a culture and save it from itself."[25] There is an irony here. As the moral progenitor of the Folklife Center, Archie Green's voice carried the most weight in the Tenn-Tom debate. Though committed to change—to extending the work of folklorists into communities, presentation, advocacy—in the end Green worried that an expertly executed alliance with the forces of intervention and disruption would align the field of folklore with centers of power hostile to the artistry and community of America's underclass. Dorson and Paredes understood that America was not like Europe—the United States lacked the hegemonic authority of a monoculture established by shared language and an imagined heroic past. But nevertheless, folklore studies was invited into the embrace of government from time to time. Compromises were made, agencies and programs established, but the effect was small and folklore studies in America was never compromised by nationalist policy. Archie Green fought to secure the moral high ground of the folklore studies stance; Dick Dorson fought to secure the independence and integrity of an academic discipline. The two never really got along but, in the end, weren't that far apart.

I've characterized folklore studies as both venerable and underappreciated. No surprise that folklore scholars, unsurprisingly envious of the notoriety acquired by competing disciplines, have often longed for the academic spotlight. But our US situation has made the requisite conflation of research and national agendas hard to achieve. Immune, or at least highly resistant, to the excesses of romantic nationalism, folklore studies in the United States has worked piecemeal from the wings of public policy. And folklore studies never much wanted to intervene with communities to enact civilization's notion of positive change—the field has been left-leaning but free of the interventionist reflexes endemic in what Theodore Kaczynski labeled "Leftism"—the impulse to "bind together the entire world into a unified whole.[26] Folklore scholars—academic or public sector—have mostly been comfortable on the observational sidelines, sustaining a healthy suspicion of reform, recognition, and exploitation. In the dance with power, things have not gone smoothly for other disciplines. The approach of folklore studies—to observe and to understand the tales we perform for one another—is a beginning, presents an opportunity to see the world in new ways. Maybe things will be different? Perhaps the patient stance of folklore studies can get it right.

FIVE

STORIES

JUST BEFORE THE PRESIDENTIAL ELECTION OF 2016, JAMES Alefantis, owner of a family-oriented pizza shop in suburban Washington, suddenly noticed menacing messages posted by dozens of new Instagram followers. The often threatening posts cited an astonishing accusation—that his restaurant, Comet Ping Pong, was headquarters for a child abuse and abduction ring headed by Hillary Clinton and her campaign chairman, John Podesta. The claim was false, but when Alefantis searched online, he located dozens of invented newslike stories about kidnapping, trafficking, and molestation of children—all tied to Secretary Clinton, Podesta, his restaurant and its kid-friendly atmosphere.

As reporter Cecilia Kang explained in the *New York Times*, the false narrative popped up in the weeks after John Podesta's personal email account had been hacked and some of its contents organized and made public on the Wikileaks website. Podesta and Alefantis had communicated online about a possible Clinton fund-raising event, and that slender link was enough to prod users of the online message board 4Chan to invent a connection between Comet Ping Pong and long-standing right-wing speculation about the existence of a Democratic Party child-exploitation ring. The rumor spread to social media sites like Twitter and Reddit, where it launched a popular discussion thread called "Pizzagate." Despite contact with DC police and the FBI, efforts to suppress, counteract, deny, and thwart the expanding online presence of the fake story and the menacing and abusive responses it inspired were ineffective. As Kang notes in her report, "Mr. Alefantis's experience shows it is not just politicians and internet companies that are grappling with the fake news fallout. He, his staff and friends have become a new kind of private citizen bull's-eye for the purveyors of false articles and their believers."[1] Nobody could halt the progress of the online story, and in the end a deeply troubling invasion of privacy organized around an invented tale nearly produced tragedy. As the *Washington Post* reported, a few weeks after the *Times* deconstructed the fake tale of child trafficking, Edgar Maddison Welch, a twenty-eight-year-old man from North Carolina, drove to Comet Ping Pong presumably to get a firsthand look at dark backrooms, hidden tunnels, and the painted-over sign that supposedly represented an international symbol for pedophilia. Welch was armed with an AR-15 assault-style rifle and other weapons and fired shots into the floor and ceiling. The restaurant was evacuated, the Washington neighborhood locked down by police, and the subject arrested without incident. He claimed to be investigating allegations he'd encountered online.[2]

During the fall campaign, candidate Donald Trump had deployed the phrase "fake news" to challenge the credibility of established sources like the *New York Times* and *Washington Post*. That was a ploy. Real fake news has nothing to do with mainstream media. Communications scholar Russell Frank, writing in the *Journal of American Folklore*, characterizes the phrase as digital folklore: "Fake news is a story generated in a non-professional social context that uses the style of news either to parody that style, satirize issues and personalities in the news, or perpetrate a hoax or prank."[3]

From its inception, the internet was a hotbed of rumor and exaggeration of tales similar to the DC child trafficking story—narratives that sported the trappings of something *possibly* true. As online news services proliferated, fictions ginned up by pranksters and partisan activists adopted the appearance and style of legitimate outlets, disguising fictional origins while injecting parody and destructive rumors into our national political discourse. A steady stream of fake headlines tracked the range of American fears, big and small: "United States to Destroy All Nuclear Warheads"; "NASA Warns Planet X Is Headed Straight for Earth"; "Sarah Palin Calls for Invasion of Czech Republic"; "Permanent Closure at Walt Disney World Due to Hurricane Irma"; "NFL Fines Pittsburgh Steelers $1M Each for Skipping National Anthem."

A rearview-mirror examination of America's 2016 election cycle forced authorities to take their first serious look at the ways manufactured fake news targeting voters online might have influenced the conduct and outcome of the US presidential campaign. Investigation advanced methodically, but, by fall 2017, official statements and leaks from the FBI, Department of Homeland Security, and multiple congressional committees made it clear that many fake stories had not been simply humorous or annoying but had been crafted with malicious intent; by winter 2018, the US Department of Justice had issued indictments naming more than a dozen Russian conspirators involved in internet efforts to disrupt or influence the outcome of the US presidential election. Still no conclusion, but day by day emerging facts point one way—this fake news business was worse than we had feared.[4]

We've already seen the way high-level talk about the customs, traditions, and norms of democracy draws on the terminology and understandings of folklore studies—a truth that underscores the pervasive importance of rules and practices maintained not in law or regulation, but in memory, oral transmission, intergenerational respect for communal values. Fake news takes the world of oral tradition, rumor, urban legend and disguises it in the framework of legitimate online media.

This is America's angle on "post-Enlightenment reality." If the Enlightenment was enabled by print technology, our new world of magical thinking, weird combinations of fiction and reality, ISIS rants and right-wing ideology is empowered and accelerated by our own new thing—the internet. The fake news Pizzagate story had been thoroughly debunked by official sources and mainstream media. The police had investigated and determined that the item had no substance. But for Edgar Welch, none of that mattered; he was immersed in a parallel universe where the usual sources of truth were suspect, where authority could not be trusted, where internet stories that reinforced assumptions, preconceptions, and stereotypes constituted a new tribal reality sharply at odds with the understandings of civilized society.

As enlightened, civilized manners, assumptions, and behaviors are shoved aside, the folkloric part of society gains authority. While many folklore scholars have continued to collect and analyze the genres that first defined the field—folksong, folktale, myth, joke, material culture—emphasis on process is increasing: how jokes are performed, how personal experience is shaped into coherent narratives, how the internet transforms and accelerates transmission. As attention shifted from the *what* of folklore to the *how* and even *why*, the hard boundaries separating clearly defined genres from simple personal narrative began to fade. Fake news was suddenly, well, in the news, and folklore scholars quickly spotted something familiar—media-accelerated stories that were high-tech renditions of rumors or urban legends, genres that had been worked on for decades. These stories, passed by word of mouth, told as true, often feature frightening tales of mayhem, the occult, or cautionary examples of business chicanery. They now had a new home, and a new legitimating context.

Folklore scholar Jan Brunvand, in his 1981 volume *The Vanishing Hitchhiker*, makes a central point about urban legends—there is a "common belief among tellers and listeners that they are truthful accounts" or an assumption that urban legends "at least are based on actual events."[5] The stories are grounded in underlying "facts," but the framework is embellished in the telling as the legend is both fleshed out and reconfigured "through repetition and creative retelling."[6] Here's an example—a simple rendition of a famous urban legend, "The Death Car," collected by one of Brunvand's students in 1969: "My friend from Los Angeles breathlessly announced that she could pick up a $5,400 Porsche Targa sports car for only $500. The reason for the reduced price was that it had sat in the middle of the Mojave Desert for one week with a dead man in it; consequently, the smell of death could not be removed from it."[7]

This is bare-bones—the desert and car brand the only specifics. But we can immediately sense why the story works, why it would be passed along. Tapping the ubiquitous role of the car in midtwentieth-century American life, the won-the-lottery allure of a fabulous bargain, tagged with a cautionary lesson: "If it seems too good to be true, it probably is." (To say nothing of the truth that death can cast its pall over anything.) Beneath a legend there is frequently some grain of truth. By applying venerable techniques of early folklore scholars, Brunvand traced a version of the legend back to mid-twentieth-century England; Richard

Dorson worked hard to connect the legend to a real event, with real, traceable people, that occurred in a Michigan town in the 1930s. But a verifiable source eluded him.[8] So an urban legend can be an exaggerated, reconfigured version referencing something that might have occurred, but framed in a way that gives the tale a metaphorical power, reinforcing preconceptions, hopes, common knowledge, motivating narrators to pass it on.

So the legend is a special kind of story—a tale that might be a tilted account of an event that once happened. But it's never told as history, the urban legend is always close at hand—last week, last month, in another city but nearby. It is a narrative believed by both teller and audience. The demands of belief place special demands on the teller; the legend must be surprising but plausible—close to what folklore scholar Elliott Oring says makes jokes funny: "appropriate incongruity."[9] It must be "credibly sourced," but since the story is elevated (incongruous) and actually *not* true, attribution must be hard to check. The source is never firsthand, rather always a specific, connected, but slightly remote figure—someone believable but not in the teller's, or listener's, daily orbit. So it's "my brother's boss told him . . ." or "Aunt Suzie's hairdresser heard . . ." This is what folklore scholars call "friend of a friend" confirmation: a validating voice, to be sure, but one too distant for easy challenge.

There's no evidence that the Grimm Brothers or William Thoms found anything like urban legends in rural villages (although nobody knows whether "Once upon a time" stories were believed). In fact, urban legends seem to be a special attribute of civilization and modernity, closely tied to the mysteries, confusions, uncertainties of contemporary life—big government, big business, impenetrable manifestations of power and control. And urban legends proliferate within the US borderland. In the 1980s, they were an exciting discovery—a fresh folklore genre that ordinary people found fascinating. For a time, Jan Brunvand brought the urban legend to something of a mass audience, publishing additional collections and licensing his book (they mostly just used the title) to a movie project. But he was writing in 1980 and analyzing texts gathered years earlier. The death-car tale was sustained in folklore's oral tradition—told as true, passed from place to place, person to person, maintaining its allure over decades. Brunvand's major contribution was made pre-internet, pre–cable news—he could assume that his material had pretty much lived in a "pure" circumstance of oral transmission.

You can sense where we are headed: the special blend of oral transmission, remote confirmation, and belief also characterizes fake news. In fact, since Brunvand's pioneering work, scholars have moved in this direction, expanding the lexicon of these "told as true" stories that tap into an expanding inventory of dreams, fears, prejudices, beliefs. He reinforced an important point: everybody has folklore; believable narratives are sustained because they engage issues that the public cares about. But Brunvand's tales were not overtly political.

Consider the welfare legend: it fits Brunvand's definition, but by reinforcing racial and societal stereotypes, the narrative is connected to, and sometimes based on, political speech. Urban legends that extend political discourse into oral tradition take us a step closer to the folklore scholar's present-day take on fake news. If Brunvand's urban legend is a story that is believed, retold, and continually modified to fit new audiences and new locales, the welfare legend is an idea or attitude that is also believed but can live in print, in media, even in the pronouncements of pundits and government officials.

A fieldwork story: In early 2011, folklore scholar Tom Mould was discussing the newly signed Affordable Care Act with a "local community member." The two agreed that a health system that forced poor people to use emergency rooms for routine medical services was far from efficient, but a deep, underlying suspicion remained. Here's the story told to Mould, as recorded in his notes:

> But poor people will still use and abuse the system when they can. I was in the grocery store not too long ago when a woman in front of me tried to buy dog food with her food stamps. She was wearing a fur coat, polished nails, designer handbag. The checkout girl told her she couldn't do that and this really made her mad. She huffed and puffed and threw the dog food down and said, "Fine, then he'll eat steak instead." She marched back to the meat counter while we're all standing there, waiting for her. The cashier is looking apologetically at us. And here she comes, sure enough, with two steaks.[10]

The first-person narrative ("I was in the grocery store") is unusual; most often the source is at a hard-to-validate, friend-of-a-friend distance.

And the purpose was new: this was not an account of a universal concern (dishonest corporations, for example) but a legend invoked to make a partisan point. Mould notes that he heard the same story as a high-school student in the 1980s, a version in which the rendition of the steak-buying woman "included a final flourish: her departure in a brand new Cadillac." But the story has resonance in a contentious discussion of the Affordable Care Act: government programs are excessive and open to fraud; food stamps and affordable care address the same recipients; behavior in the grocery store would soon be transferred to the physician's office. Not stated, but the story conveys an impression that the dog-loving woman is African American.

The welfare legend fits a larger ideological framework in which fraud-riddled social services are carelessly distributed to undeserving, ungrateful minorities. The frame fits the "welfare queen"—a staple of Ronald Reagan's early presidential campaign speeches and Guy Drake's 1970 novelty country music hit, "Welfare Cadillac." Despite continual efforts to debunk the notion of persistent abuse of the welfare system, the idea has retained its ideological resonance. As Tom Mould puts it, as late as 1996, Reagan's version of the legend "continued to influence public perception and public policy, most famously the Welfare Reform Act in place today."[11]

Let's imagine a fake-news headline, maybe "Food Stamp Regs Feed Steak to Pets" or "Food Stamp Shopper Nets Pooch a Treat!" This kind of story is all over the internet, and it works because the specifics reinforce a firmly held set of assumptions and beliefs. These urban legends are reduced to a conceptual core; they work even without the trappings of narrative detail or the need to track the story back two or three steps in the tale-telling process. Most important, this kind of knowledge—stories from the folk process that advance highly questionable assumptions about class, race, and government—has been around for decades. Folklore scholars have studied it. But the reach, impact, and pace of internet communication has today empowered traditional understanding to *displace* explanation grounded in expert knowledge, science, law, and mainstream journalism.

This kind of legendary idea can crop up as a full-blown urban legend or can just be pared down to a single phrase. ("You know, he was born in

Kenya!" "After all, the Bush team knew about the World Trade Center attacks well in advance.") These are factual statements with no basis in fact,
concise expressions of sentiments, theories, judgments, and explanations
that mesh with some overarching frame of power, wealth, influence.
When presidential candidate Donald J. Trump insists that Arab residents
of a New York City suburb danced in the streets when the Twin Towers
collapsed on 9/11, he is citing fake news, perpetuating urban legend. The
movement of folklore studies into unexplored territory—urban legend,
rumor, fake news—has been enabled by a new understanding of the
behaviors that create and maintain traditional practice.

:   :   :   :   :

The 1974 meeting of the American Folklore Society was in a memorable
spot. Portland's Benson Hotel, built in 1913, had been updated and expanded in the late 1950s, but it retained the marble floors and crystal
chandeliers that had earned the structure a place on the National Reg-
ister. With about three hundred rooms it was a good fit for a growing
AFS. Cold fall weather, shortening days, and windy rain. And special
excitement: our first days of panels and papers were haunted by hovering
government security prepping the hotel for a visit by President Gerald
Ford. On the evening he arrived, scholars and graduate students sipping
wine at a reception sponsored by the organization Women in Folklore
were startled to find themselves locked into their meeting space as the
Secret Service cleared the marbled, chandeliered lobby of the Benson so
the president could safely and efficiently get to his suite.

I wasn't sure I belonged. By the time I attended the fall AFS meeting, it was clear that my hopes for a university career had been set aside
for good. Three years in, work with the Country Music Foundation had
become a passion, the challenge of building a respected nonprofit institution around an often derided tradition in southern music a source of deep
satisfaction. Although a career as a teaching scholar had once seemed
ideal, my work with the Country Music Hall of Fame had tapped into
something I didn't know I had—a surprising reservoir of entrepreneur-
ial ambition to build a viable cultural institution in the then expanding
universe of nonprofits. I was having fun, flexing my ideas about coun-

try music and its folk roots, communing with songwriters and revered Nashville session players, absorbing some of the business expertise of a new set of Music City mentors. But folklore still felt relevant—even central—to what I was striving to achieve. Although the classroom and research library now were distant, I stayed involved.

The conference wrapped up with a banquet—white tablecloths, wine, the flushed collegiality of shared experience, learning, values. The after-dinner AFS presidential address was intended as an event highlight.[12] Society president Dell Hymes was an odd fit for this elevated role. Beloved by graduate students at the University of Pennsylvania, he was viewed in the larger folklore world as a linguist—someone with advanced ideas about speech and performance—but a scholar whose work lived for the most part on the folklore fringe. Bearded, shy, head down behind a slender lectern, exuding minimal charisma, our AFS president (ironically expert in performance) did little to sustain our interest. He further taxed the attention span of his audience by including in his talk the presentation of an entire Native American myth—"The Sun's Myth," recited by a representative of the Northwest Coast Kathlamet Chinook tribe. Attention wandered. The room was warm; eyes glazed.

The clock eased past ten. Suddenly I sat up straight. Late in the evening our AFS president was saying something important, advancing a bold vision for the essential role of folklore studies in understanding human behavior. I was transfixed.

Dell Hymes earned his scholarly reputation in the study of language in culture—the intersection of anthropology with the language-specific discipline *linguistics*. His special concern was language in social life, the way language functioned in communities. Hymes's work made him a bigger player in folklore theory than most of us understood. Fundamentally, he argued that a unity exists between what speakers do or say and the social or communal context in which the speech occurs. For Hymes, understanding language demands a close examination of both *words* and *situations*. Context and words are intertwined in every speaking occasion—parting, lecturing, lovemaking, prayer. So the combinations are culturally specific; the way we say goodbye invokes one set of words and behaviors in America, quite another combination among Hymes's objects of study, the Chinook Indians. For Hymes, the elevated realm of performance is the context that most reveals the connection between words and culture: a joke, folktale, or family story about a nightmare vacation reveals more than, say, the simple recitation of a shopping list.

Although folklore studies might appear to have been a second-tier interest for Hymes (the word *folklore* does not appear in his *New York Times* obituary), from his graduate days forward he had been engaged by the field. Hymes took classes in the Indiana University Folklore Institute (where I did my graduate work) and once he secured a position in anthropology at Penn, his appointment was crosslisted in the then lively Department of Folklore. Although not a regular attendee at AFS meetings, Hymes retained a quiet leadership role in the field and was held in the highest esteem by Penn folklore students who admired his close analysis of speech and his intense study of performed folk narrative.[13]

What did I find so exciting in our 1974 presidential address? Hymes's argument was embedded in the two-part title of his talk, "Folklore's Nature and the Sun's Myth." He was addressing the character of folklore—its "nature"—in a new way: not as text, not as artistry, not even as cultural context, but as process. Well along, Hymes looked up from his prepared text to make two related points, the first through an anecdote (I am paraphrasing here): "Suppose six people were trapped between floors in an elevator for a few hours. After rescue they would have a story—a narrative—of what had occurred. They would have talked together intensely, in a sense forming a kind of community, and when they told their story after the fact—how the accident happened, their reactions and response, the meaning of the experience—the tale would contain many shared elements, and through this process, the experience itself would have been *traditionalized*." For Hymes, this "traditionalized" story would be the stuff—incipient perhaps—of folklore. Had the event stretched over a longer time, or had it involved more people or greater danger, the traditional narrative would have been intensified, perhaps memorialized as an urban legend offering shared explanations of cause or effect, perhaps as an assemblage of cautionary proverbs, or maybe even a folksong. What was critical is the essential process of what we could call traditionalization—a process through which shared experience creates a folk, which then generates its own lore.[14]

For Hymes, the process of traditionalizing was a concept extracted from of a lifetime of folklore and language research. To traditionalize was to partake of a cultural universal, like speaking, singing, crafting alcoholic drinks. It was an elemental action found among all peoples in all societies of the world. For Hymes this is the way folklore gets made: humans together convert experience into shared narrative; this process gives us the stuff of folklore. Words are shaped within a specific set of norms, and the resulting tales, jokes, legends, or songs, when performed, constitute a projection of community understandings, assumptions, values. In addition, for Dell Hymes speaking is a social act, a performance shaped by expectations, disparities of power, ambition.[15]

Sunday morning it was still cold—Oregon early winter. In the hotel checkout line some of the society's young (mostly female) members reported that once President Ford had left the Benson for Washington and the White House, his Secret Service team had let their hair down and partied hard late into the night. I returned my rental car and airlined back to Nashville. I had never really met Dell Hymes—he was AFS president and I was a fallen folklorist directing a country music museum. But his talk inspired me. I tracked him down at the University of Pennsylvania, wrote asking for a copy of his verbatim presidential talk. He sent me a copy—blue type on slick mimeo paper. I misplaced it years ago.

The *Journal of American Folklore* published "Folklore's Nature and the Sun's Myth" a year later. The printed version seemed a bit stiff; the made-up aside about an elevator entrapment that demonstrated the way we traditionalize experience was missing, and Hymes's assertion about the centrality of folklore studies within the humanities felt dialed back. Though mild-mannered in performance, he had spoken spoke boldly behind the Folklore Society lectern—in print more tentatively—arguing that "folklore must advance a general conception of itself," attending to "some fundamental aspect of reality," to "claim a place for folklore on the plane at which major disciplines justify themselves."[16] But his important gift to folklore studies remained—Hymes's understanding that the act of organizing experience and perception into stories that can be performed is a process that occurs everywhere, in every family, every group, in all societies: "Every person, and group, makes some effort to 'traditionalize' aspects of its experience. To 'traditionalize' would seem to be a universal need."[17]

Hymes increased the reach of folklore studies by moving beyond text to a close description and analysis of the way narratives are created and performed. He advanced the idea that the impulse to traditionalize experience was a cultural universal. He not only understood how narratives were created but taught us that speech is always a social act; as Richard Bauman put it, Hymes realized that "speakers use their voices to accomplish things in the world."[18] The range of folklore studies expanded. Folkloric behavior sustained much ordinary speech; folk custom—once understood as the exclusive property of rural, unsophisticated people—dictated behaviors for leaders of industry and government. Rumor, legend, conspiracy theories, fake news fell under the gaze of prominent folklore scholars.

:   :   :   :   :

In 2003 Dave Isay launched StoryCorps. It was an idea that drew from the Writers' Project of FDR's New Deal, the oral history work of Chicago journalist Studs Terkel (who was in many ways an uncredentialed folklore scholar and remarkable proponent of the folklore stance), and of course Isay's imagination. As the StoryCorps website puts it, the project features "unscripted conversation, revealing the wisdom, courage, and poetry in the words of people you might not notice walking down the street."[19] It works this way. Two people who know each other—friends, relatives, coworkers—pay a small fee, enter a spartan recording studio; spend about an hour together, ask questions designed to stimulate discursive answers—"Can you tell me one of the most difficult moments in your life? "Do you know the story of how our ancestors came to this country?" A few minutes after the conversation ends, the studio generates two compact discs—one for the participants and one for deposit in the American Folklife Center of the Library of Congress.

The resulting recordings constitute terrific examples of "traditionalized" experiences. Condensed, often intergenerational, and framed with classic themes of ambition, work, adversity, and moral knowledge, each

StoryCorps piece exemplifies Dell Hymes's insight into folklore process and folklore performance. In Isay's collection *Callings*, conversations revolve around work. Dentist Thomas McGarvey, age 71, is interviewed by patient and friend Anne Brande, three decades his junior. "I knew that no matter what was going to happen, I was going to become a dentist.... Here I am, seventy-one years old, and I've got as much drive for dentistry as I had when I was twenty-five."[20] McGarvey's concluding assessment: "You know, life lessons are our attitudes. So get whatever it is you want in your heart, and in your gut. And once you've got it don't ever let it go."[21]

In a few hundred words, a complex work experience is framed entirely as irrepressible ambition, intuitive understanding of dentistry, achievement, tied up with an inspirational bow. Hinted realities: the early death of a parent and impoverished family life are marginalized in the collaborative creation of a coherent, purposeful story. If the Story-Corps frame is a concise metaphor for what we all must do to integrate a meaningful past into a functional present—if Hymes is right—then the folklore stance *is* central to a fundamental understanding of mankind.

By 2005, edited versions of the most interesting, heartwarming, issue-driven StoryCorps conversations were airing on NPR's "Morning Edition" every Friday. (As of this writing, this was still going on.) The Library of Congress division that houses StoryCorps interviews is the American Folklife Center—the already discussed consolation prize secured by Archie Green and collaborating advocates who came up short when pressingCongress to launch a new federal support program for folk culture in the early 1970s. This is both ironic and appropriate: StoryCorps is a very well-known project and brand name, but this kind of story does not represent a recognized folklore genre. There's no doubt that these stories—personal experience, family history, work—are by their nature highly traditionalized. So StoryCorps in the American Folklife Center makes sense, not because the collection fits what would have been considered folklore a century ago, but because Dell Hymes extended the perception of folklore studies from the exotic to the everyday, extending the meaning and potential impact of the field.

Jan Brunvand understood urban legend as a continually reconfigured told-as-true story that reinforces assumptions, elaborates fears, justifies prejudice. Contemporary folklore scholars extended Brunvand's observations into consideration of rumor and now into fake news. Journalist Walter Kirn, writing in *Harper's Magazine*, placed Donald Trump's presidential campaign in its cultural context, like others, deploying a traditional, folkloric frame: "If a hallmark of enduring fairy tales and folktales is an outsized, vivid character who overcomes impossible odds," Kirn writes, "this is one that should endure." He continues, noting that conspiracy theories were "everywhere last year, organizing and shaping confusing realities so as to make them intelligible."[22] Folklore scholar Bill Ellis defines contemporary legend in much the same way: "a proposition that may or may not be true, but which helps people interpret events during times of uncertainty."[23]

An understanding of the fundamental importance of traditionalization and the universal need for coherent life narrative has nudged folklore scholars toward the study of folklorized knowledge that frames the activities of powerful elites. There exists an unstated assumption that legends—frequently untrue—function mainly among ordinary people who lack learning. Hymes suggests no demographic category is immune to the essential effect of rumor and legend making. The 2017 annual meeting of the American Folklore Society took this on, staging three paper sessions on fake news and the related subjects of internet rumor and conspiracy theory. Legend specialist Tom Mould set the tone, arguing that folklore scholars should "drop their false modesty" when it comes to claiming ownership of the rising issues presented by traditional narrative in the digital age. "After all," Mould observed, "we've been studying this stuff for centuries."[24]

Ellis took up the challenge. Breaking with long-standing conventional wisdom that less educated people spread rumor, gossip, legend, while elite, evidence-empowered policy actors spread propaganda or disinformation, Ellis asserts that "in the wake of recent political events in the United States, it becomes less tenable to assume that influential claims made by politicians are made on the basis of secure standards of evidence."[25] He addresses three critical, war-or-peace decisions made at the level of the US presidency (or presidential candidacy), arguing that evidence underlying action was thin or nonexistent, and although there were few signs of disinformation or propaganda, legend-like narratives were pervasive: rumored looting of infant incubators by Iraqi soldiers during the invasion of Kuwait, the existence of weapons of mass destruction in Iraq, and claims of celebrating Muslims in the wake of 9/11 terrorist attacks lacked hard evidence sufficient to justify policy. Each tale had a lively presence in traditional media, online, and in what appeared to be (although Ellis doesn't explore this) an inside-Washington legend network.

As Ellis points out, each narrative, while not grounded in evidence, was still thoroughly *plausible*. "Even if a truth claim does not rely on factual truth, it takes on a reality of its own as a paradigm for motivated action." Just as Dell Hymes asserted a universal need to traditionalize experience, Ellis argues that legendry is "a valid concept for describing human social behavior . . . a universal mode of exploring ambiguous situations." And the behavior is "true at all levels, regardless of class, status, or position."[26]

Online fake news may simply relocate a widespread urban legend— the Welfare Queen reconfigured as a website headline. But it can also be a "fake legend," a made-up narrative that effectively taps into paranoia and preoccupation, insuring many clicks, many shares, wide distribution. A half-century ago, Richard Dorson coined the term *fakelore* to define tales and songs that seemed traditional but had in fact been produced by the entertainment and advertising industries. For Dorson, fakelore was usually crafted to make money by manufacturing objects, songs, narratives that capitalized on the charm of traditional expressive life without the authenticity and historical roots that give the real stuff meaning. Fake news is much the same—often produced to make money, cloaked in the appearance of institutional authenticity, but ultimately thin, weightless, deceptive. Rumor expert Pat Turner argues that folklore must advance a "doubt-centered approach" to fake news, adding that "facts are not an antidote to fake news, only *ridicule* is."[27] As folklore studies extends itself toward the traditional expressive tropes of wealth, power, and status, new challenges await. Folklore's enlightened, romantic heritage suggests that lore is always positive, communal, nurturing. But, as Ellis puts it, to see legend-making as a "universal human imperative," we must admit that some traditional narrative can be "wedge-driving and potentially sociopathic," even "evil."[28]

:   :   :   :   :

The journey of folklore studies in the United States (its "progress," in Enlightenment-speak), has been a transition from the collection and study of folklore "stuff," to the discovery of tradition as a marker of identity in a borderland society, then finally to an understanding that folklore making—the process of traditionalizing experience—is a fundamental human need, a cultural universal. The expressive lives of neighbors not like us, the narratives of marginalized peoples in other lands, can be sources of alternative knowledge—motivation, creative excellence, the refreshing sidelong look into someone else's alien, angled sense of order. Jan Brunvand, and especially Dell Hymes, extended our understanding of the ways oral narratives work in society. Hymes revealed that all people, in all places, at all times, traditionalize experience in order to impose a coherent, shareable framework of meaning on the incoherence of random experience. As our coherent side—the scientific, statutory, official wisdom of the Enlightenment—has stumbled, the capacity of folklore studies to explain where people are "coming from," what they want, what they think, has steadily increased.

In a borderland lacking a hegemonic, shared-language monoculture, legendary narrative is empowered. The pace and effect of rumor and legend are accelerated by social media and the internet; doubt undermines established sources of trusted information. For Walter Kirn, Pizzagate will be with us "throughout Trump's term. . . . Its theme of organized ritual pedophilia among the political illuminati is a perfect metaphoric vehicle for generalized suspicion of all insiders."[29] Or, as a folklore scholar might put it, a usable narrative perfectly adjusted to render borderland life coherent. Stories have meaning; it's time to *listen*.

SIX

LISTENING

THE KEN BURNS AND LYNN NOVICK PBS TELEVISION SERIES *The Vietnam War* produced a spate of commentary on television and in print: surprisingly little historical recrimination, but plenty of worries about present-day foreign affairs and the way America's dismal history of engagement with Southeast Asia is metaphor for what we now face in North Korea, Afghanistan, Syria. Donald Gregg, a former ambassador to South Korea and CIA station chief interviewed in episode 1, put it this way in a letter to the *New York Times*.

> I can't help thinking about the lessons from Vietnam that might apply today to North Korea. I fear that we are headed down a 2017 version of "ignorance alley" in our dealings with Pyongyang; we do not know what North Korea wants today, because we have not asked its leaders that question directly in several years.
>
> When we assume that we are always right, and our opponents always wrong, we overlook the need to ask questions. And as Vietnam demonstrated, in such a scenario, misguided decisions result.[1]

Amid the inflammatory online pronouncements of President Donald Trump, and the equally over-the-top responses from Kim Jong-un, North Korean officials invited a small group of American reporters to visit the closed-off country. *New York Times* columnist Nicholas Kristoff returned to report "a hard line toward the United States," that the "most totalitarian state in the world" is "steeped in the idea that they repeatedly defeated the US—and can do so again." Kristoff acknowledges that both North Korea and America are "on a hair trigger"—an atmosphere in which the smallest accidental engagement could set off a nuclear exchange. He concludes his report with recommendations: "First, Trump should stop personalizing and escalating the conflict." Fine. "Second, we need talks without conditions, if only talks about talks." Kristoff suggests a secret, senior-official visit. Okay. "Third, human rights have to be part of the agenda, backed by the threat of suspending North Korea's credentials at the United Nations."[2]

Whoa! That one stopped me. It's fine to have "talks without conditions," even "talks about talks." But human rights "have to be part of the agenda"? Doesn't that seem, well, a bit *colonial*?

As we have seen, the set of bracing universalist ideas advanced by Enlightenment thinkers provided a framework for a generous, open, respectful way for research and public policy to engage difference at home and around the world. If every life had value, every society standing, if government required the participation of many voices, many minds, then the inspiring set point of a new kind of engagement would be a generous curiosity about the values, aspirations, and ways of life of the multitudes previously excluded from the benefits of civilization. Read directly, abstract Enlightenment values seemed to imply a two-way conversation connecting wealth, power, literacy, and sophistication with the public—with the customs, artistry, and thick communal life of venerable peasant villages and ancient tribal peoples. A new understanding of the human condition would result.

Seen in this rosy light, the original enlightened promise proffered a real dialogue between civilization and previously suppressed cultures—a two-way conversation that was neutral and egalitarian. But history tracks only stark reality: this mutually adventurous and potentially advantageous interaction never occurred. Instead, as we have seen again and again, high ideals and intellectually inclusive rhetoric were conjured in the salons of Europe and America, then reconfigured as instruments of the selfish, expansionist ambitions of governments and markets. It seems that the Enlightenment's embrace of rational thought and scientific method actually precluded listening and learning from everyday experience: multitudes arrayed beneath the veneer of civilization were simply slotted into categories; assigned attributes based on race, geography, social organization; and then dealt with through imposed frameworks of law, education, language, and trade. The act of listening implies respect, but respect was never extended to individuals and communities perceived, a priori, as existing somewhere beneath civilization's accomplishments. Although the Enlightenment managed to conquer much of the world, the West never listened, never learned, and in a sense never really left home.

Richard Dorson highlighted the importance of understanding folk groups and lore by being present in communities over time. It was *fieldwork* that allowed face-to-face communication and real reciprocity; fieldwork placed research in the heart of the unfamiliar, forcing a measure of cultural humility. It was patient fieldwork that allowed the outsider-scholar to not only gather stories and songs, but also understand the human dynamic that sustains traditionalized experience. "Complete" folklorist Henry Glassie describes the work this way: "In fieldwork we patiently listen to other people. We give them all the time in the world they want to make their point. We learn about turn taking and exchange and a kind of gentility. We even hold back when we hear things we don't like."[3]

As US secretary of defense, Donald Rumsfeld famously observed, there are things you know, things you don't know, and things you don't know you don't know.[4] Because we live *in* it at the same time we talk *about* it, our understanding of our present era—its culture, cultural trends, changing cultural values—all too often resides in the realm of unknown unknowns. As serious and scientific as we might be, as attuned as we appear to be to the objective realities we face, there remains a sensation that today we *just don't understand what's going on in the world*. We don't because we don't listen.

I began my argument many pages ago by quoting Neil Gabler's lament that big ideas had become a thing of the past. But Gabler's accurate observation has an exception—over the past two decades, public intellectuals committed to understanding global conflict have striven to explain our current situation, both around the world and in the United States. Once the decades-long nuclear standoff between the United States and the Soviet Union ended and the Middle East and China emerged as vexing challenges, experienced students of national and international affairs tried to map the conceptual, architectural power structure of the current scene. They have outlined the essential contours of the international environment, addressing the two big "whats" of national and world affairs: "What the situation is; what should be done." On these pages, I've advanced my own understanding of the problem—we have reached the end point of the global influence of the Enlightenment idea. The vision of universal human rights, participatory government, equality, justice has been undermined by a long-term failure to deliver. While millions are better off, disease pushed back, the most obdurate aspects of human societies mitigated, two centuries of Enlightenment-inspired interventions in world affairs have today generated a powerful resistance: the emergence of non-state actors, the worldwide advance of religious fundamentalism, the rejection of established authority, and the suspicion of scientific knowledge fit together as the essential problem facing the United States and the world. That is my view. Further, it is my contention that the unique stance of folklore scholarship offers an essential, alternative way of reanimating the Enlightenment dream. What have others said?

In late summer 2017, Kurt Andersen—journalist and public-radio host—published "How America Lost Its Mind," a concise rendition of the core argument of a new book, *Fantasyland: How America Went Haywire—A 500-Year History*. Like me, Andersen senses that the Enlightenment has run out of steam:

> The idea that progress has some kind of unstoppable momentum, as if powered by a Newtonian law, was always a very American belief. However, it's really an article of faith, the Christian fantasy about history's happy ending reconfigured during and after the Enlightenment as a set of modern secular fantasies. It reflects our blithe conviction that America's visions of freedom and democracy and justice and prosperity must prevail in the end. I really can imagine, for the first time in my life, that America has permanently tipped into irreversible decline, heading deeper into Fantasyland.[5]

I'm with him to a point. But Andersen's argument is firmly stuck at home; the problem is all about America. He finds the nation "untethered from reality," its core values undermined by the excesses of individualism, relativism, and the growing hegemony of youth culture empowered by digital technology. He grounds the American experience in Enlightenment values but argues that the Enlightenment focus on intellectual freedom has allowed "the subjective to entirely override the objective," that imagination and free will, the "exciting parts of the Enlightenment idea, have swamped the sober, rational, empirical parts."[6]

So far so good. But Andersen ignores the global reaction against imposed Enlightenment-rationalized frameworks of law, governance, language, education. He cites instead the failure of American thought leaders and the downward spiral of what might be called American intellectualizing—a process that has led to an irredeemable loss of national self-control. Andersen argues that America entered "a national nervous breakdown" in the 1960s and never fully recovered. He traces America's growing infatuation with "fantastical beliefs" to the mid-twentieth century—conspiracy theories of the right, self-actualization programs, cultural relativism, a self-involved, irresponsible counterculture, Michel Foucault's critique of scholarly method, crime and punishment, and the treatment of mental illness together paving the way to a political culture of Trumpism, "truthiness," and "fake news."[7]

Andersen's inventory of US symptoms is fine. Easy for me to agree; his observations fit my folklore-studies frame. But it's hard to believe worldwide attacks on established Western authority and ideas got their start here. In fact, as I have argued, the spread of antiscience, internet fakery, magical (or religious) thinking, contempt for participatory government and for the norms of civil society didn't show up first in the United States, but in Southeast Asia, the postcolonial Middle East, and in countries like France and Germany—places where arrogant, nationalist power used ideology built on Enlightenment principles to insult and repress resident minority groups (who then pushed back!). Yes, America's media environment has reconfigured and accelerated these global trends, but in terms of impact, America's disrupters lag far behind the likes of ISIS.

The notion of cultural conflict as the essential driver of international affairs was not entirely ignored. The catch phrase "clash of civilizations" suggested a contest driven by beliefs and values rather than a quest for territorial or economic advantage.[8] But each of these arguments was framed within the model of competing nation-states, grounded in the belief that outcomes would be determined as in the past—through the application of conventional military advantage, threat of nuclear destruction, the weight of economic power.

To know where you are one must understand the deep forces that frame everyday reality, and current attempts to frame fundamental arguments fall short—they live innocently in the unhelpful world of *known* unknowns. To ask whether we are witnessing the triumph of liberalism, the emergence of a multipolar international order, or experiencing the effects of a new era of competition driven by national values does nothing more than reshuffle a tired deck of twentieth-century understandings and assumptions.

Our unknown unknowns are the deep residue of Enlightenment-inspired isms—the nineteenth-century ideologies that define, explain, assume. These are the hidden but self-imposed limitations on the West's ability to listen and really hear. The hegemony of economic, societal, psychological explanation produces superficial, off-target understanding: ISIS messages draw in young men who would resist if only they had had happy childhoods and a decent job; the Gates Foundation strives to make everybody healthy, so they have a "chance" to attain "productive lives."9 This kind of thinking is mired in deep unknown unknowns that produce wrongheaded analysis and ineffective policy. To understand where we are today we must acknowledge the reemergence of the tribal, the magical, the spiritual, and all the dysfunctional actions that follow when Enlightenment values are cast aside.

Kurt Andersen is a new but by no means solitary voice among experts set on explaining a disrupted world, a disoriented and drifting America. Since the late twentieth century, a gaggle of experts in international affairs have engaged in a spirited competition to explain the character of our post–Cold War world. Some have argued that the US-Soviet deadlock created an essentially unstable international order. In that view, absent bilateral hegemony, the world will return to the undisciplined competition among nation-states that created an environment that fostered the outbreak of World War I. Others interpreted the collapse of the Soviet empire as the triumph of liberal democracy, a historical transformation so profound that history itself would be transformed—history would "end."

The watershed end of the Cold War nudged experts in global affairs toward speculation about what was to come—the shape of international relations after the decades-long standoff between the United States and the Soviet Union had ended with what seemed a startling victory for

America, participatory democracy, and capitalism. The work of these thinkers engaged the challenge presented by this volume: How can we best characterize and comprehend the deep forces that are shaping our current reality? What set of basic understandings is sufficiently convincing and inclusive to provide a foundation for future action? Once we understand where we are, what then must we do?

: : : : :

How well have experts in foreign affairs handled even the *known* unknowns? As Jessica Mathews wrote in the *New York Review* in 2017, there are three overarching principles that postwar American foreign-policy actors agreed on: first, our international military and political alliances are critical to America's security; second, the global economy is not a dog-eat-dog zero-sum game, but a mutually beneficial growth system; third, over the long term, democracy will prove a superior form of governance. While we wait for democratic capitalism to take hold, "Dictators have to be tolerated, managed, or confronted, not admired." Mathews identifies (there is consensus on this) three groups of foreign policy experts with "radically different views." They are neoconservatives, liberal internationalists, and realists. For our purposes, it is only important to understand that each group sees current challenges primarily residing in the actions of established nation-states. "Neocons" might be quick to use American might to advance our (Enlightenment) values within other countries; liberal internationalists also stress engagement, but emphasize the nurturing of a cooperative international order. Realists envision a world divided among powerful states; "The US should concentrate on its relations with the other great powers and on the balance of power in the most important regions."[10]

As disparate as their analyses might be, none of these intellectual frameworks steps outside the established playing field of state action and military and economic competition. None of the three schools of foreign-affairs thinking sees a world order that is being transformed; none anticipates the Enlightenment's demise; none sees subnational and transnational actors as strong enough to reconfigure global reality. But several big-idea strategists must be considered besides—thinkers who see a modern world deeply transformed, whose ideas bump up against my post-Enlightenment frame.

Francis Fukuyama was quick to assert big change at the Cold War's end. His essay "The End of History?" was published in the *National Interest* in the summer of 1989, just as the Soviet empire was coming apart. In that year it appeared that not only was the Soviet empire collapsing, but the old nation of czars and borscht was sinking gently into the embrace of the West, constructing its own version of Euro-American market democracy. Despite its tentative question mark, Fukuyama's title introduced an essay of remarkable confidence and optimism. Citing the "total exhaustion of viable systematic alternatives to Western liberalism," he understood the spread of "consumerist culture" as central to democracy's reach.[11] Fukuyama's description of the ahistorical post–Cold War state is a confident invocation of by-now-familiar Enlightenment language: "The state that emerges at the end of history is liberal insofar as it recognizes and protects through a system of law man's universal right to freedom, and democratic insofar as it exists only with the consent of the governed."[12]

Frances Fukuyama was right, just not in the way he had hoped. His thesis, that progressive transformation in the structure of governments had ended in 1989, represented a profound commitment to the ultimate hegemony of enlightened democratic government. But by the 1990s, Fukuyama's triumph of liberal democracy would turn on itself as a cruel joke. We *are* at the "end of history" in one sense, or at least witnessing the demise of the driver of historical change that has dominated policy, war making, social intervention for two centuries. Fukuyama interpreted the collapse of the Soviet empire as a watershed transition, reconfiguring global reality, anointing liberal democracy as a permanent global system. But that "end" never occurred; instead, what we are witnessing is the final, final end of the Enlightenment—the exhaustion and rejection of social justice, elites, secularism, science, and political participation as permanent underpinnings securing progressive modernism.

Immediate and bold interpretation of rapidly changing circumstances in governments and the international system always runs the risk of being dead wrong. Such was the case with Fukuyama, who envisioned a world emerging from the Cold War into a stable, democratic order free of aggressive competition among states. Celebrating the US triumph, focused on the nation-state as the context in which human conflict is framed and worked out, he ignored or underestimated both the exhaustion of presumptively permanent Enlightenment values and the bubbling-under intensity of the looming pushback from two directions: first, from ordinary people—the folk—who bought into the elite's vision of justice, equality, and participation, but felt its effects only through intervention, exploitation, disruption; and second from China, a nation burdened by its own heritage of values, rights, and hierarchies—a society that *had* experienced the Enlightenment, but only through a series of abusive imperial interventions from the West.

Ironically, even as he assembles his "end-of-history" argument, Fukuyama gently touches on forces that would in the end define our post–Cold War era—the importance of "consciousness and culture"[13] in shaping human behavior, the threat posed by rising nationalism and "other forms of ethnic consciousness," and "religious fundamentalism."[14] In passing, Fukuyama notes that "men have proven themselves able to endure the most extreme material hardships in the name of ideas that exist in the realm of the spirit alone, be it the divinity of cows or the nature of the Holy Trinity."[15] The observation would prove ironic, foreshadowing the quests of Osama bin Laden and ISIS, acknowledging but quickly dismissing the tribal, religious, self-effacing heroic dreams that inspired thousands not only to kill perceived elite and powerful oppressors, but also to sacrifice themselves. Even as he writes of liberal democracy triumphant, Fukuyama seems to sense the latent, looming power of *real* differences in heritage, belief, identity—insight that never redirects his understanding of a world that tilts toward a permanent Enlightenment consensus.

Harvard scholar Samuel Huntington didn't buy Fukuyama's argument: he took a look at the post–Cold War order and saw a "clash of civilizations." Huntington's now-famous phrase encompasses a collapse of traditional state actors and their power centers, and the disruption of ideologies and economic systems that served as the arena of international affairs in in past. "The fault lines between civilizations will be the battle lines of the future," he argued, with competition played out among cultures that each feature fundamental values that lead to profound differences.[16] For Huntington, cultures can be not only characterized, but actually *defined* by one or two overarching characteristics that are the source of fundamental understandings within a population but are inevitably antagonistic to outsiders. (The West, for example, is basically "Christian.")

Huntington intellectualizes civilized suspicion of "the other" (the masses; ordinary people), elevating shorthand cultural stereotypes to traits that make conflict inevitable and difference nonnegotiable. He sees no present or future value in engaging cultural difference as a source of alternative knowledge to be mined for mutual benefit As François Jullien notes, by grounding international conflict in irreducible cultural traits, "Huntington cannot arrive at anything other than purely defensive and, consequently reactionary, conclusions."[17] One senses that, in Huntington's view, the West should simply hunker down, re-commit to its own traditional values, stop trying to convince the world that these are universal. Huntington's argument is seductive but wrong. Cultural stereotypes are useful (they always hold a measure of truth), but when accepted as interpretation and made real through foreign policy, irreconcilable fears of subnational groups who ground their aggression in fundamentalist identities are given too much weight.

Richard Haass is a respected public intellectual—a writer and pundit well known on the Washington stage. He heads the Council on Foreign Relations. The title of Haass's book *A World in Disarray* shorthands his argument: "History at any moment or in any era is the result of the interaction between forces of society and anarchy, of order and disorder. It is the balance between the two, between society and anarchy, that determines the dominant character of any era."[18] But anarchy is not an ideology—not an ism. Substitute *civilization* for *society*, and *the public* for *anarchy*, and Haass's notion of a world in disarray finds more solid footing. Haass would be more correct to view history as moving from periods in which international affairs are dominated by the rules of civilization, into periods when ordinary people assert autonomy, different values, contrary ambition.

Each formulation of a new order in international affairs has a fatal blind spot. It is the assumption that no matter how unsettled the global order, no matter how effectively subnational or transnational groups assert their ambition, in the end, resolution of conflict will remain in the hands of civilized authorities—nation-states, armies, the World Trade Organization, the World Economic Forum (Davos). The future will be set by men in suits armed with military might and economic power, posturing around tables bedecked with tiny flags and skimpy flower arrangements. But the assumption that the give-and-take of inevitable conflict resides permanently in the realms of state power, international trade, and assertion of legal and regulatory authority begs a critical question: Shouldn't inheritors of the residue of enlightened power consider the real possibility that ways of life grounded in traditional societies of ordinary people will overwhelm the Enlightenment consensus? Isn't it possible that the center has shifted to village-centered societies? Internet writer Christy Rodgers again: "The 'primitives' have not become extinct, and have been speaking for themselves the whole time. And . . . the language in which they speak is resonant with the tropes of myth."[19]

Thus the modern nation—assumed by policy experts to be the key actor in international affairs—is vulnerable to stateless, borderless actors hostile to elites, governments, history, and scientific knowledge. Religion, legend, traditional practice trump reason. What would a foreign-policy perspective grounded in the insights of folklore studies look like? How would a folkloric stance resuscitate universal values and human rights? The folklore scholar asks her own questions: Why are they like that? How are they different from us? What do they really want? What can they teach; what can we learn? Answers are not found in stated, official positions, in economic analysis, in military exercises or diplomatic exchange, but rather in a close look at the central, frequently hidden beliefs and understandings that shape actions. Can we look at, and listen to, traditional expression to map assumptions and beliefs; can we determine what fixed perspectives and likely responses are sustained by tradition; finally, can we develop interventions tailored to belief in specific settings, to specific populations? If we move beyond our own confidence in economics, psychology, and a universal desire for progress to *listen* and map what is true, then critical parts of the Enlightenment dream can be preserved.

This is not about control or manipulation, but listening. It is the nurturing of a genuine cosmopolitan spirit that looks at subnational groups in a new way, leaving our tools of analysis, categorization, explanation behind.

:   :   :   :   :

"To see what is in front of one's nose needs a constant struggle," wrote George Orwell in a short political essay published just after World War II.[20] In many ways this has been the struggle—the stance—of folklore scholarship from its earliest days. How do we pay close attention to ways of life quite unlike our own in order to exchange artistry, understanding, meaning? How must cultures interact? How do we look hard enough, long enough, at difference to be able to honor what is best in the lives of everyday people while pushing back against truly obdurate behaviors?

Folklore scholars have listened by living in communities—observing, sometimes working, patiently seeking out often hidden understandings, knowledge, artistry. From the earliest days of US research, fieldwork has been the path to learning. Henry Glassie describes the folklore studies stance this way: "Folklorists come into fragile worlds composed of mortal flesh, of memory and words, and the folklorist's great and pressing responsibility is recording exactly, completely, permanently the texts people weave to give their thought and culture presence."[21] This is a special kind of interaction and, as we have seen, a way of encountering difference that requires a degree of humility and self-reflection all too rare in the centuries-old implementation of the Enlightenment dream. Glassie epitomizes the folklore scholar's approach to difference. Although a generation younger than Dorson, Paredes, and Green, Henry Glassie could pass as a folklore old-timer. Apparently endowed with an enthusiasm for the study of traditional expressive life at birth, he was collecting folksongs and documenting rural architecture while in high school. In the late 1960s, while still working on his PhD, Glassie took on the new position of state folklorist for Pennsylvania. When he appeared for a guest lecture at the Indiana University Folklore Institute, I and my fellow grad students were shocked and intimidated; here was a senior folklore scholar who was *our age!*

Once employed in the academy, Glassie's path was predictable: he took on large projects, engaging traditional communities and folk artists to understand heritage, values, the creative impulse as lived in societies unlike our own. He and his family moved to Ireland, then Turkey, then Bangladesh for extended periods, learning new languages, living a "deep engagement," closely observing the words and actions of ordinary people. To date, Henry Glassie has written twenty books, achieved recognition within the humanities, and most important, set a clear model of the folklore scholar's stance—that the job of the visitor is not to talk, but to *listen.*

Patient listening, understanding, are also essential to American diplomacy in the world. There exists no more direct connection between the stance of folklore studies and public policy than the attitude we should bring to international affairs. John Paton Davies Jr., Foreign Service "China hand" and rising foreign-service star in the 1930s, 1940s, and 1950s, posits "discrimination" as essential in foreign engagements:

> Discrimination in the conduct of foreign relations starts with a native perceptiveness and sensitivity. If these inborn qualities are absent, no amount of training or experience will compensate. As a subsequently developed faculty, it embraces a knowledge and sense of history; an insight into diverse foreign psychologies gained through experience; a developing sense of proportion, and thereby a sense of humor about relations among peoples and governments and from these, some understanding of the limits of power, the fallibility of one's own judgments, the stubbornness of traditional ways and beliefs, the greater persuasiveness of example over words, the uses of implicit rather than explicit force, the value of frequent silence, the worth of occasional inaction, and the need for constant patience.[22]

Henry Glassie is the archetypal field-working folklore scholar; Davies was America's model insider diplomat. Son of missionaries, expert in language, and adept at the nuances of Chinese behavior and belief, Davies was especially well equipped to serve as an expert on-the-ground witness at a critical juncture in China-US relations. With other expert "China hands"—John Stewart Service, Edmund Clubb—Davies fed acute observations about the state of Chinese politics up the line, intended to be raw material informing policy-making within the US Department of State. Davies's sense of the diplomat's creed, so close to Glassie's sense of fieldwork's modest, patient stance, enabled the diplomat's accurate assessment of China in the late 1940s—the strength of Mao Zedong, the weakness of Chiang Kai-shek, the likelihood of a communist victory.

As Davies wrote in his memoir, *China Hand*, he and other "Americans in varying degrees concluded that Chiang's Kuomintang was decadent and that the Chinese Communists were a virile, rising force, the China Lobbyists and their confederates charged those Americans with disloyal collusion. The accusations were, in effect, that what we independently reported and predicted was what we willed and plotted to bring about."[23] Davie's cables, sent back to Washington, had been accurate, but flew in the face of widespread support for (Christian, English-speaking) Chiang and rattled a State Department enduring repeated hostile investigation by congressional right-wingers who stirred the fears of a nation caught up in "an anxiety neurosis about China, Russia, and Communism."[24] The principle villain was the demagogic Wisconsin Senator Joseph McCarthy, who placed Davies name on a list of twenty-six State Department staffers suspected of communist sympathies. Knowledge of the China situation, and a willingness to pay attention and report unfiltered observation was deemed to be somehow subversive. As John Finney wrote in the *New York Times Magazine* in the late 1960s, Davies "was too honest and foresighted in describing developments in China during 1943 and 1944. . . . For his outspoken but accurate reports . . . he was made a political scapegoat."[25]

Henry Glassie's patient observation fueled a brilliant career; Davies—proponent of patient listening—was fired. His fate shadows our Department of State and US diplomacy to this day. The lesson to young foreign service officers was clear: there is little career benefit in telling truth to power, and a distinctly negative effect if your field observations contradict policy that has already been fixed by higher-ups. Critical expertise had been punished, and Washington fell back on uninformed assumptions and political anxiety. The failure of observation and insight extended over decades. As David Halberstam put it, absent the insights of John Paton Davies and other Southeast Asia experts, "each new Administration became increasingly susceptible to blackmail from any small oligarchy which proclaimed itself anti-Communist."[26] We misunderstood the new China, invaded North Korea, blundered into a colonial war in Vietnam.

Today we are stuck in an anti-diplomatic "war on terror," a miserable military dodge that demands neither empathy nor special knowledge: to make war on a noun you need listen to nobody; understand nothing. As journalist Steve Coll commented in a 2018 interview, when it comes to the situation in Afghanistan, "we can't handle the facts."[27] In the 1950s, John Paton Davies was accused of "lack of judgment, discretion, and reliability" not disloyalty; certainly not treason. "In an organization with a tradition of factual reporting and independence of judgment, the new standard was thus to be conformity."[28] The steady decline of State Department influence began then, in the era of Joe McCarthy and the nation's reckless anti-communism. America gave up the capacity to listen and learn; as a result, every conflict over the past half-century has been an exercise in ignorance and wishful thinking. In the mid-twentieth-century, "China hands" were demeaned, ignored, moved out of the way. As Coll points out, it has been much the same for present-day specialists who master the languages and cultures of the Middle East, only to have insights ignored, recommendations pushed aside. Diplomatic capacity has dimmed; military solutions advanced. As Coll makes clear, after 9/11 the US Department of State lost funding and authority. The face of America in areas of conflict was steadily transformed from civilian diplomats, to the military, then to a secretive, drone-besotted CIA, and finally to "contractors"—muscular, ex-military bullies armed with Glocks, menacing and anonymous behind wraparound sunglasses. Emerging populations might be dangerous but are never culturally serious. By the era of Middle-East wars, whole societies were reduced to a demeaning and dismissive military shorthand—"human terrain."[29]

In 2017, Secretary of State Rex Tillerson, confirmed early in the Donald Trump administration, made "no secret of his belief that the State Department is a bloated bureaucracy and that he regards much of the day-to-day diplomacy lower-level officials conduct as unproductive."[30] Nothing new, just a reformulation of Washington's firmly established assumption that diplomacy was mere message-sending, a posture sustained by a corrosive disdain for expertise, truth, and the peaceful execution of international relations. American diplomats, once reliable cultural middle-men, teasing out essential knowledge close to the ground, have been permanently transformed into sales agents, charged with promoting the official policy of the moment, reinforcing what officials who have never left home already believe.

The new reality: When I began regular visits to China in the fall of 2007, my first stop was the public affairs office of the lurking, fortresslike US embassy in Beijing. I was seeking insider knowledge. After all, embassy staffers were our modern-day "China hands," experts in local politics, capable in language, aware of the nuances of culture and custom. But I was disappointed. Post-9/11, our embassy was tightly sealed off from the rest of the newly built international district. Staff moved through the city only as required; most were housed in a dedicated high-rise, with access to special services geared to the needs and tastes of Americans who were temporary—serving three-year postings and devoting the last year to insider politics aimed at securing the best reassignment possible.

Far from being a source of local knowledge, staffers appeared permanently on "send," executing publications and programs designed to tell the American story in a patriotic manner. Before I headed across the bleak interior courtyard of our embassy, I was handed a packet of bookmarks—English on one side, Chinese the other—headlining, then defining, key values and principles of America's democracy: "freedom of expression," "freedom of association," "checks and balances," "civil society." "How nice," I thought. But then, What Chinese citizen would use these? Who would dare mark place in a volume of Chinese history with such a blatant assertion of American ideals? How would American visitors to China's Washington embassy receive an English-language pamphlet promoting Xi Jinping Thought? What are *we* thinking?

:   :   :   :   :

To extend Donald Rumsfeld's notorious known and unknown unknowns, we know that terrorist groups distrust and disdain our values; we *think* we know that violent acts are often committed by disaffected young men who are adrift, unemployed, bereft of economic hope; we *think* we know that violent extremists flourish in ungoverned territories of collapsed nation-states. Implied in our understanding—grounded or without substance—is the assumption that the Enlightenment construct of economy, governance, human aspiration is permanent, universal, and holds a priori claim on collective understanding and imagination.

The present is disappearing moment to moment, it is the future we care most about. But the future will rest on the present: some things remaining and others dropping away. Even though we are likely to fall short, we must do our best to figure out where we are now in the hope that speculation about what is to come springs from a true and sturdy understanding of what is happening today. And further, if we plumb the unknown unknowns of where we are today, what new knowledge and what new ways of thinking and living can help us cope with the perils of conflict, distrust, power, and aggression on a globalized international stage?

There is general agreement that the West, and in fact the entire globe, is transitioning, in a time of change. But it is one thing to understand that you are straddling a watershed, quite another to define its character and divine a set of strategies through which society can cope with an environment that in some ways is all new. We can look back with confidence to discern the outlines of the Renaissance, the Reformation, the Industrial Revolution: time orders reality. In place of a sophisticated implementation of the Enlightenment dream, America's worldview has been reduced to a few tropes that retain broadly sketched elements of each ism—tropes that live in the region of Donald Rumsfeld's things "we don't know we don't know." In this case, the things we don't know we don't know are powerful enough to define beliefs while limiting imagination.

But we can still act. Listening is an essential skill of borderland life, where engagement with difference is key. It is hard but practical, for it clears a path to mapping and acquiring new knowledge, exploring places where we can yield to conceptions held by others, marking those where our own choices and beliefs must stand. Essential within the borderland, indispensable around the world. François Jullien's argument resists the authority of any pre-established universality—if the Enlightenment is to prevail, it must be first subjected to a determined critical scrutiny. If any elements of Sharia law are to gain standing in the world, each must withstand a true critical gaze.

Of course, there exists an alluring alternative. We can decide all on our own, in the manner of Huntington, that cultures ("civilizations" for him) are defined by their most problematic and overarching feature (in Europe, for example, it is "Christianity"). Acting confidently on the basis of our known knowns, we can assert our preset place in an international order shaped by an inescapable antagonism. Aggression, defense, are inevitable, cultural accommodation difficult or impossible.

But, as David Brooks wrote in August 2017,

> The most powerful answer to fanaticism is modesty. Modesty is an epistemology directly opposed to the conspiracy mongering mind-set. It means having the courage to understand that the world is too complicated to fit into one political belief system. It means understanding there are no easy answers or malevolent conspiracies that can explain the big political questions or the existential problems. Progress is not made by crushing some swarm of malevolent foes; it's made by finding balance between competing truths—between freedom and security, diversity and solidarity. There's always going to be counter-evidence and mystery. There is no final arrangement that will end conflict, just endless searching and adjustment.[31]

For Henry Glassie, modest listening reveals the complexity of truth: "If the goal is to construct a comprehensive narrative, conceived from the present backward, but told from the past forward and proceeding along a single line, too many places, too many people, too many varieties of human endeavor will prove unfit, and what does fit will be beaten out of shape to meet the needs of the narrative. . . . When the tale is held together by sequences of cause and effect, and governed by a single temporal energy, the story will never be complicated enough to account for the current state of affairs, much less the past."[32]

By listening respectfully to the voices of others, can we extract Enlightenment values from their corrupt alliance with repression, exploitation, and the reductionist gaze of social science? In short, if we *listen* first, can we begin again?

BEGINNING AGAIN 2018

IN APRIL 2016, US AMBASSADOR TO THE UNITED NATIONS Samantha Power was hurrying from Marona Airport to meetings in Mokolo, in northern Cameroon. Her speeding motorcade—"shiny vehicles filled with important people, encased in air-conditioning"—drew a fascinated roadside crowd as the fourteen-car procession sped through tiny settlements dotted along the highway. In the village of Mokong, the motorcade struck and killed a six-year-old boy. No one stopped. *New York Times* reporter Helene Cooper, in the press van, wrote about the incident months later. Despite her sentiments and sensibilities, Cooper realized that she "was stationed securely on the other side of the great divide that separates the powerful from the powerless. That all-encompassing machine that projects American might around the world." She had become "one of the people whose lives are deemed so important that we need millions of dollars spent to protect us from people so poor they have no shoes on their feet and wear hand-me-down Chelsea football shirts. . . . The people who are so important that they don't have to stop when they hit and kill a young boy."[1]

Ambassador Power later returned to apologize and commiserate with Toussaint Birwe's father, but the question is unavoidable: Is a globalized world that "disenfranchises the vast majority and empowers a technocratic elite" any more enlightened than the colonial administration that undid tribal societies of Kenya?[2] Can the human-rights objectives of the West—now enshrined in programs of the United Nations, UNESCO, numerous international foundations and NGOs—maintain any hold on the hopes of everyman if the stain of arrogance and

disrespect remains? Can America really navigate alternative understandings of different worlds if we never question our own fundamental beliefs? Is it right or even smart to send an ethnicized "Sesame Street" and
its Muppets to the Middle East, promoting "inclusion and respect, and
gender equity" for young Syrian refugees?[3]

Don't get me wrong; science and commerce have advanced material
well-being. While confidence in shared human progress has stumbled,
two hundred years of Enlightenment influence have made many things
better: Chinese foot-binding is gone, many millions have been lifted out
of absolute material scarcity, Saudi women have begun to drive. Steven
Pinker, in *Enlightenment Now*, has added up multiple positive effects of
the movement—a movement that still stands as what Vincenzo Ferrone called "the emancipatory project of modernity."[4] But as we have
seen, enabling ideologies and the tenacious habits of colonialism and
imperialism are still in play. No surprise that the West's compromised
engagement with cultural difference has handed us resistance and rejection—not just of external authority, but of the underlying values and
methods used to justify imposed law, language, values. Alain Peyrefitte
puts it this way: "For their part, the dominated countries were inevitably
outraged by the brutality with which the West ravaged their traditions.
They had pride, and rightly so, for a people without pride loses its taste
for life, especially if, like India or China, their home is the hearth of an
ancient, refined civilization."[5] If conceits of the West have spawned a
highly original cultural sin pervasive enough to guarantee that scientists,
philosophers, universities, government agencies are no longer trusted; if
America has failed to sustain the curiosity, openness, sympathy essential
to life in a vibrant borderland; gains of the past two hundred years will
collapse in the face of empowered suspicion, anger, violence. If what
might be called the "first rendition" of Enlightenment values out in the
world has ended—the version empowered by colonialism and imperialism, the one sanctified by sociology, psychology, market democracy—
what can we do, or what *must* we do?

Folklore studies was an early result of eighteenth-century Enlightenment thought. Curiosity about the expressive lives of ordinary people
living on the edge of the authority of civilization's literate tastes, wealth,
and refined mores was a natural product of a new interest in human

rights, participatory government, and a secular, worldly understanding of what constituted "the good life." Unlike Enlightenment-inspired social-science disciplines, however, folklore studies maintained a reluctance to employ scientific methods to analyze, categorize, administer, or reform rural and tribal people. Folklore scholars tended to be observant rather than intrusive. Folklore studies navigated in the uncomfortable territory between the hard rationality of science and a less prescriptive engagement of the Enlightenment's romantic side. It is significant that the field never fully embraced the smug prescriptions of sociology, psychology, economics, nor has its American rendition been swept up in the nationalist political enthusiasms of imagined monocultural national identities. As we have seen, the approach has been observational and only lightly intrusive, more tentative, less prescriptive, more willing to seek out alternative knowledge, open to taking in other ways of thinking and living. The field's most accomplished practitioners were above all patient *listeners*. Recall Henry Glassie's approach to working in "the field": "I have learned by vulnerability, by arriving alone and surrendering to the direction of the local people while the way to communicate evolved slowly and friendship grew."[6]

Historian Odd Arne Westad observes that twenty-first century America has taken a different course:

> As America entered a new century, its main aim should have been to bring other nations into the fold of international norms and the rule of law, especially as its own power diminishes. Instead, the United States did what declining superpowers often do: engage in futile, needless wars far from its borders, in which short-term security is mistaken for long-term strategic goals. The consequence is an America less prepared than it could have been to deal with the big challenges of the future: the rise of China and India, the transfer of economic power from West to East, and systemic challenges like climate change and disease epidemics.[7]

Westad might have added, "the growing influence of ISIS, the Taliban, crusaders for ethnic and religious hegemony, and other sub-national or transnational non-state actors." As we have seen, the West in general and the United States in particular have been anything but immune to the growing profile of angry outsider groups, and Donald Trump's 2016 campaign channeled and focused our home-grown frustration with worn-out Enlightenment promises that, for the average citizen, led no-where. As in Egypt, Syria, and countries like Germany and France, a star-tling number of Americans were drawn to an inexperienced change agent dedicated to reshaping the size, character, objectives of government.

No surprise: once in office this new US administration was like no other. From the outset, the president disdained the long-accepted tra-ditions of democratic process. The result was a series of unpredictable and unconventional White House actions. Staff changes, news leaks, startling presidential "tweets," growing antagonism between the admin-istration and Republican insiders moved to the foreground. Trump at-tacked established news outlets while embracing, and retweeting, urban legend–style fake news. Critical big ideas—big issues—of foreign and domestic policy were pushed to the side, replaced by talking-head analy-ses of administration personalities, speculation about the deep meaning of scripted and off-the-cuff presidential remarks, brushfires of anger, personal invective.

These distractions were unsettling, dismaying, occasionally amus-ing, but the administration's instability and tweeting inconsistency pre-vented both leaders and government critics from deep consideration of the North Korean threat, environmental decay, endless Middle East war. Washington's disarray has been a gift to me and my discipline, folklore studies. Bombarded by a punditry suddenly fascinated by "customs," "traditions," "norms," and "fake news," an observant citizen might get the impression that, in stressful times, Americans revert to the comfort of traditional explanation, to a folklorized view. In fact, as folklore studies has learned, human beings mostly live within informal culture. This is the underlying truth legitimating the inquisitive, sympathetic stance of the humanities' premier listening discipline. The stories that explain us, and the underpinnings of our beliefs and actions, reside in traditional lifeways, not in laws, written accounts, or official rules of behavior. Tradi-tionalized experience is always important, always with us, but when thin conceits of civilization weaken, the communal reassurance of sustaining folk belief and practice becomes especially important.

My objective has been to convince the reader that the explanations and actions derived from Enlightenment rhetoric, the ideological enthu-siasms that made them real, the scientific constructs that fitted mankind into predetermined slots have stopped working. The alternative stance offered by folklore studies, a venerable approach to understanding ordinary people and their ways of life, offers another way—a new, convincing, encompassing *explanation* for the watershed-unsettled disarray of global power. I believe that the end of the Enlightenment explains our unsettled present—the collapse of old assumptions, the decline of government authority, disdain for science and received wisdom.

But a worthy big idea must suggest a way forward, it must provide not only prediction, but *prescription* for a new way of engaging challenging new realities. Henry Glassie's approach to engaging difference—through vulnerability and surrender—must be fleshed out and formalized if the insights of folklore studies are to offer policy actors a bold new way to audition Enlightenment values for a mistreated and skeptical audience. What are the components of the folklore studies stance that can help to navigate a post-Enlightenment world?

The old way has failed—Achebe's imagined district commissioner, UN ambassador Power in a rush to negotiate the narrow streets of a village in Cameroon—the assumption of civilization's superiority, authority, entitlement can no longer shape relationships between power and the masses. Through imperial reach and colonial occupation, the presumed superiority of Western ways and Western people was perpetually set on *send.* How do educated leaders apply understanding to a world in disarray? The challenge, the question, according to philosopher Francois Jullien, is not just to listen, but to listen in a way that engages difference.

> Cultures are still somewhere undoubtedly (irreducibly) committed to dialogue with one another. Obliquely, to the point of extinction, in a stubborn way: through borrowings, contaminations and influences, but also through misunderstandings, resistances, twistings, dissidences, or simply through the traces and testimony buried beneath the ruins uncovered by History. . . . Moreover, the culture that has become dominant over these past centuries (the "Western" one) has been forced to recognize that its sovereign position is being chipped away and it can no longer assert its pre-established legitimacy so dogmatically.[8]

Jullien has converted a shared understanding that cultural relations have failed into a set of specific actions that can encourage mutual comprehension, respect, new wisdom. In *On the Universal,* Jullien argues that societies must first comprehend one another. This action requires a close look at difference—at the way a distinctive set of perceptions and assumptions diverge from our own. What does a culture emphasize; what are the deep ideas that are undiscussed—"implicit and largely buried choices" that limit and configure what is thinkable and doable?[9] Such interaction demands curiosity, sympathy, and a relentless skepticism about both what we comprehend and the limits of our own tools of perception. The goal is critical dialogue that interrogates themes operative in both an alien society and in our own.

As we have seen, the American way of engaging difference defaults to hegemonic impulses to force others to talk, act, and even think in our terms. We mostly send messages and listen only to hear things we expect, already know, or desire. Nicholas Kristoff proposes open-ended meetings with North Korean officials: "talks about talks," but throws in a deal-breaker—honoring enlightened Western presumption, such talks must take on "human rights."[10] Jullien's dialogue is not this kind of exchange, but instead aims to rethink and decategorize our own assumptions, to reconfigure the limits of what is conceivable, doable. Dialogue has a specific objective: to get beyond our home-base thinking and the homogenization of universal conventional wisdoms. Dialogue can uncover divergence—legitimate areas in ethics and politics in which one culture resists another. Divergence can be as profound as basic understandings of right and wrong, or as obvious as acknowledgment. "Why are they like that; why did they say that; what do they really want?" And "why do I talk this way?" Attention must be paid to alternative understandings. Consider that, for the West, the year 2000 was "celebrated as a world festivity," but what meaning did the event offer once we step away from our Christian calendar? The aim of dialogue is to take engaging cultures "back to a mutual drawing board," a place where respect can soften the intense resistance that faces once dominating nations today.[11]

To Jullien's dialogue and divergence I would add Michel Foucault's concept of *critique*. A commonplace term to be sure but Foucault uses it in a specific way. Critique is "a certain way of thinking, speaking and acting, a certain relationship to what exists, to what one knows, to what one does, a relationship to society, to culture and also a relationship to others that we could call, let's say, the critical attitude." Critique is a way of standing outside the frame, distanced from your ideas and preconceptions—an act of resistance to a dogmatic sense of truth, the application of a clear sense of the limits of our knowledge. Critique is an antidote to the scientific positivism of our inherited Enlightenment and to our assumptions of economic, sociological, psychological motives and explanations. Critique challenges the legitimacy of hegemonic power relationships in cross-cultural dialogue. To me, it is critique of our own way of knowing that is most important as we move through the process of dialogue to grasp essential divergence. For Foucault, critique is a moral stance, a way of moving in the world that is aware of the obvious and hidden forces which, uncontested, dictate understanding and action.[12]

Critique, dialogue, divergence can help focus the attentive stance of folklore studies when the civilized folklore scholar must encounter, absorb, understand cultural difference. In essence, critical dialogue engaging divergence is a respectful, even a moral, act. Great attentiveness is required if cultural divergence is to be uncovered and then acted on by scholarship or the practice of diplomacy.

America has exerted a strong normalizing influence around the world, so when torture, ethnic and religious profiling, isolationist policies come to the fore, this divergence feels new and inappropriate, generating enhanced shock. Effects on America's image are exacerbated by the ubiquity of new media, as tweets and postings take every opinion, half-truth, fake news story onto the internet and beyond. The United States, a complacent democracy dependent on the goodwill of leaders willing to govern within a complex set of constraining norms, seems especially vulnerable to power that flouts custom, instead asserting maximum control over government departments inclined to just "go along." Further, as the epicenter of new media and home to corporate giants dedicated to the unfettered expansion of Twitter, Facebook, Snapchat and the like, America is poorly equipped to push back against the accelerating and distorting capacities of the internet. But even though public intellectuals and policy actors have not yet mounted a coherent response to the social effects of media, the internet is a given; our arena of action—now and into the future. As Theodore Kaczynski pointed out in his *Unabomber's Manifesto*, "all social arrangements are transitory; they all change or break down eventually. But technological advances are permanent."[13] Today we must strive to engage the global public through real dialogue, not only mediated internet images, for just as the United States was for decades capable of leading the world toward equitable, participatory, democratic capitalism, we today may be the nation that leads the world into, as Jane Jacobs put it, the *Dark Age Ahead.*

If the world is to preserve the best ideas of the Enlightenment—the sense of common destiny, shared objectives, and common rights that gave us the United Nations; the International Space Station; and MoMa's sentimental *Family of Man* exhibition—the institutions of modern civilization must adopt the genuine cosmopolitanism of the folklore scholar. Our armies, embassies, nonprofits, global industries must see the world of everyday people as a source of challenge but also of essential wisdom and the unique communal understanding that resides in oral tradition. As America enters 2018, led by a profoundly inexperienced administration that has expressed disdain for the aspirations of the common man and contempt for government itself, we must assume that, at least for now, the insights and achievements of the Enlightenment will be walled off in the past.

This volume has argued that we are living in a time of great, global transformation, and that in the short run our era can be best understood as the end of the Enlightenment. Evidence of the Enlightenment's collapse is widespread; in the long view this failure can be laid at the feet of civilized leaders who saw the common man as someone to be exploited or reformed, leaders who never listened to oral societies, never seriously engaged the lessons available from tradition, overarching myth, face-to-face learning, communal knowledge. If we are to rescue and sustain key Enlightenment values—human rights, social justice, government through consent, confidence in science, philosophy, history—we must begin again, forging a new relationship between the sophistication, knowledge, and global vision of literate civilization and the capacities and aspirations of ordinary people. Folklore studies offers a way to reengage.

By the mid-nineteenth century, when the term *folklore* was coined, the Enlightenment had already captured the imagination of middle-class intellectuals and leaders in the West and was transforming the work of governments, scientists, and philosophers. Over the next 150 years, imperialism, colonialism, and wars to expand or defend democracy spread a vision of popular government and human rights around the world. Giving the lie to lofty language, interactions between civilization and ordinary people were almost always intrusive, exploitative, and violent. Even as the brutal implementation of change gradually eroded the influence of Enlightenment thinking, folklore studies quietly developed an increasingly inclusive understanding of the essential, universal role of tradition and orality in life. Its nineteenth-century formulation posited a broad assumption that traditional custom, belief, and ceremony were the exclusive domain of rural, mostly illiterate communities. Today there is an equally wide understanding that all people participate in the human activity of traditionalizing experience. The physician, lawyer, college professor, journalist—even elected officials—all live through beliefs, practices, understandings that are not conveyed through printed lessons or formal rules but are preserved in memory and passed along through word of mouth (and, increasingly, though social media).

As Dell Hymes understood, everybody has folklore and everyone traditionalizes experience. Folklore scholars know that bank presidents, university professors, emergency-room nurses inherit, create, sustain, and pass along traditional narratives. In addition to jokes—always an acknowledged oral form—there are corporate legends, stories about boardroom antics and the hidden tricks sure to sway the boss. Powerful customs also exist among elites—established and accepted ways of doing things that are not written down in law or regulation. These are the norms—the unwritten rules—that direct behavior in government, business, and family life. Today, in our disrupted political world, the way things get done feels more like the workings of a folk community than a polished, regulated, elite social machine.

:   :   :   :   :

In the early 1960s when I was a teen, popular history ruled the airwaves. Sunday afternoon television offered *Victory at Sea*, a triumphalist account of US naval power in World War II; *Air Power* and *The Twentieth Century* (both shows introduced and narrated by already-fatherly Walter Cronkite) presented less-militarized but no-less-chauvinistic accounts of America's unquestionable impact on the modern world. Television

Westerns like *Bonanza, Rawhide, Have Gun—Will Travel* celebrated individual mastery of challenges encountered on the imagined American
frontier. This was easy: back then only a few advisers had been deployed
to Vietnam, and despite the menacing subtext of Cold War brinksman-
ship, the Eisenhower-to-Kennedy era progressed within the comforting
bubble of what seemed a righteously earned *Pax Americana*.

But as the Vietnam war widened and deepened, and the civil-rights
movement exposed a society laced with unacknowledged and unre-
solved racism, popular analysis shifted from the communitarian tilt of
the humanities toward the harder edge of social science—psychology,
sociology, economics. As I have argued, these academic disciplines are
the minions of Marxism, Freudianism, capitalism. Standing at the ready
to serve policymakers, assigning economic and psychological motives
to demographically defined groups, these disciplines were a perfect fit
for the collective mindset of what we now can see as our late Enlightenment age. Steadily pushing history, philosophy, the arts to the side, these
disciplines offered the security of numbers—how many women married
at a certain age, how many Chinese immigrants achieved a specified
income, how many black teens graduated from high school or college,
how many felons came from nasty neighborhoods or broken, presumably
dysfunctional homes. Politicians, reformers, television pundits, conservative cultural critics, crime-chasing documentarians loved this stuff.
Today, economics and demography combine to probe society's ills while
informing public policy, social scientists and their pollsters (minions of
minions) continually probe public opinion, even boldly asserting futur-
ist predictions of ballot-box choices. Just as robotic rhetoric sustains an
enlightened vision, social science has arrogantly invaded every corner
of life:

> We are living in an age in which the behavioral sciences have become inescap-
> able. The findings of social psychology and behavioral economics are being
> employed to determine the news we read, the products we buy, the cultural and
> intellectual spheres we inhabit, and the human networks, online and in real life,
> of which we are a part. Aspects of human societies that were formerly guided by
> habit and tradition, or spontaneity and whim, are now increasingly the intended
> and unintended consequences of decisions made on the basis of scientific theo-
> ries of the human mind and human well-being.[14]

Other ways of knowing—even our homegrown alternative knowledge—have been drained of authority. Over the late decades of the twentieth century, the once-revered humanities were pushed to the margins, statistical models replaced qualitative understanding of who and where we are. Television Westerns gave way to the *CSI* and *Law and Order* franchises—resilient crime series that tracked the perpetual dangers of an urban frontier shaped by greed, sexual aggression, psychological need. Documentaries chronicled human suffering, featuring material, psychological, or social deficiencies as the definers and determinants of quality of life.

A prediction: the authority of social-science thinking wanes. I have argued that the a priori authority bestowed on the Enlightenment consensus two centuries ago has been validated and sustained through the years by the movement's spawned ideologies—influence sustained by ideology's great enabler, social science. But that power to maintain has absorbed a recent series of shocks—duly noted but not yet transformative. Recall that macro economists failed to predict the global financial collapse of 2007; sociologists failed to anticipate, and failed to analyze, the profound social impact of digital technology; psychology can't tell us who will convert to terror or engage in mass murder. Although policy actors and the public have not yet turned on the data collectors, the authority of social science was wounded in the US presidential election of 2016, when the data-enthralled Clinton campaign knew—just *knew*—the way midwesterners would vote. How could so many experts organizing so many numbers get things so wrong? My social-scientist friends argue, "It isn't a conceptual failing; we just didn't have the right data to figure out how key states, key groups, critical demographic units would behave that November." Maybe. But it's just as likely—*more* likely, really—that social science finally hit the limits of its scientific claims. After all, Isaac Newton's gravity exhibits both standing and permanence: here today, here tomorrow, *true*. Drop the apple, it falls. A psychologist's assertion that an abused prisoner will exhibit learned helplessness, an economist's forecast of stable markets, a pollster's assertion that a sidelined worker in Detroit will vote for Hillary Clinton represent a qualitatively different notion of scientific capability. Despite flash and fireworks, we've learned that too many conclusions are too often wrong. And the untruth of social science does not arise from bad data, it's the bad underlying assumption that if we can measure the external forces that press in on the human mind, we can map identity, reveal motivation, predict behavior.

And what is the future of Enlightenment values? If we are to embrace Jullien's notion of *dialogue*, what must change if we listen to and learn from other cultures, from ordinary people? China, Southeast Asia, the Korean Peninsula—modernized societies, venerable cultures, edgy interactions with the enlightened West—offer hints. We've known for centuries that outside the West, outside elite enclaves, it is not the individual, but the family or clan that is the central unit engaged by authority. In most of the world, the notion of individual rights is modified by—even subsumed under—obligations to family and community. In fact, the excesses of individualism, a commensurate decline in the vitality of community and family, are recurrent themes of homegrown social critique. We know that public services, counseling, education often work best when applied to families, not just individuals. And of course, while in the United States only individuals are investigated, tried, punished (corporations aside) by our legal system, we somehow sense that bad behavior often has a sibling-intergenerational character. For Madoffs and Trumps and Kardashians, acting out just feels like a family affair. In this sense Kurt Andersen has it right: indulgence of the individual has helped knock America off its rocker. After all, in most societies the very idea of human rights contains a strong element of responsibility to community, family, nation—in most places a right is trumped by obligation.

In dialogue with the rising East other Western values will likely step back. China exhibits a relaxed engagement with the spiritual world—a world of deceased relatives, nature, life beyond death, the notion of a universe that has its own tendencies, its own sense of efficacy. It is an informal order of belief that challenges the highly organized but often ineffectual religious practice in Europe and America. Our Western enthusiasm for the commoditization of culture—the assignment of economic worth to every costume, ritual, and utterance and even to one's ethnicity, sex, race—fuels the breakdown of communities and clans, encouraging claims of appropriation and cultural theft. African American culture has punched above its weight in part because black creativity was readily imitated and adapted by other groups and by the larger society.

Yes, there has been outright theft of creative work here and around the world, but the general practice of cultural borrowing adds vitality to the borderland and verve to the international scene. Honest dialogue will challenge the practice of pricing every expressive act.

In critique and dialogue we can begin again, and my big-idea argument is made: the Enlightenment consensus must compromise with difference; our folklore stance can help. But what else can we actually do? First, we can accept America's borderland identity and make it strong. That means vigorous, top-to-bottom public education that forces convergence around difference in race, ethnicity, religion, gender, and sexual orientation; it means zoning policies that discourage gated "gilded ghettos." Civics must come back into schools, not only to teach government, politics, citizen responsibility, and financial literacy, but to equip young people with a critical skepticism strong enough to distinguish internet truth from online fakery. Second, we must be an inspiring nation—not only an attractive, inclusive democratic borderland, but an America that once again "boldly goes," revitalizing our Peace Corps, restarting our manned space program, maintaining a United States able to satisfy the human drive toward quest and adventure. Third, America must reverse the conflation of international affairs with national defense. Generals should not rule, and our Department of State must be reconfigured—less a compliant loudspeaker, more our empathetic eyes and ears out in the world. That means longer postings for our foreign-service officers, deeper immersion in the language and alternative knowledge of other countries, and the creation of mechanisms to protect both people and their ideas when painful truth is conveyed to Washington.

Kurt Andersen posed the question that lurks beneath my big idea: "Why should modern civilization's great principles—democracy, freedom, tolerance—guarantee great outcomes?" The answer is easy: there is no guarantee; even the smallest steps toward re-enlightenment will falter absent political will. Can either American party lead? I am a Democrat, but today my party feels mired in narrow, tactical policy-making, averse to unifying possibilities of big ideas. The Republican Party, perpetually torn between communitarian generosity and a heartless, Ayn Rand cynicism has, in the distracting shadow of a posturing, incompetent president, recommitted itself to dismantling every program that nurtures the nation's shared quality of life. I still believe in the fundamental inclusiveness and generosity that inspires fellow Democrats. So I side with my party, and fervently hope my progressive compatriots will wake up, advance a powerful collective vision, and lead. But today, in the critical task of listening to each other and the world in new ways, neither party holds a clear upper hand.

I have argued that as we engage in genuine dialogue here and around the world, folklore scholarship can help. The stance of folklore studies is patient, humane, curious in the face of difference and alternative knowledge. It is a humanities view, one that I believe will advance as the authority of social science yields its present-day grip on public policy. All who seek to understand the human experience must now encourage a gradual turning from the quantitative to a qualitative approach to the human situation—human motivation, human behavior, humanity itself. This new understanding will not simply be a return to history and literature and their critical windows into the soul. It will take something from history as we have known it, and, yes, even elements of psychology, economics, sociology (after all, they tell us *something*, just not *everything*).

Dell Hymes's 1974 address to the American Folklore Society appeared in the *Journal of American Folklore* the next year. As I've recalled here, Hymes's Benson Hotel talk included elements that never made it to print: an imagined shared narrative crafted from an elevator mishap, the assertion that the impulse to traditionalize experience is a cultural universal—an aspect of behavior that is found in groups of every size in every circumstance in every part of the world. In Portland, Hymes offered an argument that was so aggressive, so bold, that on reflection it was thought best not memorialized in his published AFS presidential address.[15]

That argument—that assertion—was simple: folklore studies is a primary discipline, one that must stand proudly beside literature, history, philosophy. The basic human need to continually traditionalize experience, and the need to perform traditionalized stories to assert identity, secure a place in community, connect with the past is sufficient to give folklore studies a way of understanding that is unique and uniquely valuable in our Enlightenment-empowered quest to engage difference and distance.

Acknowledgments

Late in 2015, Indiana University Press Director Gary Dunham asked me to "write something about folklore and public policy." I accepted his invitation. Six months later I was deep into what my one-time teacher Marilynne Robinson labeled a "sober delight"—a strenuous but rewarding journey into the Enlightenment, the development of folklore studies, and the role of informal culture in current affairs.

I have been encouraged and helped along the way. I am grateful to fellow folklore scholars Elliott Oring and Timothy Lloyd, who helped think through initial features of my argument. Ray Cashman and John MacDowell of Indiana University pointed me toward the pioneering work of Américo Paredes, expanding my understanding of America's "borderland" metaphor, and master fieldworker Henry Glassie patiently explained his commitment to listening with care to the voices of traditional communities. A special thanks to my China folklore colleagues—Song Junhua, Chao Gejin, Xi Chen, and Gang Zhu.

My agent Sarah Lazin of Sarah Lazin Books, and her staffer, Margaret Shultz, have provided support throughout the project. Every writer is lucky if they have an agent, and Sarah is a good one. The Indiana University Press Team—Gary Dunham, Janice Frisch, David Hulsey, Michelle Sybert, Kate Schramm, Peggy Solic, Pam Rude–have been engaged and enthusiastic. Jamie Armstrong completed a helpful first-pass copy edit. I am especially grateful to Nancy Lila Lightfoot, whose relentless, generous, and intelligent editing made certain the final pieces were properly set in place. And thanks to my friend and former NEA colleague Victoria Hutter for advising on press and promotion.

The staff of Nashville's shared workplace—E/Spaces—provided friendship and essential technical support. They are Justin Ostlin, Chloe Adams, Lanier Daniel, Mallory Woods, McKenna Staley, Landry Lowrimore, Jon Pirtle. E/Spaces compatriots John Moen, Phil Gibbs, and Michael Heard provided internet wizardry and patient soundboarding.

Four years ago, Darren Walker and the Ford Foundation supported my research into culture, public policy, and philanthropy; that project became an essential component of my argument about the power of tradition and alternative renditions of expressive life. Over more than a decade, the Henry Luce Foundation and the American Folklore Society gave me a unique opportunity to work, study, and write with colleagues—inspiring sources of alternative knowledge—in many parts of China.

And especially warm thanks to Susan Keffer for patience and encouragement as my journey played out.

Notes

PROLOGUE

1. RonNell Andersen Jones and Sonja R. West, "Don't Expect the First Amendment to Protect the Media," *New York Times*, January 25, 2017.

2. Steven Levitsky and Daniel Ziblatt, "Is Donald Trump a Threat to Democracy?," *New York Times*, December 16, 2016. See also Amanda Taub, "Comey's Firing Tests Strength of the 'Guardrails of Democracy,'" *New York Times*, May 12, 2017. In her account of President Trump's tradition-flouting behavior, Taub deploys the term "norms" twenty-four times!

3. Greg Weiner, "The President's Self-Destructive Disruption," *New York Times*, October 11, 2017.

4. Lynne S. McNeill, *Folklore Rules: A Fun, Quick, and Useful Introduction to the Field of Academic Folklore Studies* (Logan: University of Utah Press, 2013), 3.

5. David Brooks, "A Return to National Greatness," *New York Times*, February 3, 2017.

6. Weiner, "The President's Self-Destructive Disruption."

7. Neal Gabler, "The Elusive Big Idea," *New York Times*, August 13, 2011.

8. James Davison Hunter, "Liberal Democracy and the Unraveling of the Enlightenment Project," *Hedgehog Review* 19, no. 3 (Fall 2017): 22–37. Hunter's excellent essay frames the "Enlightenment Con-sensus," labeling it the "Enlightenment Project," a phrase also deployed by columnist David Brooks in his column "The Enlightenment Project," *New York Times*, February 28, 2017.

9. An edited version of my American Folklore Society presidential address was published as "Values and Value in Folklore" (AFS Presidential Plenary Address, 2007), in the *Journal of American Folklore* 124, no. 491 (Winter 2011): 6–18.

10. Francois Jullien, *On the Universal, the Uniform, the Common and Dialogue between Cultures*, trans. Michael Richardson and Krzysztof Fijalkowski (Cambridge, UK: Polity Press, 2014), viii.

11. The Family of Man was an exhibition organized by Museum of Modern Art director of photography Edward Steichen, January 24–May 8, 1955. See also Edward Steichen, ed., *The Family of Man*, 60th anniversary ed., prologue by Carl Sandburg (New York: Museum of Modern Art, 2015).

12. Beverly Gage, "How 'Un-American' Became the Political Insult of the Moment," *New York Times Magazine*, March 26, 2017, https://www.nytimes.com/2017/03/21/magazine/how-un-american-became-the-political-insult-of-the-moment.html.

13. The Big Idea frames of contemporary international affairs—Francis Fukuyama's "The End of History," Samuel

Huntington's "Clash of Civilizations," and Richard Haass's "World in Disarray"—will be discussed more fully in chapter 6. Haass's recommendations for restabilizing the world are conventional, but his analysis of international affairs post-WWII should be required reading for every American.

14. See Bau James Graves, *Cultural Democracy: The Arts, Community, and the Public Purpose* (Urbana, University of Illinois Press), 44; Richard Dorson, ed., *Peasant Customs and Savage Myths: Selections from the British Folklorists*, vol. 1 (London: Routledge, 1968), quote is from *Folkore Forum* 1 (1968): 37; Dan Ben-Amos, "Toward a Definition of Folklore in Context," *Journal of American Folklore* 84, no. 331 (January–March 1971): 14; Lynne S. McNeill, *Folklore Rules: A Fun, Quick, and Useful Introduction to the Field of Academic Folklore Studies* (Logan: University of Utah Press, 2013), 16; and Elliott Oring, "Folk or Lore? The Stake in Dichotomies," *Journal of Folklore Research* 43, no. 3 (September–December 2006): 207. McNeill's introductory volume will be especially helpful to readers who seek to learn a bit more about present-day academic folklore scholarship. For readers seeking additional information on folklore studies, see the website of the American Folklore Society: www.afsnet.org.

15. Dell Hymes, "Folklore's Nature and the Sun's Myth," *Journal of American Folklore* 88, no. 350 (October–December 1975): 349. Hymes's argument about the universality of traditionalizing action will be discussed in more detail in chapter 5.

16. Pankaj Mishra, "The Globalization of Rage: Why Today's Extremism Looks Familiar," *Foreign Affairs* 95, no. 6 (November/December 2016): 43.

17. Christy Rodgers, "The End of the Enlightenment: A Fable for Our Times," *Counterpunch*, January 14, 2016.

18. David Brooks. "The End of the Two-Party System," *New York Times*, February 12, 2018.

19. Folklorize: To describe and interpret human behavior through the observation of action within informal culture—oral tradition, customary practice, shared belief and knowledge, universal myth.

1. ENLIGHTENED

1. Barack Obama, "Remarks by the President at the Dedication of the National Museum of African American History and Culture," White House: Office of the White House Press Secretary, Washington, DC, September 24, 2016.

2. Obama, "Remarks by the President at the Dedication."

3. Gregg Easterbrook, *It's Better than It Looks: Reasons for Optimism in an Age of Fear* (New York: Public Affairs, 2018); Steven Pinker, *Enlightenment Now: The Case for Reason, Science, Humanism, and Progress* (New York Penguin Random House, 2018). Both authors celebrate the impact of science, democracy, and rational thought on life conditions around the world, while paying only side-bar attention to the social, cultural, linguistic and political disruption that accompanied the spread of Enlightenment-enabled western ideologies. Pinker's exhaustive (and exhausting) inventory of Enlightenment contributions to the modern world is strikingly uncritical.

4. Obama, "Remarks by the President at the Dedication."

5. John Robertson, *The Enlightenment: A Very Short Introduction* (Oxford: Oxford University Press, 2015), 1. See also Eric Hobsbawm, *The Age of Revolution, 1789–1848* (New York: Vintage Books, 1962), 22: "In theory its object was to set all human beings free. All progressive, nationalist and humanist ideologies are implicit in it, and indeed come out of it." The Enlightenment is a vast subject and I

have only touched its surface, relying on descriptive secondary sources (see Robertson) and contemporary interpretive works. Pankaj Mishra, *Age of Anger*, and Vincenzo Ferrone, *The Enlightenment: History of an Idea*, were especially helpful, in part because both authors wrestle with the critical perspective of Michel Foucault. The fall 2017 special issue of the *Hedgehog Review* includes a half-dozen fine articles.

6. Vincenzo Ferrone, *The Enlightenment: History of an Idea* (Princeton, NJ: Princeton University Press, 2015), 11.

7. Pankaj Mishra, *Age of Anger: A History of the Present* (New York: Farrar, Straus and Giroux, 2017), 52.

8. Mishra, *Age of Anger*, 326.

9. Ferrone, *The Enlightenment*, 109.

10. There exists a clear distinction between observers who see Rousseau and Romanticism as a reaction to the Enlightenment and those who see Rousseau as part of the movement. To me, Rousseau's lifespan (1712–1778) places him within the Enlightenment. According to Hobsbawm, "His influence was pervasive and strong," and those who he influenced "regarded him as part of the Enlightenment" (*The Age of Revolution*, 248).

11. Paul Krugman, "When the President is Un-American," *New York Times*, August 14, 2017.

12. Obama, "Remarks by the President at the Dedication."

13. Lindy West, "Republicans, This Is Your President," *New York Times*, August 16, 2017.

14. John Hughes, writer/director, *Ferris Bueller's Day Off* (Los Angeles, CA: Paramount Pictures, 1986).

15. "Word of the Year 2015," Merriam-Webster.com, accessed February 15, 2018, https://www.merriam-webster.com /words-at-play/woty2015-top-looked-up -words-ism.

16. Michel Foucault, "What is Enlightenment?," in *The Foucault Reader*, edited by Paul Rabinow (New York: Pantheon Books, 1984), 35.

17. Eric Foner, "Evolutionary Wars," review of *The Book that Changed America*, by Randall Fuller, *New York Times Book Review*, January 22, 2017. See also Randall Fuller, *The Book That Changed America* (New York: Viking, 2017).

18. Daniel Victor, "The National Geographic Accepts Findings That Its Past Coverage Was Racist," *New York Times*, March 14, 2018. For an excellent critique of the *Geographic* and its role in defining difference, see Catherine A. Lutz and Jane L. Collins, *Reading National Geographic* (Chicago: University of Chicago Press, 1993).

19. Hobsbawm, *The Age of Revolution*, 234.

20. Lisa Appiganesi, "Freud's Clay Feet," review of *Freud: The Making of an Illusion*, by Frederick Crews, *New York Review of Books*, 64, no. 16 (October 26, 2017), http://www.nybooks.com/articles/2017 /10/26/freuds-clay-feet/.

21. Chinua Achebe, *Things Fall Apart* (London: William Heinemann, 1959), 115.

22. Achebe, *Things Fall Apart*, 147.

23. Edmund S. Morgan, "Slavery and Freedom: The American Paradox." *Journal of American History* 59, no. 1 (June, 1972): 5. For a good summary of US government policy toward native peoples, see Sebastian Junger, *Tribe: On Homecoming and Belonging* (New York: Hachette, 2016), and Nicholas Guyatt, *Bind Us Apart: How Enlightened Americans Invented Racial Segregation* (New York: Basic Books, 2016).

24. David S. Reynolds, "Our Ruinous Betrayal of Indians and Black Americans," review of *Bind Us Apart: How Enlightened Americans Invented Racial Segregation*, by Nicholas Guyatt, *New York Review of Books*, December 22, 2016, http://www .nybooks.com/articles/2016/12/22/our -ruinous-betrayal-of-indians-and-black -americans/.

25. Allen J. Greenberger, *The British Image of India: A Study in the Literature of Imperialism 1880–1960* (New York: Oxford University Press, 1969), 42.

26. Alain Peyrefitte, *The Immobile Empire*, translated by John Rothschild (New York: Alfred A. Knopf, 1992), 545.

27. Quotes are from a modern translation: Jacob Grimm and Wilhelm Grimm, *The Original Folk and Fairy Tales of the Brothers Grimm: The Complete First Edition*, translated and edited by Jack Zipes, illustrated by Andrea Dezsö (Princeton, NJ: Princeton University Press, 2014), 69, 77; "Cinderella," directed by Clyde Geronimi, Wilfred Jackson, and Hamilton Luske, produced by Walt Disney (Burbank, CA: The Walt Disney Company, 1950), won three Academy Awards. A new version of the film was released in 2015 to generally positive reviews.

28. Grimm and Grimm, *The Original Folk and Fairy Tales*, 70, 76.

29. For an excellent and complete account of the *Athenaeum* and William Thoms's defining contribution to folklore studies, see Duncan Emrich, "Folklore: William John Thoms," *California Folklore Quarterly* 5, no. 4 (October 1946): 355–74.

30. Emrich, "Folklore," 360.

31. Emrich, "Folklore," 363, 362.

32. Until now! The subtitle of this volume is *Folklorizing*.

33. At a joint meeting of the American Folklore Society and the International Society for Folk Narrative Research (ISFNR) on October 22, 2016, in Miami, Florida., president Ulrich Marzolph characterized early folklore research in "Big Data: 19th-Century Folk Narrative Research and Their Relevance for the Discipline's Future." For Marzolph, early scholarship sought to "amass, classify, compare."

34. Richard M. Dorson, *Bloodstoppers and Bearwalkers: Folk Traditions of the Up-per Peninsula*, 3rd ed. (Madison: University of Wisconsin Press, 2008), 6–8.

35. Mishra, *Age of Anger*, 64.

2. IDENTITY

1. David Rutz, "Forty-Six Times President Obama Told Americans 'That's Not Who We Are,'" a video montage edited by the *Washington Free Beacon* (a conservative journalism website), November 30, 2015, http://freebeacon.com/politics/46-times-president-obama-told-americans-thats-not-who-we-are/.

2. Tim Dowling, "'This Is Not Who We Are' is American for: 'This Is Sort of Who We Are,'" *Guardian*, March 10, 2015, https://www.theguardian.com/commentisfree/2015/mar/10/this-is-not-who-we-are-american-lindsay-graham.

3. Max Fisher and Amanda Taub, "What if We Tried to Explain America's Afghanistan Policy the Way We Explained Other Countries' Behavior?," Interpreter Newsletter, *New York Times*, August 30, 2017, https://www.nytimes.com/newsletters/2017/08/30/the-interpreter?nlid=78801897.

4. Mishra, *Age of Anger*, 129.

5. Krugman, "When the President is Un-American." See also Lynn Vavreck, "The Great Divide over American Identity," *New York Times*, August 2, 2017, https://www.nytimes.com/2017/08/02/upshot/the-great-political-divide-over-american-identity.html.

6. Gage, "How 'Un-American' Became the Political Insult of the Moment."

7. Ross Douthat, "Who Are We?," *New York Times*, February 4, 2017, https://www.nytimes.com/2017/02/04/opinion/who-are-we.html.

8. Samuel P. Huntington, *Who Are We? The Challenges to America's National Identity* (New York: Simon & Shuster, 2004), 9.

9. Huntington, *Who Are We?*, 336.

10. Folklore scholar Dorothy Noyes titled her important collection of articles *Humble Theory*. A strain of rhetorical humility runs through folklore studies.

11. It is unfortunate that no biography of Richard Dorson exists. See C. Gerald Fraser, "Richard M. Dorson, Historian Focused on Folklore of U.S.," *New York Times*, September 23, 1981, http://www .nytimes.com/1981/09/23/obituaries /richard-m-dorson-historian-focused-on-folklore-of-us.html; Ann T. Keene. "Dorson, Richard Mercer," American National Biography, accessed March 9, 2018, http:// www.anb.org/view/10.1093/anb /9780198606697.001.0001/anb -9780198606697-e-1401172; and Nikolai Burlakoff, "Richard Mercer Dorson (1916– 1981): A Memorate," *Journal of American Folklore* 131, no. 519 (Winter 2018), 91–97.

12. Constance Rourke, *American Humor: A Study of the National Character* (Tallahassee: Florida State University Press, 1959).

13. Richard M. Dorson, *Jonathan Draws the Long Bow* (Cambridge: Harvard University Press, 1946).

14. Richard M. Dorson, "A Theory for American Folklore," in *American Folklore and the Historian*, edited by Richard M. Dorson (Chicago: University of Chicago Press, 1971), 43.

15. William Bernard McCarthy, "Richard Dorson in Upper Michigan," *Folklore Historian* 17 (2000), 23–33.

16. Dorson, *Bloodstoppers & Bearwalkers*, 6–7. Quotes are on page 7.

17. Aaron Shapiro, *The Lure of the North Woods: Cultivating Tourism in the Upper Midwest* (Minneapolis: University of Minnesota Press, 2013). Shapiro documents the extent to which ethnicity and folk and folk-like tales were used to advance tourism as a substitute for static timber and declining mining industries.

18. B. A. Botkin, *A Treasury of American Folklore: The Stories, Legends, Tall Tales, Traditions, Ballads and Songs of the American People* (New York: Crown Publishers, 1944). Ben Botkin compiled multiple popular collections of American folklore, worked as an editor in the Roosevelt-era Federal Writers' Project. Uncritical of his sources, Botkin came to symbolize popularized, sentimentalized, folk-like stuff. To Dorson much was "fakelore," and Botkin was criticized by Dorson and other scholars dedicated to the special significance of stories passed through oral tradition, face-to-face, in folk communities.

19. Dorson, *Bloodstoppers*, 3.

20. Dorson, *Bloodstoppers*, 272.

21. Dorson, *Bloodstoppers*, 23–24.

22. Dorson, *Bloodstoppers*, 11.

23. John Holmes McDowell, "Transnationality: The Texas-Mexican Border as Barrier and Bridge," in *Border Folk Balladeer: Critical Studies on Américo Paredes*, ed. Roberto Cantu (Newcastle: Cambridge Scholars Publishing, forthcoming).

24. NBC News/Wall Street Journal Poll, March 10–14, 2018. http://www .nbcnews.com/politics/first-read /americans-are-ready-protest-here-s -what-s-got-n861296.

25. Américo Paredes, *With His Pistol in His Hand: A Border Ballad and Its Hero*, (Austin: University of Texas Press, 1958), 242.

26. Paredes, *With His Pistol*, 13.

27. Ramón Saldívar, *The Borderlands of Culture: Américo Paredes and the Transnational Imaginary* (Durham, NC: Duke University Press, 2006), 345.

28. Edward J. Blakely and Mary Gail Snyder, "Divided We Fall: Gated and Walled Communities in the United States," in *Architecture of Fear*, edited by Nan Ellin (New York: Princeton Architectural Press, 1997), 98.

29. Rich Benjamin, "The Gated Community Mentality," *New York Times*, March 30, 2012, http://www.nytimes.com

/2012/03/30/opinion/the-gated
-community-mentality.html.

30. Valdimar Hafstein, *El Condor Pasa and Other Stories from UNESCO* (Bloomington: Indiana University Press, 2018). Based at the University of Iceland, Hafstein has exhibited a strong interest in American folklore scholarship and in the interactions among research, commerce, and government policy.

31. Bari Weiss, "Three Cheers for Cultural Appropriation," *New York Times*, August 30, 2017, https://www.nytimes.com /2017/08/30/opinion/cultural -appropriation.html.

3. UNDERSTANDING

1. Laleh Khadivi, *A Good Country: A Novel* (New York: Bloomsbury USA, 2017), 79.

2. Roger Cohen, "The Power of Ariana Grande," *New York Times*, May 26, 2017, https://www.nytimes.com/2017/05/26 /opinion/manchester-ariana-grande -salman-abedi.html.

3. Richard A. Friedman, "Psychiatrists Can't Stop Mass Killers," *New York Times*, October 12, 2017, https://www .nytimes.com/2017/10/11/opinion /psychiatrists-mass-killers.html.

4. Comment posted by pharaoh, October 17, 2016, in response to Arie W. Kruglanski, "Joining Islamic State Is about 'Sex and Aggression,' Not Religion," Reuters .com, October 16, 2016, http://blogs.re-uters.com/great-debate/2014/10/16 /joining-islamic-state-is-about-sex-and -aggression-not-religion/.

5. Odd Arne Westad, "The Cold War and America's Delusion of Victory," *New York Times*, August 28, 2017, https://www .nytimes.com/2017/08/28/opinion/cold -war-american-soviet-victory.html.

6. Denice Turner, *Writing the Heavenly Frontier: Metaphor, Geography, and Flight Autobiography in America, 1927–1954* (Amsterdam-New York: Rodopi, NPD), ix.

7. Benjamin Dueholm, "Return of the King," *Aeon*, June 30, 2015, https://aeon .co/essays/the-appeal-of-isis-isn-t-so-far -from-that-of-tolkien.

8. Graeme Wood, "What ISIS Really Wants," *Atlantic*, March 2015, https:// www.theatlantic.com/magazine/archive /2015/03/what-isis-really-wants/384980/.

9. Dueholm, "Return of the King."

10. Joseph Campbell, *The Hero with a Thousand Faces* (Princeton, NJ: Princeton University Press, 1949); George Lucas quoted in Stephen Larsen and Robin Larsen, *Joseph Campbell: A Fire in the Mind: The Life of Joseph Campbell* (New York: Doubleday, 1991), 541. Larsen and Larsen's *Joseph Campbell* includes an interesting interview with Lucas on pages 541–43.

11. *Star Wars*, a.k.a. *Star Wars, Episode IV—A New Hope*, written and directed by George Lucas, rev. 4th draft, January 15, 1976. The film was released by 20th Century Fox in the spring of 1977.

12. For Vogler's original, fascinating Disney memo, framed by the author's tale of how his argument navigated the complexities of a giant entertainment corporation, see Christopher Vogler, "The Memo That Started It All." Vogler's 1985 memorandum was entitled, "A Practical Guide to Joseph Campbell's The Hero with a Thousand Faces," Livingspirit.typepad.com /files/chris-vogler-memo-1.pdf.

13. Christopher Vogler, *The Writer's Journey: Mythic Structure for Writers*, 3rd ed. (Studio City, CA: Michael Wiese Productions, 2007).

14. Larsen and Larsen, *Joseph Campbell*, all quotes are on page 229.

15. Elliott Oring, "Back to the Future: Questions for Theory in the Twenty-First Century," *Journal of American Folklore*, forthcoming.

16. For a discussion of Campbell versus Jung, see Robert A. Segal, "Campbell as a Jungian," in *Joseph Campbell: An Intro-*

duction, revised ed. (New York: Penguin Books USA, 1990), 244–63.

17. David Brooks paraphrasing Eric Hoffer (in his book *The True Believer*), "How ISIS Makes Radicals," *New York Times*, December 8, 2015, https://www.nytimes.com/2015/12/08/opinion/how-isis-makes-radicals.html.

18. John Graham, "Who Joins Isis and Why?," *Huffington Post*, accessed December 27, 2015, https://www.huffingtonpost.com/john-graham/who-joins-isis-and-why_b_8881810.html.

19. Graham, "Who Joins Isis and Why?"

20. Larsen and Larsen, *Joseph Campbell*, 541.

21. Vogler, "A Practical Guide."

22. Graeme Wood, "True Believers: How ISIS Made Jihad Religious Again," *Foreign Affairs* 96, no. 5 (September/October 2017): 138.

23. Joseph Campbell discusses "following your bliss" in *The Hero's Journey: Joseph Campbell on His Life and Work*, edited by Phil Cousineau (San Francisco: Harper & Row, 1990), 110–13; see also Joseph Campbell, *Myths to Live By* (New York: Penguin, 1993).

24. Ann O'Neil and Bob Ortega, "The Unknowable Stephen Paddock and the Ultimate Mystery: Why?," CNN, October 7, 2017, https://www.cnn.com/2017/10/06/us/unknowable-stephen-paddock-and-the-mystery-motive/index.html. See also Sabrina Tavernise, Serge F. Kovaleski, and Julie Turkewitz, "Who Was Stephen Paddock? The Mystery of the Nondescript 'Numbers Guy,'" *New York Times*, October 7, 2017, https://www.nytimes.com/2017/10/07/us/stephen-paddock-vegas.html.

25. O'Neil and Ortega, "The Unknowable Stephen Paddock."

26. Tavernise, Kovaleski, and Turkewitz, "Who Was Stephen Paddock?"

27. Dave Phillips, "Father's History Could Offer Insight into Mind of Las Ve-

gas Gunman," *New York Times*, October 13, 2017, https://www.nytimes.com/2017/10/13/us/stephen-paddock-father-vegas.html.

28. Sheri Fink, "Las Vegas Gunman's Brain Will Be Scrutinized for Clues to the Killing," *New York Times*, October 26, 2017, https://www.nytimes.com/2017/10/26/us/las-vegas-shooting-stephen-paddock-brain.html.

29. Joseph Campbell with Bill Moyers, *The Power of Myth*, 1st Anchor ed. (New York: Anchor, 1991), 81.

30. Luke O'Brien, "The Making of an American Nazi," *Atlantic* 320, no. 4 (December 2017), https://www.theatlantic.com/magazine/archive/2017/12/the-making-of-an-american-nazi/544119/.

31. Tamsin Shaw, "Invisible Manipulators of your Mind," review of *The Undoing Project: A Friendship that Changed Our Minds*, by Michael Lewis, *New York Review of Books* 64, no. 7, April 20, 2017, http://www.nybooks.com/articles/2017/04/20/kahneman-tversky-invisible-mind-manipulators/, opening quote.

4. NEGOTIATION

1. Tamsin Shaw, "The Psychologists Take Power," *New York Review of Books* 63, no. 3 (February 25, 2016), http://www.nybooks.com/articles/2016/02/25/the-psychologists-take-power/.

2. James Risen, "American Psychological Association Bolstered C.I.A. Torture Program, Report Says," *New York Times*, April 30, 2015, https://www.nytimes.com/2015/05/01/us/report-says-american-psychological-association-collaborated-on-torture-justification.html. See also James Risen, "Outside Psychologists Shielded U.S. Torture Program, Report Says," *New York Times*, July 10, 2015, https://www.nytimes.com/2015/07/11/us/psychologists-shielded-us-torture-program-report-finds.html; Daniel Engber, "The Bush Torture Scandal Isn't

Over," *Slate: Science*, September 5, 2017, http://www.slate.com/articles/health _and_science/science/2017/09/should _psychologists_take_the_blame_for _greenlighting_bush_era_enhanced .html.

3. Shaw, "The Psychologists Take Power."

4. William A. Wilson, "Herder, Folklore and Romantic Nationalism." *Journal of Popular Culture* 6, no. 4 (1973): 820.

5. Bill Nicolaisen, "Folklore in the Third Reich," review of *The Nazification of an Academic Discipline: Folklore in the Third Reich*, edited and translated by James R. Dow and Hannjost Lixfield, *Letters to Ambrose Merton #1* (1995): http:// ambrosemerton.org/?cat=14. See also Joel F. Harrington, "Himmler's Aryan Witch Project: Germanic Folklore Meets Nazi Bureaucracy," forthcoming; Christa Kamenetsky, "Folktale and Ideology in the Third Reich," *The Journal of American Folklore* 90, no. 356 (April–June 1977), 168–78.

6. Richard M. Dorson, "Folklore and the National Defense Education Act," *The Journal of American Folklore* 75, no. 296 (April–June, 1962): 163.

7. Dorson, "Folklore and the National Defense Education Act," 162, 164, 163, 164.

8. Alan Lomax, *The Land Where the Blues Began* (New York: Dell, 1993). Quotes are from John Szwed, *Alan Lomax: The Man Who Recorded the World* (New York: Penguin, 2010), 49, 53. See also Joe Klein, *Woody Guthrie: A Life* (New York: Dell, 1980).

9. Richard A. Reuss with JoAnne C. Reuss, *American Folk Music and Left-Wing Politics, 1927–1957* (Lanham, MD: The Scarecrow Press, 2000), 34; see also R. Serge Denisoff, *Great Day Coming: Folk Music and the American Left* (New York: Penguin, 1973); David Hadju, *Positively 4th Street: The Lives and Times of Joan Baez, Bob Dylan, Mimi Baez Farina and Richard*

Farina (New York: Farrar, Straus and Giroux, 2001).

10. Reuss and Reuss, *American Folk Music*, 60.

11. Szwed, *Alan Lomax*.

12. Fred Bartenstein, ed., *Lucky Joe's Namesake: The Extraordinary Life and Observations of Joe Wilson* (Knoxville: University of Tennessee Press, 2017).

13. For interesting observations regarding the interaction between academic folklore scholars and the folk song revival see Dave Van Ronk with Elijah Wald, *The Mayor of MacDougal Street: A Memoir* (Cambridge: Da Capo Press, 2005).

14. Sean Burns, *Archie Green: The Making of a Working-Class Hero* (Urbana: University of Illinois Press, 2011).

15. Dillon Ripley, congressional testimony quoted in Sandra Gross Bressler, *Culture and Politics: A Legislative Chronicle of the American Folklife Preservation Act* (PhD diss., University of Pennsylvania, 1995), 14.

16. Ralph Rinzler, quoted in Bressler, *Culture and Politics*, 17.

17. Much of the story of the American Folklife Preservation Act recounted here is based on Bressler, *Culture and Politics*.

18. Dillon Ripley, congressional testimony quoted in Bressler, *Culture and Politics*, 48.

19. Richard Dorson, congressional testimony quoted in Bressler, *Culture and Politics*, 62.

20. Archie Green, congressional testimony quoted in Bressler, *Culture and Politics*, 63.

21. Michael Straight, *Nancy Hanks: An Intimate Portrait* (Durham and London: Duke University Press, 1988), 275.

22. Alan Jabbour, interview with the author, September 23, 2016.

23. Wayland Hand, quoted in Bressler, *Culture and Politics*, 165.

24. Peggy Bulger, "Looking Back, Moving Forward: The Development of

Folklore as a Public Profession" (AFS Presidential Plenary Address, 2002), *Journal of American Folklore* 116, no. 462 (Autumn 2003): 387. See also Michael Ann Williams, "After the Revolution: Folklore, History, and the Future of Our Discipline" (American Folklore Society Presidential Address, October, 2015), *Journal of American Folklore* 130, no. 516 (Spring 2017): 129. Both Bulger and Williams disagree with me, arguing that rejecting participation in the Tenn-Tom project was a lost opportunity and a setback for the field.

25. Daniel Patrick Moynihan quoted in Steven R. Weisman, ed., *Daniel Patrick Moynihan: A Portrait in Letters of an American Visionary* (New York: Public Affairs, 2010), 3.

26. Theodore Kaczynski, *The Unabomber Manifesto: Industrial Society and Its Future* (Berkeley, CA: Jolly Roger Press, 1995), 72.

5. STORIES

1. Cecilia Kang, "Fake News Onslaught Targets Pizzeria as Nest of Child-Trafficking," *New York Times*, November 21, 216, https://www.nytimes.com/2016/11/21/technology/fact-check-this-pizzeria-is-not-a-child-trafficking-site.html.

2. Faiz Siddiqui and Susan Svrluga, "N.C. Man Told Police He Went to DC Pizzeria with Gun to Investigate Conspiracy Theory," *Washington Post*, December 5, 2016, https://www.washingtonpost.com/news/local/wp/2016/12/04/d-c-police-respond-to-report-of-a-man-with-a-gun-at-comet-ping-pong-restaurant/?utm_term=.2e173427e7bb.

3. Russell Frank, "Caveat Lector: Fake News as Folklore," *Journal of American Folklore* 128, no. 509 (Summer 2015): 317.

4. US Department of Justice, "Grand Jury Indicts Three Russian Companies for Scheme to Interfere in the United States Political System," Justice News, February 16, 2018, www.justice.gov/opa/pr/grand-jury-indicts-thirteen-individuals-and-three-russian-companies-scheme-interfere.

5. Jan Brunvand, *The Vanishing Hitchhiker: American Urban Legends and Their Meanings* (New York and London: W.W. Norton & Company, 1981), 21.

6. Brunvand, *The Vanishing Hitchhiker*, 14.

7. Brunvand, *The Vanishing Hitchhiker*, 20.

8. Brunvand, *The Vanishing Hitchhiker*, 20, 22.

9. Elliott Oring has deployed the phrase in the study of jokes and humor for decades. He introduced it in, "'Hey, You've Got No Character': Chizbat Humor and the Boundaries of Israeli Identity," *Journal of American Folklore* 86, no. 342 (October–December 1973) 358–66.

10. Tom Mould, "The Welfare Legend Tradition in Online and Offline Contexts," *Journal of American Folklore* 129, no. 514 (Fall 2016): 384.

11. Mould, "The Welfare Legend," 385.

12. Hymes, "Folklore's Nature."

13. For a summary of Hymes's contributions to folklore studies and linguistics, see Margaret A. Mills, "Dell H. Hymes (1927–2009)," *Journal of American Folklore* 124, no. 491 (Winter 2011): 88–89; Margalit Fox, "Dell Hymes, Linguist with a Wide Net, Dies at 82," *New York Times*, November 22, 2009, http://www.nytimes.com/2009/11/23/us/23hymes.html.

14. Barbara Johnstone and William Marcellino, "Dell Hymes and the Ethnography of Communication" (Pittsburgh: Carnegie Mellon University *Research Showcase@CMU*, 2010), 4.

15. Fox, "Dell Hymes."

16. Hymes, "Folklore's Nature," 353.

17. Hymes, "Folkore's Nature," 353.

18. Richard Bauman, "Dialogue and Discover in Ethnopoetics," in *The Legacy of Dell Hymes*, edited by Paul V. Kroskrity

and Anthony K. Webster (Bloomington: Indiana University Press, 2015), 177.

19. StoryCorps Podcast, https:// storycorps.org/podcast/, accessed March 5, 2018.

20. Dave Isay, *Callings: The Purpose and Passion of Work* (New York: Penguin Random House, 2016), 50.

21. Dave Isay, *Callings*, 51.

22. Walter Kirn, "A Grim Fairy Tale," *Harper's Magazine*, February 2017, 6.

23. Bill Ellis, "'Fake News': Propaganda, Disinformation, or Contemporary Legend?," paper presented at the 129th Annual Meeting of the American Folklore Society, Minneapolis, MN, October 20, 2017. Ellis's paper and comments by Tom Mould and Patricia Turner are part of a panel discussion: "Fake News, Part IV: The Politics of Knowledge in a Crisis of Trust," AFS Annual Meeting, October 20, 2017. Papers presented in four fake news special sessions held during the 2017 AFS Annual Meeting will be published as a special issue of the *Journal of American Folklore*, Spring 2019 (quoted by permission).

24. Mould, "Comments," 2.

25. Ellis, "'Fake News,'" 2.

26. Ellis, "'Fake News,'" 1.

27. Turner, "Comments," 2.

28. Ellis, "'Fake News.'"

29. Kirn, "A Grim Fairy Tale," 8.

6. LISTENING

1. Donald P. Gregg, "The Vietnam War, Revisited," Sunday Review: Letters, *New York Times*, September 24, 2017, https://www.nytimes.com/2017/09/23/opinion/sunday/vietnam-war-ken-burns.html.

2. Nicholas Kristoff, "Inside North Korea, and Feeling the Drums of War," *New York Times*, October 5, 2017, https://www.nytimes.com/2017/10/05/opinion/sunday/nuclear-north-korea.html.

3. Gregory Hansen, "An Interview with Henry Glassie," *Folkore Forum* 31, no. 2 (2000): 111.

4. Donald Rumsfeld, "As we know, there are known knowns; there are things we know we know. We also know there are known unknowns; that is to say we know there are some things we do not know. But there are also unknown unknowns—the ones we don't know we don't know." Department of Defense News Briefing (with General Richard Myers) February 12, 2002.

5. Kurt Andersen, "How America Lost Its Mind," *Atlantic* 320, no. 2 (Sept. 2017), https://www.theatlantic.com/magazine/archive/2017/09/how-america-lost-its-mind/534231/. The *Atlantic* piece summarized the argument of Andersen's book, *Fantasyland: How America Went Haywire—A 500-Year History* (New York: Random House, 2017).

6. Andersen, "How America Lost Its Mind."

7. Andersen, "How America Lost Its Mind."

8. The dramatic phrase, "Clash of Civilizations," introduced by Samuel P. Huntington (see, e.g., "The Clash of Civilizations?," *Foreign Affairs* 72, no. 3 [Summer 1993]: 22–49) simultaneously elevates the importance of cultural difference while reducing the complexity of cultural identity to one or two stereotypical tropes.

9. The wording of the Gates Foundation credit line has varied over the years. Here's the most frequent formulation, heard regularly on NPR programs such as "Morning Edition" and "All Things Considered": "the Bill and Melinda Gates Foundation, dedicated to the idea that all people deserve a chance to live healthy, productive lives." Reduced to basics, the foundation's aim seems to be to offer a lottery-shot at participation in a globalized workforce. A good example of the way enlightened interventions are framed within the objectives of power and markets.

10. Jessica T. Mathews, "What Trump Is Throwing out the Window," *New York Review of Books* 64, no. 2 (February 9,

2017), http://www.nybooks.com/articles /2017/02/09/what-trump- throwing-out -the-window/.

11. Francis Fukuyama, "The End of History?," *The National Interest* 16 (Summer 1989): 3.

12. Fukuyama, "The End of History?," 5.

13. Fukuyama, "The End of History?," 7.

14. Fukuyama, "The End of History?," 14.

15. Fukuyama, "The End of History?," 8.

16. Samuel P. Huntington, "The Clash of Civilizations?," in *The Clash of Civilizations?: The Debate*, 20th anniv. ed., ed. Gideon Rose (New York: Foreign Affairs Publishing, 2013), 3.

17. Jullien, *On the Universal,* 159.

18. Richard Haass, *A World in Disarray: American Foreign Policy and the Crisis of the Old Order* (New York: Penguin, 2017), 20.

19. Rodgers, "The End of the Enlightenment."

20. George Orwell, "In Front of Your Nose." *Tribune*, March 22, 1946.

21. Henry Glassie, *Irish Folk History: Tales from the North* (Philadelphia: University of Pennsylvania Press, 1998), 16.

22. John Paton Davies, *Foreign and Other Affairs* (New York: W.W. Norton & Company, 1966), 195–96.

23. John Paton Davies Jr., *China Hand: An Autobiography* (Philadelphia: University of Pennsylvania Press, 2012), 327.

24. Davies, *China Hand*, 300.

25. John W. Finney, "The Long Trial of John Paton Davies; A Former Diplomat's Ordeal Shows How McCarthyism Still Haunts Us," *New York Times Magazine*, August 31, 1969, https://timesmachine .nytimes.com/timesmachine/1969/08/31 /103475805.pdf.

26. David Halberstam, *The Best and the Brightest* (New York: Fawcett Crest Books, 1973), 149.

27. Steve Coll on MSNBC, Breaking News, February 6, 2018. Transcript available at https://buzzybuzz.info/news /breaking-news-7am-2-6-18-donald -trump-news-today-february-6–2018/, accessed March 7, 2018.

28. Finney, "The Long Trial."

29. Gen. David Petraeus et al., *The Petraeus Doctrine: The Field Manual on Counterinsurgency Operations* (Washington, DC: Joint Chiefs of Staff Joint Publication 3–24, 2009). "Understanding cultural forms of the relevant population can be key to understanding the OE [Operating Environment] in COIN [Counterinsurgency]." See also Myron Varouhakis, "Challenges and Implications of Human Terrain Analysis for Strategic Intelligence Thinking." Political Studies Association, *Differences* 20, no. 2–3 (2015): 250–78.

30. Gardiner Harris, "Diplomats Sound the Alarm as They Are Pushed Out in Droves," *New York Times*, November 24, 2017, https://www.nytimes.com/2017/11 /24/us/politics/state-department -tillerson.html.

31. David Brooks, "How to Roll Back Fanaticism," *New York Times*, August 15, 2017, https://www.nytimes.com/2017 /08/15/opinion/fanaticism-white -nationalists-charlottesville.html.

32. Henry Glassie, *The Stars of Ballymenone*, new ed. (Bloomington: Indiana University Press, 2016), 130.

AFTERWORD

1. Helene Cooper, "I Was in the Motorcade That Struck and Killed 6-Year-Old Toussaint Birwe," *New York Times*, January 6, 2017, https://www.nytimes.com /2017/01/05/insider/i-was-in-the -motorcade-that-struck-and-killed-6-year -old-toussaint-birwe.html.

2. R. R. Reno, "Republicans Are Now the 'America First' Party," Sunday Review, *New York Times*, April 28, 2017, https:// www.nytimes.com/2017/04/28/opinion /sunday/republicans-are-now-the -america-first-party.html.

3. Daniel Victor, "MacArthur Grant Will Create 'Sesame Street' for Syrian Refugees," *New York Times*, December 23,

2017, https://www.nytimes.com/2017/12/21/world/middleeast/macarthur-sesame-street-refugees.html.

4. Ferrone, *The Enlightenment*, 26.

5. Alain Peyrefitte, *The Immobile Empire*, 545–46.

6. Henry Glassie, *Art and Life in Bangladesh* (Bloomington: Indiana University Press, 1997), 7.

7. Westad, "The Cold War."

8. Jullien, *On the Universal*, viii.

9. Jullien, *On the Universal*, 144.

10. Kristoff, "Inside North Korea."

11. Jullien, *On the Universal*, 162.

12. Quote is from Michel Foucault, "What is Critique?," in *The Essential Foucault: Selections from the Essential Works 1954–1984*, edited by Paul Rabinow and Nikolas Rose (New York: The New Press, 1994), 263. See also Judith Butler, "What is Critique? An Essay on Foucault's Virtue," *eipcp.net*, May 2001, http://eipcp.net/transversal/0806/butler/en. Because Foucault's ideas were frequently expressed through lectures and interviews rather than books or journal articles, his main points seem especially open to interpreta-

tion and reconfiguration. I have chosen to use *critique* as a stance or attitude that applies to both observer and subject. Thus, we must continually critique both the actions of our subject and our own presumptions, even if those presumptions proceed from Foucault's somewhat cynical understanding of the pervasive societal deployment of power and control. For a sense of the way "Foucauian critical caution" can apply to folklore studies and research its UNESCO equivalent, Intangible Cultural Heritage, see Valdimar Tr. Hafstein. "Protection as Dispossession: Government in the Vernacular," in *Cultural Heritage in Transit: Intangible Rights as Human Rights*, edited by Deborah Kapchan, 25–57 (Philadelphia: University of Pennsylvania Press, 2014).

13. Theodore Kaczynski, *The Unabomber Manifesto*. Just as we would pay attention to a *fatwah* composed by Osama bin Laden, we need to consider the ideas of our homegrown, anti-modern terrorists.

14. Shaw, "Invisible Manipulators of Your Mind," 65.

15. Hymes, "Folklore's Nature ."

Works Referenced and Consulted

Achebe, Chinua. *Things Fall Apart*. London: William Heinemann, 1959.

Adams, James Truslow. *The Epic of America*. New York: Triangle Books, 1941.

Allen, Danielle. "Equality and American Democracy: Why Politics Trumps Economics." *Foreign Affairs* 95, no. 1 (January/February 2016): 23–28.

Andersen, Kurt. "How America Lost Its Mind." *Atlantic* 320, no. 2 (September 2017): 76–91.

Appiah, Kwame Anthony. *Cosmopolitanism: Ethics in a World of Strangers*. New York: W.W. Norton, 2006.

Appigranesi, Lisa. "Freud's Clay Feet." Review of *Freud: The Making of an Illusion*, by Frederick Crews. *New York Review of Books*, October 26, 2017, 37–39.

Avins, Jenni. "The Dos and Don'ts of Cultural Appropriation." *Atlantic*, October 20, 2015. https://www.theatlantic.com/entertainment/archive/2015/10/the-dos-and-donts-of-cultural-appropriation/411292/.

Bakewell, Sarah. *At the Existentialist Café: Freedom, Being, and Apricot Cocktails*. New York: Other Press, 2016.

Bartenstein, Fred. *Lucky Joe's Namesake: The Extraordinary Life of Joe Wilson*. With a foreword by Barry Bergey. Knoxville: University of Tennessee Press, 2017.

Bauman, Richard. *Verbal Arts as Performance*. Long Grove, IL: Waveland Press, 1977.

Bauman, Richard, ed. *Verbal Art as Performance*. Rowley, MA: Newbury House, 1978.

Bauman, Richard, and Joel Sherzer, eds. *Explorations in the Ethnography of Speaking*. London: Cambridge University Press, 1974.

Ben-Amos, Dan. "The Idea of Folklore: An Essay." In *Fields of Offerings: Studies in Honor of Raphael Patai*, edited by Victor D. Sanua, 57–63. Rutherford, NJ: Fairleigh Dickenson University Press, 1983.

———. "Toward a Definition of Folklore in Context." *The Journal of American Folklore* 84, no. 331 (January–March): 3–15.

Bendix, Regina. "Diverging Paths in the Scientific Search for Authenticity." *Journal of Folklore Research* 29, no. 2 (May–August 1992): 103–32.

Benhabib, Seyla. *Another Cosmopolitanism: The Berkeley Tanner Lectures*. Edited by Robert Post. New York: Oxford University Press, 2006.

Benjamin, Rich. "The Gated Community Mentality," *New York Times*, March 29, 2012. http://www.nytimes.com/2012/03/30/opinion/the-gated-community-mentality.html.

Bennett, Gillian, and Paul Smith, eds. *Urban Legends: A Collection of Interna-*

tional *Tall Tales and Terrors*. Westport, CT: Greenwood Press, 2007.

Berman, Sheri. "Populism Is Not Fascism: But It Could Be a Harbinger." *Foreign Affairs* 95, no. 6 (November–December, 2016): 39–44.

Betts, Richard K., ed. *Conflict After the Cold War: Arguments on Causes of War and Peace*. 2nd ed. New York: Pearson Education, 2005.

Blakely, Edward J., and Mary Gail Snyder. "Divided We Fall: Gated and Walled Communities in the United States." In *Architecture of Fear*, edited by Nan Ellin, 85–99. New York: Princeton Architectural Press, 1997.

Boggs, Ralph Steele. "Folklore: Materials, Science, Art." *Folklore Americas* 3, no. 1 (June 1943): 1–8.

Boot, Max. *The Road Not Taken: Edward Lansdale and the American Tragedy in Vietnam*. New York: Liveright Publishing Corporation, 2018.

Botkin, B. A., ed. *A Treasury of American Folklore: The Stories, Legends, Tall Tales, Traditions, Ballads and Songs of the American People*. With a foreword by Carl Sandburg. New York: Crown Publishers, 1944.

Botstein, Leon. "American Universities Must Take a Stand." *New York Times*, February 8, 2017.

Bressler, Sandra Gross. "Culture and Politics: A Legislative Chronicle of the American Folklife Preservation Act." PhD diss., University of Pennsylvania, 1995.

Brooks, David. "After the Women's March." *New York Times*, January 24, 2017.

——. "The End of the Two-Party System." *New York Times*, February 13, 2018.

——. "The Enlightenment Project." *New York Times*, February 28, 2017.

——. "The Four American Narratives." *New York Times*, May 26, 2017.

——. "How to Roll Back Fanaticism." *New York Times*, August 16, 2017.

——. "In Praise of Equipoise." *New York Times*, September 1, 2017.

——. "The Internal Invasion." *New York Times*, January 20, 2017.

——. "A Return to National Greatness." *New York Times*, February 3, 2017.

——. "This Century Is Broken." *New York Times*, February 21, 2017.

Bruni, Frank. "God Bless America." *New York Times*, October 4, 2017.

Brunvand, Jan Harold. *The Mexican Pet: More "New" Urban Legends and Some Old Favorites*. New York and London: W.W. Norton, 1986.

——. *The Study of American Folklore*. New York: W.W. Norton, 1968.

——. *The Vanishing Hitchhiker: American Urban Legends and Their Meanings*. New York and London: W.W. Norton, 1981.

Bulger, Peggy. "Looking Back, Moving Forward: The Development of Folklore as a Public Profession" (AFS Presidential Plenary Address, 2002). *Journal of American Folklore* 116, no. 462 (Fall 2003): 377–90.

Burchell, Graham, Colin Gordon, and Peter Miller, eds. *The Foucault Effect: Studies in Governmentality*. Chicago: University of Chicago Press, 1991.

Burlakoff, Nikolai. "Richard Mercer Dorson (1916–1981): A Memorate." *Journal of American Folklore* 131, no. 519 (Spring, 2018): 91–97.

Burns, Sean. *Archie Green: The Making of a Working-Class Hero*. Urbana: University of Illinois Press, 2011.

Butler, Judith. "What is Critique? An Essay on Foucault's Virtue." *Eipcp multilingual web journal* (Institute Europeen pour des Culturelles en Devenir), May 2001. http://eipcp.net/transversal /0806/butler/en.

Callimachi, Rukmini. "Not 'Lone Wolves' After All: How ISIS Guides World's

Terror Plots from Afar." *New York Times*, February 5, 2017.

Campbell, Joseph. *The Hero's Journey: Joseph Campbell on His Life and Work*. Edited by Phil Cousineau. San Francisco: Harper & Row, 1990.

——. *The Hero With a Thousand Faces*. New York: Pantheon, 1949.

——. *The Masks of God: Occidental Mythology*. New York: Penguin, 1976.

——. *Myths to Live By*. New York: Penguin, 1993.

Campbell, Joseph, with Bill Moyers. *The Power of Myth*. New York: Anchor, 1991.

Cohen, Roger. "The Power of Ariana Grande." *New York Times*, May 26, 2017.

Coll, Steve. *Directorate S: The C.I.A. and America's Secret Wars in Afghanistan and Pakistan*. New York: Penguin, 2018.

Cooper, Helene. "I Was in the Motorcade That Struck and Killed 6-Year-Old Toussaint Birwe." *New York Times*, January 6, 2017.

Cousineau, Phil, and Stuart L. Brown. *The Hero's Journey: The World of Joseph Campbell*. New York: Harper & Row, 1990.

Crews, Frederick. "Freud: What's Left?" Review of *Freud: In His Time and Ours*, by Élisabeth Roudinesco, translated by Catherine Porter. *New York Review of Books* 64, no. 3 (February 23, 2017). http://www.nybooks.com/articles/2017/02/23/freud-whats-left/.

Cronin, Audrey Kurth. "ISIS Is Not a Terrorist Group: Why Counterterrorism Won't Stop the Latest Jihadist Threat." *Foreign Affairs* 94, no. 2 (March–April 2015): 87–98.

Danner, Mark. "The Real Trump." Review of *Trump Revealed: An American Journey of Ambition, Ego, Money, and Power*, by Michael Kranish and Marc Fisher. *New York Review of Books* 63, no. 20 (December 22, 2016). http://www.nybooks.com/articles/2016/12/22/the-real-trump/.

Davies, John Paton, Jr. *Foreign and Other Affairs*. New York: W.W. Norton, 1966.

Debord, Guy. *Society of the Spectacle*. Detroit: Black & Red, 1977.

Deneen, Patrick J. "The Tragedy of Liberalism." *Hedgehog Review* 19, no. 3 (Fall 2017): 38–51.

Dick, Ernest S. "The Folk and Their Culture: The Formative Concepts and the Beginnings of Folklore." In *The Folk: Identity, Landscapes and Lores*, edited by Robert J. Smith and Jerry Stannard, 11–28. Lawrence: Department of Anthropology, University of Kansas, 1989.

Dominus, Susan. "When the Revolution Came for Amy Cuddy," *New York Times Magazine*, October 22, 2017.

Dorson, Richard M., ed. *America Begins: Early American Writing*. New York: Pantheon Books, 1950.

——. *American Folklore*. Chicago: University of Chicago Press, 1977.

——. *American Folklore and the Historian*. Chicago: University of Chicago Press, 1971.

——. *Bloodstoppers and Bearwalkers: Folk Traditions of the Upper Peninsula*. Cambridge, MA: Harvard University Press, 1952.

——. *The British Folklorists: A History*. Chicago: University of Chicago Press, 1968.

——. "Fakelore." *Zeitschrift fur Volkskunde*, 1969, 287–89.

——. "Folklore and the National Defense Education Act." *The Journal of American Folklore* 75, no. 296 (April–June 1962): 160–64.

——. *Jonathan Draws the Long Bow*. Cambridge, MA: Harvard University Press, 1946.

——, ed. *Peasant Customs and Savage Myths: Selections from the British Folklorists*, vol. 1. London: Routledge, 1968.

——. "A Theory for American Folklore." In *American Folklore and the Historian*, edited by Richard M. Dorson, 15–48.

Chicago: University of Chicago Press, 1971.

Douthat, Ross. "Our House Divided." *New York Times*, August 16, 2017.

———. "Who Are We?" *New York Times*, February 5, 2017.

Dueholm, Benjamin. "Return of the King." Essay, *Aeon Magazine*, June 30, 2015. https://aeon.co/essays/the-appeal-of-isis-isn-t-so-far-from-that-of-tolkien.

Dundes, Alan, ed. *Folklore: Critical Concepts in Literary and Cultural Studies.* 4 vols. London: Routledge, 2005.

———. *The Study of Folklore.* Englewood Cliffs, NJ: Prentice-Hall, 1965.

Dunn, Susan. "Ho Chi Minh and Thomas Jefferson." *The History Reader: Dispatches in History from St. Martin's Press.* August 19, 2011. http://www.thehistoryreader.com/modern-history/ho-chi-minh-thomas-jefferson/.

Easterbrook, Greg. *It's Better Than It Looks: Reasons for Optimism in an Age of Fear.* New York: Public Affairs, 2018.

Egan, Timothy. "The National Crackup," *New York Times*, October 27, 2017.

Ellis, Bill. "'Fake News': Propaganda, Disinformation, or Contemporary Legend?" Unpublished conference paper presented at the annual meeting of the American Folklore Society, October 18–21, 2017, Minneapolis, MN.

Emrich, Duncan. "'Folklore: William John Thoms.'" *California Folklore Quarterly* 5, no. 4 (October 1946), 355–74.

Engber, Daniel. "The Bush Torture Scandal Isn't Over," *Slate*, September 5, 2017. http://www.slate.com/articles/health_and_science/science/2017/09/should_psychologists_take_the_blame_for_greenlighting_bush_era_enhanced.html.

Federal Writers' Project. *Michigan: A Guide to the Wolverine State.* New York: Oxford University Press, 1941.

Feintuch, Burt, ed. *The Conservation of Culture: Folklorists and the Public Sector.* Lexington: University of Kentucky Press, 1988.

Ferrone, Vincenzo. *The Enlightenment: History of an Idea.* Translated by Elizabetta Tarantino. With a new afterword. Princeton, NJ: Princeton University Press, 2015.

Fine, Gary Alan. *Manufacturing Tales: Sex and Money in Contemporary Legends.* Knoxville: University of Tennessee Press, 1992.

Fine, Gary Alan, and Bill Ellis. *The Global Grapevine: Why Rumors of Terrorism, Immigration, and Trade Matter.* New York: Oxford University Press, 2010.

Fine, Gary Alan, and Patricia A. Turner. *Whispers on the Color Line: Rumor and Race in America.* Berkeley: University of California Press, 2001.

Fink, Sheri. "Las Vegas Gunman's Brain Will Be Scrutinized for Clues to the Killing," *New York Times*, October 26, 2017.

Finney, John W. "The Long Trial of John Paton Davies," *New York Times Magazine*, August 31, 1969.

Fisher, Max, and Amanda Taub. "Why Afghanistan's War Defies Solutions," The Interpreter, *New York Times*, August 24 2017.

Foner, Eric. "Evolutionary Wars." Review of *The Book That Changed America: How Darwin's Theory of Evolution Ignited a Nation*, by Randall Fuller. *New York Times Book Review*, January 22, 2017.

Foucault, Michel. *The Essential Foucault: Selections from Essential Works of Foucault, 1954–1984.* Edited by Paul Rabinow and Nikolas Rose. New York: The New Press, 2003.

Foucault, Michel. *The Foucault Reader.* Edited by Paul Rabinow. New York: Pantheon Books, 1984.

Fox, Margalit. "Arthur Janov, 93, Dies: Psychologist Caught World's Attention with 'Primal Scream.'" *New York Times*, October 4, 2017.

——. "Dell Hymes, Linguist with a Wide Net, Dies at 82." *New York Times*, November 22, 2009.

Frank, Russell. "Caveat Lector: Fake News as Folklore." *Journal of American Folklore* 128, no. 509 (Summer 2015): 315–32.

Fraser, C. Gerald. "Richard M. Dorson, Historian Focused on Folklore of U.S." *New York Times*, September 23, 1981.

Freytas-Tamura, Kimiko de. "For Dignity and Development, East Africa Curbs Used Clothes Imports." *New York Times*, October 12, 2017.

Friedman, Richard A. "Psychiatrists Can't Stop Mass Killers." *New York Times*, October 12, 2017.

Friedman, Thomas L. "If Only Stephen Paddock Were a Muslim," *New York Times*, October 3, 2017.

Fukuyama, Francis. "American Political Decay or Renewal? The Meaning of the 2016 Election." *Foreign Affairs* 95, no. 4 (July/August 2016): 58–68.

——. "The End of History?" *The National Interest* 16 (Summer 1989): 3–18.

Gabler, Neal. "The Elusive Big Idea." *New York Times Sunday Review*, August 13, 2011.

Gage, Beverly. "How 'Un-American' Became the Political Insult of the Moment." *New York Times Magazine*, First Words, March 26, 2017.

Galston, William A. "What Is to Be Done?" *Hedgehog Review* 19, no. 3 (Spring 2017): 80–90.

Gessen, Masha. "Lessons From Russia: Verify Everything, Don't Publish Rumors." *New York Times*, January 14, 2017.

Geva-May, Iris, ed. *Thinking Like a Policy Analyst: Policy Analysis as a Clinical Profession*. New York: Palgrave Macmillan, 2005.

Glassie, Henry. *All Silver and No Brass: An Irish Christmas Mumming*. Philadelphia: University of Pennsylvania Press, 1983.

——. "Architects, Vernacular Traditions, and Society." *TDSR* 1 (1990): 9–21.

——. *Art and Life in Bangladesh*. Bloomington: Indiana University Press, 1997.

——. *Irish Folk History: Texts from the North*. Philadelphia: University of Pennsylvania Press, 1982.

——. *Irish Folktales*. New York: Pantheon Books, 1985.

——. *Material Culture*. Bloomington: Indiana University Press, 1999.

——. *The Potter's Art*. Bloomington: Indiana University Press, 1999.

——. *The Spirit of Folk Art: The Girard Collection at the Museum of International Folk Art*. New York: Harry N. Abrams, 1989.

——. *The Stars of Ballymenone*. New Edition. Bloomington: Indiana University Press, 2016.

Goffman, Erving. *Interaction Ritual: Essays on Face-to-Face Behavior*. Garden City, NY: Doubleday, 1967.

——. *The Presentation of Self in Everyday Life*. New York: Anchor Books, 1959.

Gopnik, Adam. "Americanisms." Comment, *New Yorker*, February 13 and 20, 2017, 29–30.

——. "Jane Jacobs's Street Smarts: What the Urbanist and Writer Got So Right about Cities—and What She Got Wrong." *New Yorker*, September 26, 2016. https://www.newyorker.com/magazine/2016/09/26/jane-jacobs-street-smarts.

Gore, Al. *The Assault on Reason*. New York: Penguin, 2007.

Gottlieb, Anthony. *The Dream of Enlightenment: The Rise of Modern Philosophy*. New York: Liveright Publishing Corporation, 2016.

Graham, John. "Who Joins ISIS and Why?" *Huffington Post*, The World Post, accessed December 27, 2015. https://www.huffingtonpost.com/john-graham/who-joins-isis-and-why_b_8881810.html.

Graves, Bau James. *Cultural Democracy: The Arts, Community, and the Public Purpose*. Urbana: University of Illinois Press, 2005.

Green, Archie. *Only a Miner: Studies in Recorded Coal-Mining Songs*. Urbana: University of Illinois Press, 1972.

Greenberger, Allen J. *The British Image of India: A Study in the Literature of Imperialism 1880–1960*. New York: Oxford University Press, 1969.

Grimm, Jacob, and Wilhelm Grimm. *The Original Folk and Fairy Tales of the Brothers Grimm: The Complete First Edition*. Translated and edited by Jack Zipes. Illustrated by Andrea Dezsö. Princeton, NJ: Princeton University Press, 2014.

Griswold, Wendy. *Cultures and Societies in a Changing World*. 3rd ed. Los Angeles: Pine Forge Press, 2008.

Gutting, Gary. "Rethinking Our Patriotism." Opinion: The Stone, *New York Times*, February 6, 2017. https://www.nytimes.com/2017/02/06/opinion/rethinking-our-patriotism.html.

Guyatt, Nicholas. *Bind Us Apart: How Enlightened Americans Invented Racial Segregation*. New York: Basic Books, 2016.

Haass, Richard. *A World in Disarray: American Foreign Policy and the Crisis of the Old Order*. New York: Penguin, 2017.

———. "World Order 2.0: The Case for Sovereign Obligation." *Foreign Affairs* 96, no. 1 (January/February 2017): 2–9.

Hafstein, Valdimar. *El Condor Pasa and Other Stories from UNESCO*. Bloomington: Indiana University Press, 2018.

Halberstam, David. *The Best and the Brightest*. New York: Fawcett Crest Books, 1973.

Hansen, Gregory. "An Interview with Henry Glassie." *Folklore Forum* 31, no. 2 (2000): 91–113.

Harris, Gardiner. "Diplomats Sound the Alarm as They Are Pushed Out in Droves," *New York Times*, November 24, 2017.

Harrison, Lawrence E. "Promoting Progressive Cultural Change." In *Culture Matters: How Values Shape Human Progress*, edited by Lawrence E. Harrison and Samuel Huntington, 296–307. New York: Basic Books, 2000.

Harrison, Lawrence E., and Samuel P. Huntington, eds. *Culture Matters: How Values Shape Human Progress*. New York: Basic Books, 2000.

Hayes, Christopher. *Twilight of the Elites: America After Meritocracy*. New York: Crown Publishers, 2012.

Hobsbawm, Eric. *The Age of Capital: 1848–1875*. New York: Vintage Books, 1975.

———. *The Age of Empire, 1875–1914*. New York: Vintage Books, 1987, 1989.

———. *The Age of Revolution: 1789–1848*. New York: Vintage Books, 1962.

———. *On Empire: America, War, and Global Supremacy*. New York: Pantheon, 2008.

———. *On History*. London: Abacus, 1997.

———. *Uncommon People: Resistance, Rebellion and Jazz*. London: Abacus, 1999.

———. *Workers: Worlds of Labor*. New York: Pantheon, 1984.

Hughes, John, writer/director. *Ferris Bueller's Day Off*; Los Angeles, CA: Paramount Pictures, 1986.

Hunter, James Davison. "Liberal Democracy and the Unraveling of the Enlightenment Project." *Hedgehog Review* 19, no. 3 (Fall 2017): 22–37.

Huntington, Samuel P. "The Clash of Civilizations?" in *The Clash of Civilizations? The Debate*, 20th anniv. ed., edited by Gideon Rose, 3–27. New York: Foreign Affairs Publishing, 2013.

———. *Who Are We? The Challenges to America's National Identity*. New York: Simon & Schuster, 2004.

Hymes, Dell. "Folklore's Nature and the Sun's Myth (AFS Presidential Address, 1974)." *Journal of American Folklore*

88, no. 350 (October–December 1975): 345–69.

Inglehart, Ronald. "Inequality and Modernization: Why Equality Is Likely to Make a Comeback." *Foreign Affairs* 95, no. 1 (January/February 2016): 2–10.

Isay, Dave, ed. *Callings: The Purpose and Passion of Work*. New York: Penguin, 2016.

——. ed. *Listening is an Act of Love*. New York: Penguin, 2008.

——. ed. *Listening is an Act of Love: A Celebration of American Life from the StoryCorps Project*. New York: Penguin, 2007.

Isenberg, Nancy. *White Trash: The 400-Year Untold History of Class in America*. New York: Viking, 2016.

Ivey, Bill. *Arts, Inc.: How Greed and Neglect Have Destroyed Our Cultural Rights*. Berkeley: University of California Press, 2008.

——. *Handmaking America: A Back-to-Basics Pathway to a Revitalized American Democracy*. Berkeley: Counterpoint Press, 2012.

——. "Values and Value in Folklore" (AFS Presidential Plenary Address, 2007). *Journal of American Folklore* 124, no. 491 (Winter 2011): 6–18.

Jacobs, Jane. *Dark Age Ahead*. New York: Vintage Books, 2004.

——. "Downtown Is for People." Fortune Classic, 1958. Edited by Nin-Hai Tseng. *Fortune*, September 18, 2011. http:// fortune.com/2011/09/18/downtown-is -for-people-fortune-classic-1958/.

Jacobs, Joseph. "The Folk." *Folk-Lore* 4 (1893): 233–38.

Jeffrey, James F. "Why Counterinsurgency Doesn't Work: The Problem Is the Strategy, Not the Execution." *Foreign Affairs* 94, no. 2 (March/April 2015): 178–80.

Johnson, Maisha Z. "What's Wrong with Cultural Appropriation? These 9 Answers Reveal Its Harm." *Everyday Feminism Magazine*, June 14, 2015. https://

everydayfeminism.com/2015/06 /cultural-appropriation-wrong/.

Johnstone, Barbara, and William Marcellino. "Dell Hymes and the Ethnography of Communication." Pittsburgh: Carnegie Mellon University, *Research Showcase @ CMU*, January 2010. http:// repository.cmu.edu/cgi/viewcontent .cgi?article=1013&context=english.

Jones, Robert P. "The Collapse of American Identity." *New York Times*, May 2, 2017.

Jones, RonNell Andersen, and Sonja R. West. "Don't Expect the First Amendment to Protect the Media." *New York Times*, January 25, 2017.

Judt, Tony, with Timothy Snyder. *Thinking the Twentieth Century*. New York: Penguin, 2012.

Jullien, Francois. *On the Universal, the Uniform, the Common and Dialogue between Cultures*. Translated by Michael Richardson and Krzysztof Fijalkowski. Cambridge: Polity Press, 2014.

——. *The Propensity of Things: Toward a History of Efficacy in China*. Translated by Janet Lloyd. New York: Zone Books, 1995.

Junger, Sebastian. *Tribe: On Homecoming and Belonging*. New York: Hachette, 2016.

Kaczynski, Theodore. *The Unabomber Manifesto: Industrial Society and Its Future*. Berkeley: Jolly Roger Press, 1995.

Kahl, Colin, and Hal Brands. "Trump's Grand Strategic Train Wreck." *Foreign Policy*. January 31, 2017. http://foreign policy.com/2017/01/31/trumps-grand -strategic-train-wreck/.

Kahneman, Daniel, Paul Slovic, and A. Tversky, eds. *Judgement under Uncertainty: Heuristics and Biases*. New York: Cambridge University Press, 1982.

Kamenetsky, Christa. "Folklore as a Political Tool in Nazi Germany." *Journal of American Folklore* 85, no. 337 (July–September 1972): 221–35.

Kang, Cecilia. "Fake News Onslaught Targets Pizzeria as Nest of Child-Trafficking." *New York Times*, November 21, 2016.

Katzenstein, Peter J., ed. *Civilizations in World Politics: Plural and Pluralistic Perspectives*. London: Routledge, 2010.

Kazin, Michael. "Trump and American Populism: Old Whine, New Bottles." Comment, *Foreign Affairs* 95, no. 6 (November/December 2016): 17–24.

Keene, Ann T. "Dorson, Richard Mercer (1916–1981), Folklorist and Historian." American National Biography Online. http://oxfordindex.oup.com/view /10.1093/anb/9780198606697.article.14 01172?rskey=FYEPEs&result=25.

Kerry, John. "What We Got Right." *New York Times*, January 19, 2017.

Khadivi, Laleh. *A Good Country: A Novel*. New York: Bloomsbury USA, 2017.

Kilcullen, David. *Counterinsurgency*. Oxford, UK: Oxford University Press, 2010.

Kirn, Walter. "A Grim Fairy Tale." Easy Chair, *Harper's Magazine*, February 2017, 5–7.

Kipling, Rudyard. *Kim*. With an introduction and notes by Jeffrey Meyers. New York: Barnes & Noble Classics, 2003.

Kissinger, Henry A. *A World Restored: The Politics of Conservatism in a Revolutionary Age*. New York: Universal Library, 1964.

Klein, Joe. *Woody Guthrie: A Life*. New York: Alfred A. Knopf, 1999.

Knight, Peter. *Conspiracy Nation: The Politics of Paranoia in Postwar America*. New York: New York University Press, 2002.

Kristoff, Nicholas. "Inside North Korea, and Feeling the Drums of War." *New York Times*, October 5, 2017.

Kroskrity, Paul V., and Anthony K. Webster, eds. *The Legacy of Dell Hymes: Ethnopoetics, Narrative Inequality, and Voice*. Bloomington: Indiana University Press, 2015.

Kruglanski, Arie W. "Joining Islamic State Is About 'Sex and Aggression,' Not Religion. Reuters.com, October 16, 2014.

Krugman, Paul. "Ignorance Is Strength." *New York Times*, February 13, 2017.

———. "When the President is Un-American." *New York Times*, August 14, 2017.

Larsen, Stephen, and Robin Larsen. *A Fire in the Mind: The Life of Joseph Campbell*. New York: Doubleday, 1991.

Leach, MacEdward, and Henry Glassie. *A Guide for Collectors of Oral Traditions and Folk Cultural Material*. Harrisburg, PA: Pennsylvania Historical and Museum Commission, 1968.

Lears, Jackson. "Technocratic Vistas: The Long Con of Neoliberalism." *Hedgehog Review* 19, no. 3 (Fall 2017): 70–78.

Lederer, William J., and Eugene Burdick. *The Ugly American*. New York: W.W. Norton & Company, 1958.

Leibovich, Mark. *Citizens of the Green Room: Profiles in Courage and Self-Delusion*. New York: Plume, 2014.

Leland, John. "Harry Belefonte Knows a Thing or Two about New York." *New York Times*, February 3, 2017.

Letizia, Angelo J. "End of Enlightenment? Not If We Fight It." Philosophers for Change, November 19, 2013. https:// philosophersforchange.org/2013/11/19 /end-of-enlightenment-not-if-we-fight -for-it/.

Levinson, Marc. "End of a Golden Age." *Aeon*, February 22, 2017. https://aeon .co/essays/how-economic-boom-times -in-the-west-came-to-an-end.

Levitsky, Steven, and Daniel Ziblatt. "Is Donald Trump a Threat to Democracy?" *New York Times*, December 16, 2016.

Lomax, Alan. *The Land Where the Blues Began*. New York: Dell Publishing, 1993.

———. *Mister Jelly Roll: The Fortunes of Jelly Roll Morton, New Orleans Creole and "Inventor of Jazz."* New York: Grosset & Dunlap, 1950.

Lukacs, John. *A Thread of Years*. New Haven, CT: Yale University Press, 1998.

Lutz, Catherine A., and Jane L Collins. *Reading National Geographic*. Chicago: University of Chicago Press, 1993.

Lyons, Jonathan. *The Society for Useful Knowledge*. New York: Bloomsbury Press, 2013.

MacCannell, Dean. *The Tourist: A New Theory of the Leisure Class*. Berkeley: University of California Press, 1999.

Malka, Ariel, and Yphtach Lelkes. "In a New Poll, Half of Republicans Say They Would Support Postponing the 2020 Election If Trump Proposed It." Monkey Cage, *Washington Post*, August 10, 2017.

Mandelbaum, Michael. *The Ideas That Conquered the World: Peace, Democracy, and Free Markets in the Twenty-First Century*. New York: Public Affairs, 2002.

Martin, Benjamin G. "'European Culture' Is an Invented Tradition." Ideas, *Aeon*, January 23, 2017. https://aeon.co/ideas/european-culture-is-an-invented-tradition.

Mathews, Jessica T. "What Trump Is Throwing out the Window." *New York Review of Books* 64, no. 2 (February 9, 2017): 11–13.

McCann, Erin. "The Coin: Gold. The 'Real Value': Lady Liberty Is Black." *New York Times*, January 14, 2017.

McCarthy, William Bernard. "Richard Dorson in Upper Michigan." *Folklore Historian* 17 (2000): 23–33.

McDowell, John Holmes. "Transnationality: The Texas-Mexican Border as Barrier and Bridge." In *Border Folk Balladeers: Critical Studies on Américo Paredes*, edited by Roberto Cantu. Newcastle: Cambridge Scholars Publishing, 2018.

McNeill, Lynne S. *Folklore Rules: A Fun, Quick, and Useful Introduction to the Field of Academic Folklore Studies*. Logan: University of Utah Press, 2013.

Mearsheimer, John J., and Stephen M. Walt. "The Case for Offshore Balancing: A Superior U.S. Grand Strategy." *Foreign Affairs* 95, no. 4 (July/August 2016): 70–83.

Mills, Margaret. "Dell H. Hymes (1927–2009)." *Journal of American Folklore* 124, no. 491 (Winter 2011): 88–89.

Mishra, Pankaj. *Age of Anger: A History of the Present*. New York: Farrar, Straus and Giroux, 2017.

———. *From the Ruins of Empire: The Revolt Against the West and the Remaking of Asia*. New York: Farrar, Straus, and Giroux, 2012.

———. "The Globalization of Rage: Why Today's Extremism Looks Familiar." *Foreign Affairs* 95, no. 6 (November/December 2016): 46–54.

Mould, Tom. "The Welfare Legend Tradition in Online and Off-line Contexts." *Journal of American Folklore* 129, no. 514 (Fall 2016): 381–412.

Nagel, Thomas. "How They Wrestled with the New." Review of *The Dream of Enlightenment: The Rise of Modern Philosophy*, by Anthony Gottlieb. *The New York Review of Books* 63, no. 14 (September 29, 2016). http://www.nybooks.com/articles/2016/09/29/hobbes-spinoza-locke-leibniz-hume-wrestled-new/.

Nagl, John A. *Learning to Eat Soup with a Knife: Counterinsurgency Lessons from Malaya and Vietnam*. Chicago: University of Chicago Press, 2002.

Niblett, Robin. "Liberalism in Retreat: The Demise of a Dream." *Foreign Affairs* 96, no. 1 (January/February 2017): 17–24.

Nichols, Tom. "How America Lost Faith in Expertise: And Why That's a Giant Problem." *Foreign Affairs* 96, no. 2 (March/April 2017): 60–73.

Nixon, Ron. "Homeland Security Goes Abroad. Not Everyone Is Grateful." *New York Times*, December 26, 2017. https://www.nytimes.com/2017/12/26/world

/americas/homeland-security-customs
-border-patrol.html.

Noyes, Dorothy. *Humble Theory: Folklore's Grasp on Social Life.* Bloomington: Indiana University Press, 2016.

Obama, Barack. "Farewell Address to the American People," Chicago, Illinois. White House: Office of the White House Press Secretary, January 10, 2017. https://obamawhitehouse.archives .gov/the-press-office/2017/01/10 /remarks-president-farewell-address.

———. "Remarks by the President at the Dedication of the National Museum of African American History and Culture," Washington, DC. White House: Office of the White House Press Secretary, September 24, 2016. https://obamawhitehouse.archives.gov/the-press -office/2016/09/24/remarks-president -dedication-national-museum-african -american-history.

O'Brien, Luke. "The Making of an American Nazi." *Atlantic* 320, no. 5 (December 2017): 54–67.

Oinas, Felix J. "The Problem of the Notion of Soviet Folklore." In *Folklore Today: A Festschrift for Richard M. Dorson,* edited by Linda Degh, Henry Glassie, and Felix J. Oinas, 379–97. Bloomington: Indiana University Press, 1976.

O'Neill, Ann, and Bob Ortega. "The Unknowable Stephen Paddock and the Ultimate Mystery: Why?" CNN, October 7, 2017. https://www.cnn.com/2017 /10/06/us/unknowable-stephen -paddock-and-the-mystery-motive /index.html.

Oring, Elliott. "Back to the Future: Questions for Theory in the Twenty-First Century." *Journal of American Folklore,* forthcoming.

———. "Folk or Lore? The Stake in Dichotomies." *Journal of Folklore Research* 43, no. 3 (September–December 2006): 205–218.

———. "'Hey, You've Got No Character': Chizbat Humor and the Boundaries of Israeli Identity." *Journal of American Folklore,* 86, no. 342 (October-December, 1973): 358–66.

Pally, Marcia. *Commonwealth and Covenant: Economics, Politics, and Theologies of Rationality.* Grand Rapids, MI: William B. Eerdmans, 2016.

Parades, Américo. *With His Pistol in His Hand: A Border Ballad and Its Hero.* Austin: University of Texas Press, 1958.

Petraeus, Gen. David, et al. *The Petraeus Doctrine: The Field Manual on Counterinsurgency Operations.* Washington, DC: Joint Chiefs of Staff Joint Publication, 3–24, 2009.

Peyrefitte, Alain. *The Immobile Empire.* Translated by Jon Rothschild. New York: Alfred A. Knopf, 1992.

Pfaff, William. *The Bullet's Song: Romantic Violence and Utopia.* New York: Simon & Schuster, 2004.

———. *The Irony of Manifest Destiny: The Tragedy of America's Foreign Policy.* New York: Walker Publishing Company, 2010.

Phillips, Dave. "Father's History Could Offer Insight into Mind of Las Vegas Gunman," *New York Times,* October 13, 2017.

Pinker, Steven. *Enlightenment Now: The Case for Reason, Science, Humanism, and Progress.* New York: Viking, 2018.

Porterfield, Nolan. *The Last Cavalier: The Life and Times of John A. Lomax, 1867–1948.* Urbana: University of Illinois Press, 1996.

Priestland, David. "What's Left of Communism." Sunday Review, *New York Times,* February 24, 2017.

Rabin, Roni Caryn, and Rachel Rabkin Peachman. "Parents View New Peanut Guidelines with Guilt and Skepticism." *New York Times,* January 12, 2017.

Risen, James. "American Psychological Association Bolstered C.I.A. Torture

Program, Report Says." *New York Times*, April 30, 2015.

——. "Outside Psychologists Shielded U.S. Torture Program, Report Finds." *New York Times*, July 10, 2015.

Robertson, John. *The Enlightenment: A Very Short Introduction*. Oxford, UK: Oxford University Press, 2015.

Robinson, Marilynne. "What Are We Doing Here?" *New York Review of Books* 64, no. 17 (November 9 2017): 28, 35–36.

Rodgers, Christy. "The End of the Enlightenment: A Fable for Our Times." *Counterpunch*, January 14, 2016. https://www.counterpunch.org/2016/01/14/the-end-of-the-enlightenment-a-fable-for-our-times-2/.

Romero, Simon. "Deep in Brazil's Amazon, Exploring the Ruins of Ford's Fantasyland." *New York Times*, February 21, 2017.

Rosanvallon, Pierre. "How to Create a Society of Equals: Overcoming Today's Crisis of Inequality." *Foreign Affairs* 95, no. 1 (January/February 2016): 16–22.

Rose, Gideon, ed. *The Clash of Civilizations? The Debate*. Twentieth Anniversary Edition. New York: Foreign Affairs Publishing, 2013.

Rose, Nikolas. *Inventing Ourselves: Psychology, Power, and Personhood*. Cambridge, UK: Cambridge University Press, 1998.

Rourke, Constance. *American Humor: A Study of the National Character*. Tallahassee: Florida State University Press, 1959.

Ruskin, John. *The Lamp of Beauty: Writings on Art*. Selected and edited by Joan Evans. London: Phaidon Press, 1980.

Sachs, Jeffrey D. *The Price of Civilization: Reawakening American Virtue and Prosperity*. New York: Random House, 2011.

Saldívar, Ramón. *The Borderlands of Culture: Américo Paredes and the Transnational Imaginary*. Durham, NC: Duke University Press, 2006.

Schaffner, Brian, and Samantha Luks. "This Is What Trump Voters Said When Asked to Compare His Inauguration Crowd with Obama's." Monkey Cage, *Washington Post*, January 25, 2017.

Schell, Orville, and John Delury. *Wealth and Power: China's Long March to the Twenty-First Century*. New York: Random House, 2013.

Schweder, Richard A. "Moral Maps, 'First World' Conceits, and the New Evangelists." In *Culture Matters: How Values Shape Human Progress*, edited by Lawrence E. Harrison and Samuel P. Huntington, 138–76. New York: Basic Books, 2000.

Seligman, Adam. *The Idea of Civil Society*. New York: The Free Press, 1992.

Shane, Scott, Matthew Rosenberg, and Eric Lipton. "Trump Pushes Dark View of Islam to Center of U.S. Policy-Making." *New York Times*, February 1, 2017.

Shapiro, Aaron. *The Lure of the North Woods: Cultivating Tourism in the Upper Midwest*. Minneapolis: University of Minnesota Press, 2013.

Shaw, Tamsin. "Invisible Manipulators of Your Mind." Review of *The Undoing Project: A Friendship That Changed Our Minds*, by Michael Lewis. *New York Review of Books* 64, no. 7 (April 20 2017): 62–65.

Shiller, Robert J. "Making America Great Again Isn't Just About Money and Power." *New York Times*, January 12, 2017.

Shriver, Lionel. "Lionel Shriver's Full Speech: 'I Hope the Concept of Cultural Appropriation Is a Passing Fad.'" *Guardian*, September 13, 2016. https://www.theguardian.com/commentisfree/2016/sep/13/lionel-shrivers-full-speech-i-hope-the-concept-of-cultural-appropriation-is-a-passing-fad.

Siddiqui, Faiz, and Susan Svrluga. "N.C. Man Told Police He Went to D.C. Pizzeria with Gun to Investigate

Conspiracy Theory." *Washington Post*, December 5, 2016.

Šmidchens, Guntis. "Folklorism Revisited." *Journal of Folklore Research* 36, no. 1 (1999): 51–70.

Smith, Mitch, Jennifer Medina, and Timothy Williams. "After Las Vegas Shooting, a Tight-Lipped Sheriff Faces a Maddening Case." *New York Times*, October 9, 2017.

Solnit, Rebecca. "Coming Apart." Easy Chair, *Harper's Magazine*, November, 2016, 5–8.

Steichen, Edward, ed. *The Family of Man*. With a prologue by Carl Sandburg. New York: Museum of Modern Art, 1955.

Stephens, Bret. "Why I'm Still a Never Trumper." *New York Times*, December 30, 2017.

Stern, Sadie. "The Art of Nonfiction No. 8: Jane and Michael Stern." *Paris Review* 215 (Winter 2015): 45–80.

Stevenson, Alexandra. "Davos Elites See an 'Abyss': The Populist Surge Upending the Status Quo." *New York Times*, January 19, 2017.

Stillman, Edmund, and William Pfaff. *The New Politics: America and the End of the Postwar World*. New York: Coward McCann, 1961.

Stohr, Karen. "Our New Age of Contempt." *New York Times*, January 23, 2017.

Straight, Michael. *Nancy Hanks: An Intimate Portrait. The Creation of a National Commitment to the Arts*. Durham, NC: Duke University Press, 1988.

Strawson, P. F. *Freedom and Resentment and Other Essays*. London: Methuen, 1974.

Szwed, John. *Alan Lomax: The Man Who Recorded the World: A Biography*. New York: Viking, 2010.

Taub, Amanda. "Comey's Firing Tests Strength of the 'Guardrails of Democracy,'" *New York Times*, May 12, 2017.

———. "The Real Story About Fake News Is Partisanship." *New York Times*, January 11, 2017.

Tavernise, Sabrina, Serge F. Kovaleski, and Julie Turkewitz. "Who Was Stephen Paddock? The Mystery of a Nondescript 'Numbers Guy.'" *New York Times*, October 7, 2017.

Titon, Jeff Todd. "Orality, Commonality, Commons, Sustainability, and Resilience." *Journal of American Folklore* 129, no. 514 (Fall 2016): 486–97.

Traver, Robert (John Voelker). *Danny and the Boys: Being Some Legends of Hungry Hollow*: Cleveland: The World Publishing Company, 1954.

Trent, Deborah L., ed. *Nontraditional U.S. Public Diplomacy: Past, Present, and Future*. Washington, DC: Public Diplomacy Council, 2016.

Turner, Denice. *Writing the Heavenly Frontier: Metaphor, Geography, and Flight Autobiography in America, 1927–1954*. Amsterdam: Rodopi, 2011.

U.S. Department of Justice. "Grand Jury Indicts Thirteen Russian Individuals and Three Russian Companies for Scheme to Interfere in the United States Political System." Justice News, Justice.gov, February 16, 2018. https://www.justice.gov/opa/pr/grand-jury-indicts-thirteen-russian-individuals-and-three-russian-companies-scheme-interfere.

Vance, J. D. *Hillbilly Elegy: A Memoir of a Family and Culture in Crisis*. New York: HarperCollins, 2016.

Van Ronk, Dave, with Elijah Wald. *The Mayor of MacDougal Street: A Memoir*. Cambridge: Da Capo Press, 2005.

Varouhakis, Myron. "Challenges and Implications of Human Terrain Analysis for Strategic Intelligence Thinking." Political Studies Association, *Differences* 20, no. 2–3 (2015): 250–78.

Vavreck, Lynn. "The Great Political Divide Over American Identity." *New York Times*, August 2, 2017.

Victor, Daniel. "MacArthur Grant Will Create 'Sesame Street' for Syrian Refugees." *New York Times,* December 21, 2017.

Vierick, George Sylvester. "What Life Means to Einstein: An Interview by George Sylvester Vierick." *Saturday Evening Post,* October 26, 1929, 17, 110, 113–14, 117. http://www.saturday eveningpost.com/wp-content/uploads /satevepost/what_life_means_to _einstein.pdf.

Vogler, Christopher. *The Writer's Journey: Mythic Structure for Writers.* 3rd ed. Studio City, CA: Michael Wiese Productions, 2007.

Wakabayashi, Daisuke, and Scott Shane. "Twitter, With Accounts Linked to Russia, to Face Congress Over Role in Election." *New York Times,* September 27, 2017.

Walt, Stephen M., and John J. Mearsheimer, "The Case for Offshore Balancing: A Superior U.S. Grand Strategy." *Foreign Affairs* 95, no. 4 (July/August 2016). https://www.foreignaffairs.com /articles/united-states/2016–06–13 /case-offshore-balancing.

Warrick, Joby. *Black Flags: The Rise of ISIS.* New York: Doubleday, 2015.

Weatherford, J. McIver. *Tribes on the Hill: The U.S. Congress Rituals and Realities.* New York: Rawson, Wade Publishers, 1981.

Weiner, Greg. "The President's Self-Destructive Disruption." *New York Times,* October 11, 2017.

Weisman, Steven R., ed. *Daniel Patrick Moynihan: A Portrait in Letters of an American Visionary.* New York: Public Affairs, 2010.

Weiss, Bari. "Three Cheers for Cultural Appropriation." *New York Times,* August 30, 2017.

West, Lindy. "Republicans, This Is Your President." *New York Times,* August 16, 2017.

Westad, Odd Arne. "The Cold War and America's Delusion of Victory." *New York Times,* August 28, 2017.

Williams, Michael Ann. "After the Revolution: Folklore, History, and the Future of Our Discipline" (American Folklore Society Presidential Address, October, 2015). *Journal of American Folklore,* 130, no. 516 (Spring 2017), 129–41.

Williams, Neville, and Philip Waller. *Chronology of the Modern World, 1763 to 1992.* 2nd ed. New York: Simon & Schuster, 1994.

Wilson, William A. "Herder, Folklore and Romantic Nationalism." *Journal of Popular Culture* 6 (1973): 819–35.

Wood, Graeme. "True Believers: How ISIS Made Jihad Religious Again." *Foreign Affairs* 96, no. 5 (September/October 2017): 136–41.

———. "What ISIS Really Wants." *Atlantic.* March, 2015, 79–94.

Zakaria, Fareed. "Populism on the March: Why the West Is in Trouble." *Foreign Affairs* 95, no. 6 (November/December 2016): 9–15.

Zaretsky, Robert. "Trump and the 'Society of the Spectacle.'" Opinion: The Stone, *New York Times,* February 20, 2017.

Index

Confucian philosophy, 9

conspiracy theories, 99–101, 110, 112, 114, 119, 132

Cooper, Helene, 133

corridos, 53–54

Cortez, Gregorio, 53–54

cosmopolitanism, 37

Council on Foreign Relations, 124

country music, 8. *See also* folk music

Country Music Foundation, 106

creolization, 57

critique: defined, 138–39

Crockett, Davy, 46–47

Cultural Democracy (Graves), 13

culture: appropriation, 58–59; authority, 30; borrowing, 145; commoditization of, 144; complexity, 59; conflicts, 119; differences, 26–27, 123–24; and Enlightenment construction of identity, 44; hegemony, 31, 41, 74; and language of folklore studies, 16–17; relativism, 119; stereotypes, 124

Daily Stormer, The (website), 74

Danley, Marilou, 72

Dark Age Ahead (Jacobs), 140

Darwinism, 25–28, 40, 69–70, 75

Davies, John Patton, Jr., 127–29

Davy Crockett (film), 85

"The Death Car" (urban legend), 102–4

Declaration of Independence, 21, 42, 44

deep Marxism, defined, 58

demagogues, 17–18

democracy and democratic ideals: and borderlands, 54, 57, 60; and collapse of Soviet Union, 120–21; connection with Enlightenment values, 5–6, 17, 19–21, 23, 25, 37; and Enlightenment construction of identity, 41, 43; and failures of Enlightenment values, 18, 118, 139–40; and informal norms, 2; and post-Enlightenment world, 12–13; and prospects for "re-enlightenment," 145–46; and recent global upheavals, 11; and status of folk culture, 91, 101; and technological advances, 139; and Trump's election, 2–3, 7, 136; and US foreign policy, 121–23, 130;

and Western cultural imperialism, 134, 140–41

Democratic Party, 8, 39, 52, 99, 145–46

dialogue, 9, 40–41, 116, 137–40, 144–46; defined, 138–39

digital folklore, 100. *See also* fake news

digital media and technology, 7, 12, 100, 112, 118, 143

diplomacy, 9, 21, 125, 127–30, 139

divergence, defined, 138–39

diversity, 39

documentaries, 143

Dorson, Richard: background and education, 45–48; and Campbell, 66; and definition of folklore, 13, 34; and "fakelore" concept, 82, 113, 153n18; and folklore in public policy, 81–89, 91–93, 94, 97; and Glassie, 126; on importance of fieldwork, 117; and nature of borderlands, 45, 48–52, 59, 64; and Paredes, 52–56; and urban legends, 102–3

Douthat, Ross, 43

Dowling, Tim, 38

Drake, Guy, 105

Dueholm, Benjamin, 63–64

Dylan, Bob, 8, 67, 86

Earnest, Josh, 1

Easterbrook, Gregg, 20

Eastern Europe, 92

economics: and borderlands, 51; and causes of terrorism, 61–63, 64, 69–70, 73, 130; and "clash of civilizations" thesis, 123; and colonialism, 30; connection with Enlightenment values, 37; and cultural appropriation, 58; and Enlightenment construction of identity, 39–40, 40–41; failure to explain behaviors, 75; and folklore activism, 95; and Foucault's critique, 139; and global conflict, 125; and identity creation, 72; and influence of nineteenth century "isms," 28; influence on public policy, 13–14; and Marxist worldview, 27–28; origins in Enlightenment thought, 135; and prospects for "re-enlightenment," 146; and recent global upheavals, 11, 12; and shortcom-

ment values, 116; and shortcomings of Enlightenment principles, 120

Trump, Donald J.: and anti-Enlightenment sentiment, 6; and fake news, 106, 112, 136; and North Korea, 115–16; and Pizzagate, 100; as populist change agent, 135–36; and populist nationalism, 80–81; and power of folk beliefs, 14; and press relations, 1–2; and recent global upheavals, 9–10; and US diplomatic failures, 129

"truthiness," 119

Turner, Denice, 63

Turner, Pat, 113

Twain, Mark, 8

Twitter, 136, 139

Unabomber's Manifesto (Kaczynski), 139–40

unconscious mind, 28

UN Convention on the Preservation and Protection of Intangible Cultural Heritage, 58

UNESCO, 11, 23, 58, 133

United Nations, 11, 23, 84, 116, 133, 140

"universal cultural imperative," 63

University of California, Berkeley, 88

University of Illinois, 89

University of Pennsylvania, 87, 107, 109

University of Texas, 52, 53

Upper Peninsula (UP) of Michigan, 45–52

urban legends, 67, 101–6, 108, 111–13, 136

US Congress, 92, 95

US Constitution, 2

US Department of Defense, 77

US Department of Homeland Security, 101

US Department of State, 128, 129, 145

US Department of the Interior, 96

Vanderbilt University, 8

Vanishing Hitchhiker, The (Brunvand), 102

Vietnam War, 92, 115, 129, 142

Vietnam War, The (television series), 115

violence, 39

Vogel, Hans, 73

Vogler, Christopher, 70, 75

Volkskunde, 80

Voltaire, 22

"Wakanda," 75

Wall Street Journal, 82

Walt Disney Studios, 8, 32, 64–65, 85

war on terror, 129

Washington Free Beacon, 38

Washington Post, 100

Watson, Doc, 87

Weavers, the, 85

Weiner, Greg, 2, 3

Weiss, Bari, 58

Welch, Edgar Maddison, 100, 101

welfare legends, 104–5, 113

Welfare Reform Act, 105

West, Lindy, 24

West, Sonja, 1

Westad, Odd Arne, 63, 135

Western politics, 21

Western values, 41, 133–34, 137, 140–41, 144

White, Josh, 85–86

white supremacy, 7. *See also* racism

Who Are We? (Huntington), 44

Wilson, Bert, 79

Wilson, Joe, 87, 94, 96

With His Pistol in His Hand: A Border Ballad and Its Hero (Paredes), 52

Women in Folklore, 106

Wood, Graeme, 64, 70

Works Progress Administration (WPA), 89

World Bank, 23

World Economic Forum (Davos), 16, 125

World in Disarray, A (Haass), 124

World Trade Center, 106

World Trade Organization (WTO), 125

World War I, 120

World War II, 17, 52, 53, 141–42

Xi Jinping, 130

Yarborough, Ralph, 90, 91

youth culture, 118

zoning policies, 145

BILL IVEY was Chairman of the National Endowment for the Arts during the Clinton-Gore Administration and a Team Leader in the Barack Obama presidential transition. A former president of the American Folklore Society, he has for the past decade served that group as Senior Advisor for China. His books include *Arts, Inc.: How Greed and Neglect Have Destroyed Our Cultural Rights* and *Handmaking America: A Back-to-Basics Pathway to a Revitalized American Democracy*. Ivey is Visiting Research Scholar for the Indiana University Department of Folklore and Ethnomusicology.

CPSIA information can be obtained
at www.ICGtesting.com
Printed in the USA
BVHW03*0045300618

520519BV00001B/1/P

9 780253 029690